The Next Public Administration

Sara Miller McCune founded SAGE Publishing in 1965 to support the dissemination of usable knowledge and educate a global community. SAGE publishes more than 1000 journals and over 800 new books each year, spanning a wide range of subject areas. Our growing selection of library products includes archives, data, case studies and video. SAGE remains majority owned by our founder and after her lifetime will become owned by a charitable trust that secures the company's continued independence.

Los Angeles | London | New Delhi | Singapore | Washington DC | Melbourne

The Next Public Administration
Debates & Dilemmas

B Guy Peters
& Jon Pierre

Los Angeles | London | New Delhi
Singapore | Washington DC | Melbourne

Los Angeles | London | New Delhi
Singapore | Washington DC | Melbourne

SAGE Publications Ltd
1 Oliver's Yard
55 City Road
London EC1Y 1SP

SAGE Publications Inc.
2455 Teller Road
Thousand Oaks, California 91320

SAGE Publications India Pvt Ltd
B 1/I 1 Mohan Cooperative Industrial Area
Mathura Road
New Delhi 110 044

SAGE Publications Asia-Pacific Pte Ltd
3 Church Street
#10-04 Samsung Hub
Singapore 049483

Editor: Natalie Aguilera
Assistant editor: Delayna Spencer
Production editor: Katie Forsythe
Copyeditor: Lotika Singha
Proofreader: Bryan Campbell
Marketing manager: Susheel Gokarakonda
Cover design: Stephanie Guyaz
Typeset by: C&M Digitals (P) Ltd, Chennai, India
Printed in the UK

Library of Congress Control Number: 2017940492

British Library Cataloguing in Publication data

A catalogue record for this book is available from the
British Library

ISBN 978-1-4462-5283-3
ISBN 978-1-4462-5289-5 (pbk)

At SAGE we take sustainability seriously. Most of our products are printed in the UK using FSC papers and boards.
When we print overseas we ensure sustainable papers are used as measured by the PREPS grading system.
We undertake an annual audit to monitor our sustainability.

Contents

About the Authors

B. Guy Peters is Maurice Falk Professor of American Government at the University of Pittsburgh. He earned his PhD at Michigan State University in 1970 and has four honorary doctorates from European universities. He is founding President of the International Public Policy Association, and founding editor of *Governance* and the *European Political Science Review.* Guy Peters is associate editor of the *Journal of Comparative Policy Analysis* and also editor of a book series on public sector organizations for Palgrave/Macmillan. He is author or editor of over 80 books, including most recently *Pursuing Horizontal Management: The Politics of Policy Coordination*, and *Governance and Comparative Politics* (with Jon Pierre).

Jon Pierre is Professor of Political Science at the University of Gothenburg, Sweden and Professor of Public Governance, Melbourne School of Government, University of Melbourne. He is also Adjunct Professor at the University of Pittsburgh. His most recent books in English include *Governing the Embedded State* (with Bengt Jacobsson and Göran Sundström, Oxford University Press, 2015); *The Relevance of Political Science* (co-edited with Gerry Stoker and B. Guy Peters, Palgrave, 2015); *The Oxford Handbook of Swedish Politics* (ed., Oxford University Press, 2015); and *Comparative Governance* with B. Guy Peters, Cambridge University Press, 2017). His work has also appeared in journals such as *Administration and Society, Journal of Public Administration Research and Theory, Public Administration* and *Journal of Politics.*

1

Public Administration in Democratic Governance

Few phenomena in public life are probably more misunderstood than public administration. It is customary to think of public administration, or public bureaucracies as they are often called, as rigid organizations more concerned with promoting their own interests than catering to the needs of their clients. The more extreme images of the bureaucracy tend to portray these public organizations as essentially exoskeletons of power and control, accountable to no one. Political rhetoric, fictional literature but also a surprising amount of academic work is replete with these images of public administration. These caricatures also serve political purposes. Parties and politicians on the political right advocating extensive tax cuts and cutbacks in the public service need to instill an image of an inefficient, costly and power-minded bureaucracy to sustain their claim that taxes can be cut dramatically without any noticeable difference to the rest of society. And parties of the political left have criticized public administration for being insensitive to the needs of the disadvantaged in society.

Yet these public institutions organize public transport in cities, manage service facilities for children and the elderly, provide emergency rescue services, maintain infrastructure, and help ensure safety and security to citizens. They are charged with the fundamental task of implementing public policy and upholding legal authority. To be sure, it is difficult to think of any significant public service that is not delivered by the public bureaucracy or a private contractor working for the bureaucracy. Furthermore, while it is certainly true that administrative decisions can have a major impact on the lives of clients and citizens – from issuing a driver's license to sentencing individuals to serve time in prison or having them deported – that administrative authority is conducted under supervision and accountability.

Given this centrality of the public administration in fundamental public affairs such as policy implementation and service delivery, at least in the Western democratic world, the public administration is integral to democratic governance. However, this perspective has been overlooked for a long time, with the public bureaucracy treated to a large extent as a system of organizations on its own. For instance, in the United States, public administration and political science have become different academic disciplines; an arrangement which has prevented many observers from observing the inherently political and democratic mission of the public bureaucracy. Many political scientists now do not appear to realize that most of the work of governing is done through public administrators.

It is also a mistake to think of the public bureaucracy as a rigid, self-referential system unable or unwilling to change and modernize. There are few, if any, areas of the public sector that have undergone more extensive reform over the past couple of decades than the public administration. Public organizations have to a significant extent increased their efficiency in delivering service and to operate in closer contact with their clients. New models for measuring the performance of the bureaucracy have been developed and are today an essential instrument in the management of most public organizations. Managers have been given greater autonomy, allowing them to organize their work in an efficient and professional way. Basically all major systems in the public administration, from human resource management to budgeting and accounting, have been thoroughly modernized over the past several years.

It is fair to say that public administration scholars in general tend to be closer to their object of study than are most other political scientists or economists. The linkages between academia and public administration have historically been strong. The positive aspect of this close relationship between practitioners and scholars is that research is more likely to be relevant to practice. The main downside of this arrangement is that research may become atheoretical and mainly concerned with documenting and studying practice without wider reflection or theoretical criteria for assessment (see Bogason and Brans, 2008; Peters and Pierre, 2016). There are also examples of the opposite pattern, where we can see students of public administration deliberately removing themselves from administrative practice in order to apply abstract deductive theory. Strange as it perhaps might seem, building theory means that you have to remove context and formulate more general statements about how, in this case, public administration behaves and what might account for that behavior. What is gained in terms of generalizations is lost in the lack of attention to detail.

Public administration has for long suffered from being undertheorized. Dwight Waldo once described public administration as a 'subject matter in search of a discipline' (1968: 2), an observation that remains relevant to date. There are both positive and negative aspects of this state of affairs. The positive aspect is that an explicitly multidisciplinary research area draws on theories from a multitude of academic disciplines. The main downside is that, paradoxically, this multitude of relevant theories has led many scholars in the field of public administration away from theory altogether. There is a disturbing tendency among some public administration scholars to avoid complex theoretical or normative issues and instead rely on administrative practice as a yardstick of research quality. Instead the philosophy seems to be that as long as practitioners recognize their work in the analyses presented by scholars, this is proof of the quality of the research. Instead of deriving benchmarks and criteria for assessment from theory and investigating the degree to which practice meets those criteria, such a strategy of research runs a real risk of elevating practice to standard or even to ideals.

It is equally erroneous to think that one can gain an understanding of a public organization, or any organization, for that matter, without having at least some interaction with that organization. Although the organizations that make up a public bureaucracy operate under similar rules and management philosophies, they differ in many other respects, which means that understanding any individual organization cannot be achieved only through observations at the systemic level. We insist that public administration can and should serve both academic and practice-oriented interests and that indeed it is not possible to deliver good-quality public administration without considering both the theoretical aspects as well as the practice of public administration. Part of the reason why many scholars choose not to address conceptual and theoretical issues is that public administration is by definition a multidisciplinary area of research. Some scholars have made great efforts in separating the study of public administration from other social science disciplines. This has particularly been the case in the United States, where public administration is its own academic discipline. Meanwhile others have emphasized the close relationship to disciplines such as sociology, organization theory, economics and political science. Thus, there is no single core of defining theories in public administration.

Again, we argue that close dialogue between the study and the practice of public administration is central to the development of both. Scholars of administration cannot come up with meaningful research questions without engaging practitioners – indeed, most universities today strongly emphasize engagement as a key activity for its academic staff – and practitioners often lack the national and international overview required to design effective reform or devise models for evaluating the organization's performance. Scholars also have a role in stepping back from the object they study; in deriving yardsticks and benchmarks from conceptual and theoretical analysis; and in applying that framework to empirical cases. We need to understand public administration through a variety of analytic perspectives. This enables us to both understand the institutions involved in delivering public services and to evaluate its performance.

This book offers an advanced introduction to public administration as a field of practice and as a research field. Throughout the book we will be pursuing the argument that public administration matters a great deal, in several different ways. The institutions and people that make up the public bureaucracy are essential to policy implementation – often also policy advice – and are thus key components of democratic government and governance. Furthermore, while we as voters have an opportunity to communicate our views and opinions to the political elite only on election day, we do in fact have almost daily interactions with the public administration and may be able to influence the services we are offered by engaging the producers of that service directly instead of going via political channels. Public administration is thus the key linkage between the state and society. The public bureaucracy channels information upward from clients into the public sector and maintains continuing contact with the public as they administer government programs.

Central to government, democracy and society as these roles of the public administration are, a noticeable development over the past 20–25 years has been the denigration of public administration in public discourse and the elevation of 'public management' as the preferred way to think about the public sector. The architects of administrative reform lost interest in many of the conventional roles of public administration, such as upholding due process or ensuring legality, transparency and accountability. Instead, they focused on efficiency and the creation of competition in public service delivery. There was certainly merit in focusing on cost-cutting and efficiency issues although, we suggest, the reform agenda that was pursued during the 1990s and early years of this millennium came at a price: core aspects of public administration and its role in governance were ignored (Frederickson, 2005). It is intriguing to note that important elements of so-called 'post-NPM' or neo-Weberianism can be seen as proof of a growing awareness of these problems (Pollitt and Bouckaert, 2011).

We have also had similar comments from practitioners over the years. Public management reform involves middle and senior levels of public organizations and has shifted attention across organizations towards productivity issues and measurements. Meanwhile, large numbers of public bureaucrats still find that their workday is dominated by issues related to more conventional public administration tasks. The shift in scholarly attention from public administration to public management is thus more than a fad or a modernization of an academic discipline; it has meant a redefinition of the reform and research agenda related to public sector organizations. One important mission of the present book is to reintroduce public administration both to practitioners and to our fellow scholars and students of public sector organizations. The book will discuss these and many other aspects of public administration in detail. Each of the chapters ahead will address a dichotomy or a dilemma in public administration, for instance the tension between neutrality and responsiveness; or between autonomy and integration; or between authority and democracy. These dilemmas continue to shape how public administrative systems around the world are designed and operate.

Rediscovering Public Administration

Some 200 years ago, Alexander Hamilton wrote in the *Federalist Papers* that 'the true test of a good government is its aptitude and tendency to produce a good administration' (1788, quoted in Pierre, 2013b). There is very little to suggest that this statement is not as relevant today as it was then. In fact, recent research efforts on good governance or the 'quality of government' typically emphasize the critical role of public administration in building institutional trust and legitimacy for the political system (Rothstein and Teorell, 2008) and that, indeed, the quality of public administration is more important in these respects than the degree to which that system allows for effective political representation and accountability (Gilley, 2009; Rothstein, 2009; Peters, 2010a).

A host of literature substantiates the integral role of public administration, both in developed countries and in the developing world, in producing effective and legitimate governance (Doornbos, 2004). Public administration is essential to all aspects of good government and democratic governance (Suleiman, 2003).

Let us first go through a few definitions. A baseline definition of public administration is that it refers to those organizational structures of the public sector that are charged with service delivery, law enforcement and due administrative processes. This means that we usually do not think of state-owned companies such as public service radio and television companies or public utility companies as part of the public administration; nor do we include private contractors in public administration. Public administration refers both to particular organizational structures in the public sector charged with specific tasks that we associate with the state and governing and also to formalized processes of making decisions pertaining to clients. The former category, which relates to clients at the aggregate level, typically includes policy implementation. The latter meaning of public administration applies to due process deliberations and rulings on matters related to individual clients.

We should, however, also think of public administration as a fundamental function of governing; indeed, it is difficult to think of democratic government without a professional public administration. The public bureaucracy delivers a range of tasks that are essential to governing, from tax collection and law enforcement to providing policy advice to politicians and facilitating different exchanges between clients and public officials. This means that public administration is much more than an institutional system created to deliver public service or enforce the law; as pointed out earlier, it is integral to democratic governance. Following Alexander Hamilton, we would argue that the quality of public administration tells us much about the quality of democracy in any given country. A high-performing professional public bureaucracy enhances the quality of policy implementation and increases clients' trust in the bureaucracy, thus reducing transaction costs. By the same logic, a public bureaucracy plagued by corruption and a lack of institutional integrity in relation to policymakers and society will be detrimental not just to public service delivery but to democratic governance more broadly.

To sum up so far, public administration refers to organizational structures; to processes of deliberation and decision-making; and also to an actor or an interface connecting the citizenry with their political leaders. Perhaps most importantly, while elections are essential in deciding which party or parties should govern a country and its agenda, the public bureaucracy provides citizens with daily exchanges with the state and is therefore essential in shaping citizens' perception of government (see, for instance, Nilsson, 2004).

Public administration and its intellectual neighbors

Having provided a baseline definition of public administration, we can now delineate this somewhat nebulous phenomenon in relation to close yet significantly different phenomena such as governance and public management.

We discussed the role of public administration in governance in some detail earlier. The governance role of public administration is today beyond controversy among students in the public administration field. Just a few decades ago, however, there was more emphasis on the apolitical nature of the bureaucracy and the formal–legal nature of its deliberation and service delivery (see Peters, 2009). That perspective ultimately harked back to the Weberian and Wilsonian dichotomy between politics and administration, and the importance of keeping these spheres of government separate. Today, however, there is recognition that the public administration is indeed part of the policy process and an important link between state and society.

The relationship between public administration and public management is perhaps less obvious. Indeed, despite several fundamental differences, public management became, in many ways, used synonymously to public administration during the 1990s and early 2000s, as part of the New Public Management (NPM) reform campaign that swept across the Western world and beyond. The essence of NPM was, as the name suggests, a focus on management; the objective was to cut costs in public service delivery and to empower its clients, or customers, by providing choice among competing service providers (see Kettl, 1997; Peters, 2001). We will return to these issues later in this chapter. For now, we note that public management is primarily concerned with reforming public organizations in such a way that they become more cost-efficient. With such efficiency as the key driver of reform, conventional norms in public administration such as due process, equal treatment and accountability came under attack.

The public management 'turn' meant a reprioritization of the goals of public administration, with all that entails in terms of changing roles, decision-making processes and command lines. That having been said, we see management issues as subordinate to the bigger issues about the role of public administration in governing. Such a perspective suggests that management reform should be assessed not just in terms of its expected effects on costs or efficiency but also, and primarily, in terms of the degree to which is contributes to the core mission of public administration. Here, as we will see later, opinions tend to differ significantly as some argue that NPM reform has made a major contribution to democratic governance since it empowers citizens as customers, whereas critics maintain that political responsiveness and accountability have been damaged by reform.

Thus, in our view, governance, public administration and public management are essentially a set of *matryoshka* dolls, with public management being a subsection of public administration, which, in turn, is a subsection of governance. Attempting to understand any level of this nesting of institutions and practices without understanding their context is likely to lead to significant errors.

Critiquing public administration

As we rearticulate public administration as a practice or as an element of governance or as a field worthy of study we need to remind ourselves that this is not an uncontroversial area. Public administration has for a long time been the target of criticism. Part of this criticism against 'the bureaucracy' (here used in a very pejorative sense) is its 'irritating methods and unsatisfactory performance' (Niskanen, 1971: 18). In the early 1970s, William Niskanen launched an all-out attack on the US federal bureaucracy accusing it both for its inefficiency and its self-serving bureaucrats. Consistent with public choice theory, managers were assumed to maximize their bureau's budget, which leads to a suboptimal allocation of resources within the bureaucracy. That these were all unproven hypotheses seemed to play a minor role. Niskanen and his followers shaped, or reinforced, a discourse on the ineffective, unproductive and even undemocratic nature of the public administration, which paved the way for the NPM reform campaign that would begin in the 1990s.

Others seem less concerned with the purported inefficiency and rigidity of the public administration. Instead they suggest that bureaucrats are energetic and zealous actors, but they are driven by motives other than the public interest. The criticism here is thus that bureaucrats have an agenda of their own, and that their pursuit of those objectives puts them in opposition to elected officials and the electorate: 'the very expertise that bureaucrats and other actors enjoy, along with their structural role in the policy processes, provides them with opportunities to work against the interests of politicians and their supporters' (Huber and Shipan, 2002: 2). Much of this criticism emanated from the economic disciplines. Applying economic theories based in assumptions about rationalistic behavior on the public sector, this approach became popular among neoliberal political thinkers and part of an overall critique of the state. Public choice theory – the application of economic theory to public administration – generated a 'principal–agent' model, with politicians as 'the principal' and bureaucrats as 'agents' (Mueller, 2003 [1979]). The model was also applied to the relationship between the legislature and the bureaucracy as an institution. The model departed from the assumption of 'asymmetrical information', so that the agents always had an advantage in relation to the principal. From this analysis it was assumed that bureaucrats had incentives not always to obey the principal's instructions but rather to pursue other options that would lead to a higher degree of utility maximization (see Pierre and Peters, 2016).

Leaving aside the neoliberal orientation and high-pitched tenor of some of the most ardent critics, an intriguing question is whether they in fact had a point. Subsequent reform, to a large extent related to the public choice critique, promised to increase public sector efficiency, to cut costs and to boost customer satisfaction. Did it? The first major stock-taking analysis of some three decades of public management reform answers this question in the negative. Christopher Hood and Ruth Dixon, authors of the study, arrive at the middle-of-the-road conclusion that the UK central government 'cost a bit more and worked a bit worse' over the 30 years they had studied it (2015: 183). Thus, customers are less satisfied, costs have not decreased but rather increased and productivity has not changed significantly. However, Hood and Dixon also point out that the result is better than what the most ardent NPM critics warned would be the result of reform. Equally disturbing, NPM reform, according to critics, undermined the role of the public administration in democratic governance by portraying clients as customers, thus introducing a market-like exchange between state and society, and also by reducing the role of elected officials essentially to goal-setting and granting significant autonomy to the managers of executive institutions. In implementing NPM reforms, Suleiman argues, 'democratic societies have been following a path that leads to undermining, or even destroying, one of the central institutions on which a democratic polity depends' (2003: 18). Democratic government requires a professional and impartial executive branch, and market-based administrative reform has reduced the capabilities of public administration as well as de-professionalized and politicized the bureaucracy. Thus, a critical account of NPM would be that it has not only failed to deliver on its promise of a cheaper and more efficient public service but also that the reform significantly undermined the involvement of the public administration in democratic governance.

All is, however, not gloomy. On the positive side, there is much more attention to performance and quality of public services today compared with a few decades ago. Public administration has undergone extensive modernization in almost all defining aspects: its organizational management; budgeting and accounting; relationships both upwards with the political leadership and downwards with its clients; human resource management; information and communication technology (ICT) systems, etc. This modernization has been implemented without altering the fundamental norms and values of public administration. A recent study in the UK shows that despite decades of public management reform, the fundamental values – 'public ethos' – are still embraced by public servants (John and Johnson, 2008). A bureaucracy is a multi-functional organization, pursuing efficiency and client satisfaction at the same time as it is expected to adhere to principles of impartiality, legality, due process, equal treatment and transparency (Christensen et al., 2007). These values are deeply entrenched in the public administration and resilient to change, which also means that efficiency is not likely to become a top priority within the bureaucracy as it has to cater to a wide variety of goals.

We have already touched on the role of the public administration in democratic governance. Let us now look more closely on the types of contribution that the public bureaucracy makes to governance and governing.

Public Administration and Democratic Governance

The public bureaucracy is integral to democratic governance in several different ways. At a baseline level, we should note that the public bureaucracy ensures that core functions of the state such as law enforcement, defense and tax collection are upheld. Beyond these rudimentary functions, there are two particularly important types of democratic role that we will highlight in this introductory chapter.

The first role is related to the relationship between politicians and the public service, and the role of the bureaucracy in governing more broadly. The public service is a key source of policy advice and the chief structure in society to implement public policy, yet as we will discuss later in this chapter, they are basically a different species than elected officials. The public service can, and

should, provide expert advice with relatively little concern for the political consequences of the policies that they advocate. This raises the question of how
politicians and bureaucrats relate to each other. The literature offers many different versions of this relationship. Sometime ago now, Aberbach, Putnam and
Rockman (1981) described it as 'uneasy'. Later, one of the present authors
developed a typology of different types of relationship, ranging from consen-
sual to adversarial (Peters, 1987). Still later accounts have provided even more
polarized views about this relationship, ranging from studies that emphasize
bureaucratic loyalty toward the government of the day and mutual respect
between politicians and civil servants (Page, 2012) to the public choice-based
instrumental view that bureaucrats follow politicians' instructions only when it
is in their own interest to do so (Hood and Lodge, 2006; see also Brehm and
Gates, 1997; Pierre and Peters, 2016). This diversity in how the exchanges
between politicians and bureaucrats reflect different theoretical and normative
approaches also points to some fundamental differences between the two
groups and the interdependence that exists between them. In some instances,
the administrators and politicians may be different players on the same team
(Rose, 1980) while in others they may be in conflict with one another over
policy and over power within the public sector.

The other main role that the public administration plays in democratic governance is to function as the chief interface between state and society. The
bureaucracy daily delivers extensive service such as education, healthcare, and
public daycare for children and the elderly. It also delivers less visible services
such as environmental protection, national security, defense and legal services.
Certainly for most people in the developed world, hardly a day goes by without
some form of interaction with the state and its administration. These interactions are instrumental in forming our opinions about the public sector and the
state. In welfare states such as the Scandinavian countries, studies suggest that
the wide range of public services enjoys strong support among the citizens,
despite the high tax pressure this entails (Nilsson, 2004; Svallfors, 2015). There
is also a pattern that the more frequent the exchanges with the public sector an
individual has, the more likely it is that they will support a big public sector.
Furthermore, trust in public institutions is also shaped by citizens' perception of
impartiality, legality and due process (Rothstein and Teorell, 2008; Rothstein,
2009). This institutional trust, in turn, helps sustain the legitimacy of the state.
Thus, there are several essential linkages between the quality of public service,
our interactions with the public sector and how we as citizens value government.

An important aspect of the democratic role of the public administration, as
already mentioned, is that unlike participation in general elections, citizens
engage with the public administration on a daily basis. Election campaigns are
essential to democracy as they allow for debate among different ideas about how
to develop society, but the daily services shape our views of the state in more
concrete ways. Our evaluation of the services we receive influence both our
choice of which party we should vote for in a coming election – a party advocating an expansion of public services or one which argues for tax cuts and a
reduction in such services – as well as our perception of government in a wider
perspective. Elections, as Schmitter and Karl (1991) argue, certainly have their

place in democracy but so do other forms of engagement between elections, whether in associational, collective forms or through individual political action and reflection.

The obvious counterargument here is that as recipients of services we are just that: recipients, with little or no means of actually shaping decisions or services in the public sector. Conventional public service delivery offered clients limited opportunities to voice their opinions about the quality of those services. This is, however, no longer the case. Along with market-based reform in the public sector, clients (or 'customers') can – and to a large extent do (Dowding and John, 2012; Pierre and Röiseland, 2016) – use either 'voice' to let service providers know when they are dissatisfied with the services they receive, or use 'exit' to switch to a different provider. Thus, notwithstanding our previous tentative position on the idea of thinking of clients as customers, once markets are introduced into public service delivery we should expect the public to use the new instrument of empowerment that such reform offers.

These opportunities to communicate criticism to service providers also include talking directly with service managers. While it is fair to assume that such contacts are not new, the new models of public management are more open to direct customer–manager communication than was the conventional model of public administration. And the content of the discourse between the actors may also be different, emphasizing service and efficiency perhaps more than the law. This development has helped drive a debate about the degree to which the conventional, input-based legitimacy is now either replaced or supplemented by a legitimacy of the public sector which is the result of exchanges on the output side of the political system where service delivery takes place.

This debate has been going on for some time, dating back (at least) to the 1990s and the continuing integration of the European Union (EU) (Scharpf, 1999). The argument here was that the EU would have problems in being seen as a legitimate representative system and that instead its legitimacy would primarily be output-based, that is, the result of services delivered by the EU. Interestingly, this argument dovetailed with Bruce Gilley's (2009) research on the sources of legitimacy of advanced democratic states. He studied 72 countries across the globe, and his overall result was that the quality of democratic representation is less important than the quality of government and public administration in generating legitimacy for the political system. Again, this result fueled the debate on whether input-related factors, primarily democratic representation, or output-related factors, such as service or quality of administration, were most instrumental in fostering support and legitimacy for government. Importantly, studies on these issues in the EU context suggest that the distinction between input- and output-based legitimacy, while empirically relevant, is to some extent a false dichotomy as the strongest predictor of output-based legitimacy is a high level of input legitimacy (Lindgren and Persson, 2010). Further research will hopefully tell us more about the relationship between these two different sources of legitimacy. For now, we conclude by noting that the output side of the political system – the quality of administration and public service – is an important source of such legitimacy and that this role has been accentuated by public management reform. This pattern speaks directly to the role of public administration in democratic governance.

Against this backdrop, we now need to briefly go back to the discussion about the values of public administration and institutional trust and look more broadly at the various roles public administration plays in contemporary governing. These factors about public administration may be in a reciprocal relationship. That is, greater trust will facilitate service delivery and effective service delivery will build trust among the citizens.

The Role of Public Administration in Governing

Arguably, the key role of public administration in governing is that in relationship to policymakers. The public service is a critical component in the policy-making process; indeed, apart from setting policy goals and attempting to control public spending ,the public bureaucracy is perhaps the central institutional actor in governance. And it is also the institution within the public sector that actually delivers goods and services to citizens, and which has daily contacts with them.

Relationship to policymakers

Politicians typically enter government with an agenda of projects they want to see realized. Their agenda defines key goals in different policy sectors and specific projects they want to see carried out – in recent years not just what should be done but also with what instruments it should be done have become more important to politicians – but the finer details of those projects are rarely worked out. The public service is expected to be loyal to the government of the day and offer 'free and frank' advice on policy matters. Usually, bureaucrats are charged with the task of working out specific details of policies and programs and to issue decrees on policy application and implementation without challenging the policy goals set by politicians (Page, 2012). Thus, while politicians define goals and objectives, they rely on public servants to apply their expertise to the policy within the normative framework in which it is embedded.

We mentioned earlier that politicians and public servants are different species. The two groups of officials differ in many significant aspects. First, politicians are elected representatives for a political party. They are rarely specialized in any particular policy sector; rather, they are generalists, which means that they have baseline knowledge of most policy sectors. Public servants, by contrast, may have longstanding specialized expertise in designing and implementing public policy in a given policy sector. Second, politicians tend to focus on the election cycle and therefore favor political projects that can present results prior to the next election. Public servants, by comparison, are mainly concerned with designing sustainable problem-solving arrangements, and therefore often have a more long-term perspective. Third, politicians and public servants are subject to quite different forms of accountability. Politicians are first and foremost accountable to their voters while bureaucrats are accountable to politicians (Page, 2010).

These are the preconditions for politicians and public servants' working together in the policy process. We mentioned earlier the different perspectives which the scholarly community has offered on this relationship. We would like to emphasize not just the factors that help make this an efficient partnership, such as loyalty and mutual respect, but also the seemingly inherent disagreements that come with different roles and agendas.

Relationship to citizens

If the relationship with the political level is one of the chief concerns of the senior levels of the public service, most exchanges with citizens and clients is handled by public sector employees in local government. It is here that core public services such as education, social welfare and (in most countries) healthcare are delivered, and these are the sectors where direct contact with public employees – teachers, nurses, social workers, etc. – takes place. This face-to-face interaction with public officials facilitates client input on the service he or she is receiving. The consequences of such immediate contact with clients on the 'street-level bureaucrat' have been the topic of some scholarly debate (Lipsky, 1980; Hupe, Hill and Buffat, 2015).

The public bureaucracy in several countries has introduced new channels for citizen involvement not only in public service but also in public discourse at the pre-policy or implementation stage. These increasingly popular models of citizen involvement are often referred to as 'citizen panels', which is an umbrella concept for a variety of what M. B. Brown (2006: 203) defines as 'temporary advisory bodies that involve lay people in cooperative deliberation informed by expert advice'. This would include discursive venues such as consensus conferences, citizen juries and deliberative polls (M. B. Brown, 2006: 203). Citizen panels emerged in Europe, North America, Asia and the Antipodes during the 1970s but seem to have lost some momentum recently, at least in their conventional design (see Mann et al., 2014). Instead, new forms of facilitating citizen engagement in public affairs using social media or smartphones have emerged, often on an experimental basis. In some local governments in Victoria (Australia), for instance, a website (Yoursay) is used to enable citizens to become involved in the budgetary process.

Participatory budgeting is somewhat of a classic in bringing citizens into the policy process. First introduced in Brazil in 1989 it has since then been used in more than 1,500 cities across all continents.[1] In Porto Alegre in Brazil, to give an example, citizen panels were authorized to deliberate and decide on how to allocate 20 percent of the city's budget. Indeed, the public can engage the public administration in any number of ways. In Indonesia, for instance, anyone with a smartphone can download an app and use that to point out flaws in public services directly and instantaneously to the public bureaucracy. Coming back to a point mentioned briefly earlier, these forms of direct engagement in public service delivery are often assumed to help increase citizens' trust in the

---

[1]See www.participatorybudgeting.org

public sector and the legitimacy of public institutions. More specifically, they would be assumed to boost output legitimacy of government, as well as providing more opportunities for citizens to shape those outputs through direct inputs.

The intriguing question is to what extent citizen panels and participatory budgeting affect the legitimacy of input democracy channels such as political parties or individual candidates. Do these alternative channels of citizen input on political decisions undermine their position, or is there the opposite effect so that the political system as a whole benefits from these new forms of participation and the strengthened legitimacy they are assumed to entail? We do not know much about those potential consequences of direct citizen involvement, nor do we know a great deal about the democratic quality and sustainability of these arrangements. While it appears extremely likely that direct contact with a nurse or a social worker contributes to better public service than would otherwise have been the case, citizen panels offer a more complicated analysis. One of the strengths of the conventional model of representative democracy is that it makes accountability reasonably clear, blame games and other manipulations notwithstanding. In that conventional perspective, allowing citizens to have input on budgets or policy without being able to hold them to account poses a serious problem from a democratic point of view.

Relationship to strategic societal actors

One of the more profound developments over the past couple of decades is the intensified collaboration between the public administration and strategic actors in society. This collaboration serves in part to broaden the cast of actors involved in the governance of an increasingly complex society (see Rhodes, 1997; Pierre and Peters, 2000, 2016; Torfing et al., 2011) and in part to forge partnerships with specialized organizations and networks to assist in public service delivery. These two aspects of collaboration can be related so that partnerships over time may morph into governance instruments (Donahue and Zeckhauser, 2011).

Collaboration serves several purposes. One is obviously cost-sharing, but equally important is that working with nongovernmental organizations (NGOs) and other associations gives the public bureaucracy better access to the targets of the service. For instance, public officials may find it difficult to reach groups such as immigrant communities, people with disabilities or HIV-AIDS positive, but working with organizations and networks representing these groups will help the public service design and deliver programs more efficiently and effectively than had they tried to do it on their own.

We will delve into these issues in detail later in this book. For now, we note that together with the modernization of the public bureaucracy, the growing importance of collaborating with societal actors is perhaps the most important development in public administration. Some years ago Hjern and Porter (1981) wrote that the single lonely organization was dead, and that implementation would be conducted though collections of organizations, public and private. While true then, this perspective on public administration has become even more central as a series of reforms within the public sector, and changes in the private sector, bring the actors together around particular public problems.

Understanding Administrative Reform

As important as public administration is for governance, it is not surprising that several attempts have been made to reform its structure and its processes. Public administration may be a particularly apt target for reform because it is delivering public services and therefore should be managed for efficiency and effectiveness – along with other important values such as probity (see Chapter 2). In addition, because it is generally without direct political power, public administration can be made the scapegoat for other more fundamental failings in the public sector.

Some features of public administration also help to make it a frequent target for reform initiatives. The public image of the bureaucracy is often divided between two negative conceptions of what these organizations are like. The first view is that the bureaucracy is a Leviathan attempting to take over the rest of government and to subvert democratic rule. The second view is that the bureaucracy is inept and almost inherently inefficient and therefore requires the injection of good management from the private sector. The large-scale reforms associated with NPM were very much in this vein of addressing inefficiencies and perceived incompetence.

Although administrative reform has been ubiquitous, it has been manifested in a number of different ways in different countries (see Peters, 2001). Less developed countries, for example, are often engaged in very basic types of reform attempting to establish an effective administrative system. More developed countries have been engaged in somewhat different styles of reform, but often with the same general purposes of creating more effective and legitimate governments. And the diffusion of the ideas of NPM through organizations such as the World Bank has meant that some very similar ideas may be implemented, regardless of the nature of the administrative system. Finally, administrative reform has not been confined to any particular policy area or level of government. That said, the reforms have often been more successful at lower levels of government, in part because of their smaller size makes implementation and monitoring easier. Likewise, some central policy areas such as healthcare have been targets of reform more often than have many other sectors that are less expensive and less visible to the public. But regardless of the policy area or level of government, administrative reform continues to be a major activity in the public sector.

Summary

This chapter has pointed to a number of important roles for public administration in governance. The remainder of this book will address these underlying issues in governance, using a series of dichotomies that produce tensions within the public sector. These dichotomies each expose fundamental questions about governing, and also present the designers and reformers of the public sector with difficult choices. Each side of a dichotomy not only has some virtues but also presents potential difficulties in administration and governance.

2

Management and Administration

The first dichotomy we will discuss in this book is between public administration and public management. As was pointed out in Chapter 1, we see public management as embedded in public administration. Therefore, the dichotomy we will address in this chapter refers to the tensions between those two different perspectives – management versus administration – on fundamental issues related to the bureaucracy. These will include its relationship to elected officials and its clients, and the values and norms that are prioritized in the two perspectives. These differences are most distinct and pertinent when we confront conventional public administration with New Public Management (NPM) which is the currently dominant version of public management thinking and a neo-Weberian philosophy of public service. Thus, our discussion about public management is mainly related to NPM, although we will also trace the history of the public management school of thought.

This chapter will look more closely at the shift from public administration to public management in the scholarly literature and also in the debate among politicians and civil servants. We first discuss the different meanings and consequences of the shift from public administration to public management. After that, and as a way of further clarifying what the concepts of public administration and public management stand for, we will stylize the two different approaches to the public sector and its organizations. We then conclude the chapter by discussing whether there is today some degree of convergence between the two approaches and, if so, what that position means and the degree to which neo-Weberianism deviates from those two approaches.

The 1980s witnessed a subtle but significant change in the literature and debate on public sector reform among scholars and practitioners. 'Public administration' became used less, and was gradually marginalized while 'public management' gained rapid recognition and diffusion. Numerous books and articles were published, often in new journals devoted specifically to the study of public management (Hood, 1991; D. Osborne and Gaebler, 1993; Christensen and Laegreid, 2011a). Public administration schools and programs were renamed and new degrees were created. In an astonishingly brief period of time public administration had become a phenomenon of the past while public management was the *au courant* way to talk and write about the public bureaucracy.

Was this mainly a matter of change in jargon, an 'old wine in new bottles' process, or did the replacement of public administration with public management signify a substantive change in focus, theory and discourse? This chapter will argue the latter position. Not only do management and administration denote different organizational functions and roles, but the two concepts also denote different theoretical and normative lenses through which the public bureaucracy is observed. Management and administration highlight different organizational roles within the public service just as they prioritize different goals and norms. The almost unilateral attention to public management issues at the expense of public administration has thus meant that some empirical and normative aspects of the public service have been prioritized over others, and that indeed a discourse emphasizing efficiency and performance has taken precedence over a discourse of legality, due process and transparency.

Recently we have seen tendencies towards a convergence between the public administration and public management philosophies. The classic public administration has been found to have problems with modernizing service delivery, while costs have become a growing concern. At the same time, the public management model of administrative reform has been proven to drive fragmentation and coordination problems in the public service (see Chapter 5). Similarly, the strict focus on performance measurement has had undesirable consequences on administrative decision-making and prioritizing (Radin, 2006), and public management reform has to some extent failed to deliver on its promises of cost-cutting and customer satisfaction (Hood and Dixon, 2015). Therefore, many countries have sought to develop a model of administration that ensures responsiveness and accountability while at the same time safeguarding the gains from public management reform. Sometimes labeled 'post-NPM' or 'neo-Weberianism' (Christensen and Laegreid, 2011a; Pollitt and Bouckaert, 2011; but see Goldfinch and Wallis, 2010), this reform project has aimed at strengthening the center of the political system, ensuring that management is embedded in, and contributes to, democratic governance and, as Ramesh and his associates put it, 'rearticulating the public in public administration' (Ramesh, Araral and Wu, 2010; see also Kramer, 1999; Thomas, 1999; Halligan, 2010; Dahlström, Peters and Pierre, 2011). We will return to these issues later in this chapter.

From Public Administration to Public Management

Public administration was for long an area of academic study in its own right, devoted to the study of bureaucracies. It was, as pointed out in Chapter 1, a fragmented and eclectic field of study, drawing on several different academic disciplines, like sociology, political science, economics and organization theory.

Another fault line among public administration scholars exists between on the one hand, scholars who were mainly interested in applying theoretical arguments to the system of administration, for instance the assumption that actors are maximizing their utility, and to explore the consequences of that assumption, and on the other hand, those scholars who were primarily interested in describing the daily practice of public administration (Peters and Pierre, 2016; Pollitt, 2016).

Public management shares many of these features, drawing on largely the same disciplines as public administration and is equally torn between deductive theory and the study of administrative practice. In addition, public management is still evolving as a research field. Although 'modern' public management emerged in the 1970s and 1980s, its intellectual roots can be traced far back in time (see Hood, 2005; Noordegraaf, 2015). Although a heterogeneous field replete with potential normative tensions, public management presents itself as based in 'the scientific study of the modern state' (Lynn, 2005: 27), originally in the United States around the turn of the twentieth century. For example, Woodrow Wilson and the progressives wanted to create a more professional perspective on management in the public sector. If public administration is mainly concerned with constitutional issues, such as how public decisions are to be made, the role of the public service in relation to the political level of government, and the formal rights of citizens and clients vis-à-vis the bureaucracy, public management looks first and foremost at the management, i.e. leadership, efficiency problems, resource allocation and relationships with customers/clients.

The interesting observation as we compare the two research fields is that there is little overlap between the two. Both areas of study and practice are critical to the organization, yet given the different foci of public administration and public management there should be intellectual space to accommodate both. There are several reasons why public administration and public management have become seen as competitors in academia and among practitioners. One reason, as mentioned above, is that they focus on different aspects of public sector organization. Importantly, during the past couple of decades the issues at the heart of public management – cost-cutting, efficiency, market-based reform, etc. – have risen to prominence on the public sector reform agenda. The old POSDCORB management system (Planning, Organizing, Staffing, Directing, Coordinating, Reporting and Budgeting) was assumed to provide a template for efficient management (Gulick and Urwick, 1937). At the heart of classic public administration (see Simon, 1947) there was also concern with efficiency, albeit not in a strictly economic sense. At the same time, issues that are central to public administration – responsiveness, legality, transparency, conventional accountability, and so on – are today less at the center of attention among political and administrative leaders. These issues have had to give way to management issues.

Second, public management and public administration are related to quite different academic disciplines. Public management has its roots in economics and business management while public administration is mainly academically derived from law, political science, organization theory and sociology. These differences suggest that although the object of study is not vastly different, the two fields approach this object from distinctly different intellectual vantage points and apply different discourses to the public bureaucracy.

Third, public management gained importance and prominence during the 1980s and 1990s to some extent because it spoke more directly to the problems that were seen as the chief problems in the public sector at that time, and it advocated a novel approach to those problems. At the same time, public administration became to some extent seen as part of the problem, given its emphasis on values that did not promote efficiency, such as due process and responsiveness. Notions of 'old public administration' and 'new public management' are indicative of the erroneous idea that public bureaucracies are no longer engaged in administration but only concerned with managing. Given the ascendancy of neoliberalism to political power across the Western world during these decades, there has been growing political pressure to cut costs and increase efficiency in the public sphere. Public administration scholars and practitioners alike had very little advice to offer on these matters. Instead, management experts, often with expertise in corporate management, could respond to this demand and apply their work to the public sector.

Table 2.1 summarizes our discussions on the differences between public administration and public management. As we can see, the two research fields accord the public bureaucracy somewhat different roles and describe the organization differently.

Table 2.1   Public administration, public management and neo-Weberianism: key differences

	Public administration	**Public management**	**Neo-Weberianism**
Objectives	Legality	Efficiency	Balance
	Due process	Marketization	Political control
	Accountability	Performance	
		Customer satisfaction	
Clients	Public interest	Stakeholders	Public interest
	Citizens	Customers	Citizens
Key roles of bureaucracy	Policy advice	Service delivery	Service delivery
	Law enforcement	Contract management	Legality
	Implementation		
Relationship to political leaders	Loyalty	Autonomy	Advisors
	Responsiveness		Responsiveness
Relationship to clients	Legal security	Customer	Balancing efficiency
	Predictability	satisfaction	and legal security
Management	By command	By results	By goal setting
Source of legitimacy	Procedure	Performance	Strategic leadership

The difference between public administration and public management is thus far greater than merely focusing on different aspects of the public bureaucracy or drawing on different academic disciplines. The two disciplines essentially tell different grand stories about the public bureaucracy. Public administration departs from the political and democratic roles of the bureaucracy, defines what that perspective means for the relationships to citizens and elected officials and studies how intra-organizational processes may support or interfere with the democratic mission of the bureaucracy. Public management asks questions about how the performance of public organizations can be enhanced and how collaboration with private sector organizations or nongovernmental organizations (NGOs) can best be organized.

Neo-Weberianism has emerged in the wake of NPM and in reaction to some of the pathologies that this reform entailed (Pollitt and Bouckaert, 2011). Neo-Weberianism has, however, also been careful to preserve the positive changes that NPM brought about. We will discuss neo-Weberianism in some detail later in this chapter. For now, we should note that the overarching objective of this reform strategy has been to find the optimal balance between the values, norms and practices that were typical to the public administration model on the one hand, and the focus on efficiency and customer orientation that NPM introduced. See Table 2.1.

A key issue in shifting intellectual focus from public administration to public management was the degree of public sector specificity, that is, whether there were features of public sector organizations that set them apart from for-profit organizations or NGOs. Indeed, the import of management ideas, including internal markets and a customer focus, from the corporate sector rested on the idea that public management was essentially no different from managing private sector organizations (see Allison, 1983). The solution, often implicit, was to think of management as a 'generic' organizational function, that is, organizational leadership was the same challenge regardless of whether the organization is public or private (Peters, 2001).

To further clarify the differences between public administration and public management and what the shift from the former towards the latter has meant we will outline two stylized models. From that comparison we will be able to see more clearly the differences between the two, both in terms of their empirical organizational focus as well as the main differences between them conceptually and theoretically.

We will compare the two models and also the neo-Weberian model in more detail with regard to their perspectives and objectives on four sets of issues: normative theory, organizational structure, leadership and control; and accountability.

Public Administration

As already mentioned, we see public administration as integral to democratic governance. Indeed, this is a key point which we are pursuing throughout this book; the norms and governance tasks associated with public administration are just as salient today as they were 25 or 50 years ago. Without the public bureaucracy the elected government would not be able to implement its decisions and the large number of regulations that it issues would not be enforced. The specific organizational tasks that are associated with the bureaucracy's role in governance may or may not lend themselves to objectives such as efficiency or performance, but then again it was not created with these objectives in mind.

Normative theory

From Max Weber and Woodrow Wilson onwards, public administration as a field of academic study has elaborated the normative foundation of public administration. The tension between political loyalty and responsiveness on the one hand and legality and due process on the other has been a main theme in this debate. If the former norms are prioritized, there is a risk of excessive political control of the bureaucracy, which will jeopardize legality and equal treatment and, in the longer run, institutional trust. If, however, the values related to the internal processes in the public bureaucracy are emphasized, we may end up with a public administration that is mainly self-serving and aloof to the interests of both elected officials and the citizens. Different countries have sought to find the 'sweet spot' between these two norms and objectives, with the answers based on different political cultures and different challenges to governance.

The normative theory of public administration also includes an understanding of the role of intra-organizational processes of self-selection and socialization. According to this perspective, the public bureaucracy as an organization carries values and norms about the ethics of public service. These values are constantly reproduced within the organization, and new employees are taught what it means to be a public servant and how public employment differs from working in a private organization. As we discussed in the previous chapter, these values have proven to be quite resilient despite decades of NPM reform (John and Johnson, 2008). Thus, in this model, a public bureaucracy is to a large extent shaped by these deeply entrenched norms about the pursuit of the public interest, loyalty to elected office, and the implementation of legality and due process.

Organizational structure

Given the significance of organizational behavior and norms, public administration emphasizes structure, partly because it is structure that defines roles and the relationship between those roles, and partly because structure defines the interfaces with citizens and the elected level of government. Central to these ideas are beliefs about permanency and continuity, hierarchy, rationality and accountability. Clients' trust in a bureaucracy is to some extent dependent on a high degree of continuity, so that the client recognizes the institution and knows what services it delivers.

The Weberian model of bureaucracy, which has informed administrative development in a large number of countries, emerged in the early twentieth century. At that time, there was less concern with developing the human capital in public organizations and more emphasis on uniformity in administrative behavior. To that effect, bureaucracies were structured so as to minimize individual discretion – both for the manager and for the street-level bureaucrats. More recently there has been a growing understanding that some degree of bureaucratic discretion is not dysfunctional to the organization but, indeed, often necessary to deliver targeted and effective public service (Lipsky, 1980; Hupe, Hill and Buffat, 2015).

Leadership and control

In the public administration model, leadership is impersonal and strictly tied to office. The top administrative leadership is accountable to the political leaders. Furthermore, leadership and control in this stylized model is a fairly simple exercise as hierarchy ensures compliance with orders and instructions. There is a firm distinction between political and administrative leadership, where the latter is accountable to the former. Elected officials are accountable to the electorate in democratic regimes, thus legitimating their policy choices and their control over the bureaucracy.

Leadership in public administration has a vertical and a horizontal dimension. The vertical dimension highlights the line command systems that are typical to hierarchical organizations. The horizontal dimension of leadership is arguably as important as vertical leadership in terms of how it defines the tasks and modus operandi of public servants. Horizontal leadership is related to peer, professional guidance and coordination in administrative decision-making. Professionalism is a defining feature of public administration. Professional groups in the public service, for instance teachers, police officers, social workers and medical doctors, are socialized into norms about proper professional conduct. As Brehm and Gates point out, 'bureaucracies have cultures, where workers learn from one another about appropriate behavior' (1997: 48). Most tasks and work stations in the public service require some degree of professional skills, and in order to ensure uniformity professionals meet to discuss how different types of cases should be addressed.

Thus, leadership and control in the public administration model is exercised along different dimensions. While the organizational leadership often stresses the importance of professional deliberation, there can easily emerge tensions between organizational and professional leadership. Typically, the views held by professionals in the public administration about what constitutes good public service may often strike the organizational leadership as too costly.

Accountability

The public administration perspective recognizes that public institutions and servants exercise tremendous power over society and its citizens. These powers are ultimately delegated from elected officials and must therefore be held to close legal and democratic account. All offices in the public bureaucracy must have a distinct place in the hierarchical chain of command, which also facilitates accountability. Thus, in this framework, accountability is mainly legal; it refers to accountability in cases of malfeasance in or abuse of public office. There is also accountability in cases of legal but inappropriate behavior among public servants, which is exercised, for instance, when the public servant seeks promotion.

In addition to the legal accountability in public administration, there is also a strong strand of political accountability. Public administrators are, through the chain of hierarchy described above, ultimately accountable to their political masters in the executive, and also to the legislature. This relationship may be less clear in presidentialist systems with a separation of powers, but the political connection remains important in those cases. In presidentialist systems public administrators have to serve two sets of political leaders. Their day-to-day superiors are in the executive branch, but they must also answer to the legislature, especially when the legislature has well-developed mechanisms for oversight. Perhaps most importantly public organizations must depend on the legislature for their budgets, and the power of the purse is a crucial source of legislative power over the bureaucracy.

Public Management

The version of public management in the 1980s and 1990s – the New Public Management – prioritized a different set of objectives for the public sector. The key problems in the public sector, according to this approach, were low efficiency, low effectiveness, high costs, lack of customer orientation, an inefficient budget-making process coupled with limited knowledge or data about public spending and its outcomes, and detailed political control that stifled entrepreneurship in the public sector. The public management school argued that these problems were systemic, that is, they were directly related to the structure, the leadership and the management processes of the public sector (Hood, 1991). Politicians, it was suggested, are not good organizational managers; they often lack education and experience in management and are likely to focus more on their re-election than on managing public organizations. A key argument, against this background, was to empower the managers, 'let the managers manage', as the NPM advocates put it (D. Osborne and Gaebler, 1993), and to define the role of elected officials as setting long-term goals for service delivery. Managing organizations and contracts was believed to be an essentially similar challenge in the public and private sectors, and the public sector would learn a lot by emulating private sector management.

Thus, the public management perspective challenged the public administration model on almost all major themes. As we will see, public management either highlights issues that are of little concern to the public administration model or emphasizes arrangements that are at odds with public management. This neoliberal perspective on the state and the public sector, however, does not preclude a strictly academic approach to public service. Public management scholars have investigated principal–agent problems in service delivery (Entwistle and Martin, 2005), contract management issues (T. L. Brown, Potoski and van Slyke, 2006), efficiency problems in public sector organizations (Borghe, Falch and Tovmo, 2008), accountability problems (Hood, 1991; Barberis, 1998), issues related to shared responsibility in service delivery (Ansell and Gash, 2007; Donahue and Zeckhauser, 2011), and so on.

Normative theory

If the public administration perspective draws on sociological organization theory and political science, public management departs from economic theory. The public management focus on efficiency, cost-cutting and competition in service delivery is in many ways reflective of a distinctly different perspective on the state and collective action compared with that which sustains public administration (Bresser-Pereira, 2004). In the public management model, the state has limited inherent value. Its role is to solve collective action problems, enforce regulation and to provide public and collective goods. This is, however, not to say that public management ignores the contributions to governance that the public bureaucracy delivers. On the contrary; this perspective argues that those roles are performed better by improving the management of public organizations.

In some ways the distinctive feature of the public management perspective in terms of normative theory is not so much that it advocates a particular set of norms and values for the public sector, but more its rejection of the norms that the public administration school associates with the state (see Pollitt, 1993; Milward et al., 2016). This 'generic' and instrumental view of public institutions in and of itself represents a clear break with the conventional public administration perspective. For public management scholars, the main norms and objectives related to the public sector are concerned with economic factors, both in terms of internal resource allocation and the public sector's regulation of markets.

Organizational structure

One of main areas of interest for the emerging public management school was the organizational structure of the public sector which it believed harbored several causes of low efficiency and poor management. Perhaps the main issue in this respect was the tendency in most countries to have the 'policy' and 'operations' functions executed by the same organization. The public management perspective argued that these two functions should be divided between departments in charge of policy and autonomous, executive agencies which should be in charge of the operational element of the process (Pollitt, 1990; Pollitt and Talbot, 2004; Pollitt et al., 2005). This division would assist the development of more professional managers who should be accorded extensive autonomy in relationship to the political level of government

The agencification of government has been one the most important legacies of the managerial approach to the public sector. Even after governments have walked away from some of the other aspects of managerialism this structural feature has persisted (Verhoest et al., 2012). This has been in part because it allows an organization to focus directly on a particular policy area, and it also to some extent facilitates accountability.

Another central theme in the public management discourse was that the public sector should not have to deliver all public services itself. Given the focus on outcomes, it was argued that the bureaucracy should use contractors and competitive tendering in public service delivery. This strategy had some implications on the structure of the public service; conventional service delivery units can be scaled back while organizations devoted to contract management, tendering and procurements need to be developed (Hall, 2011).

Leadership and control

As mentioned, public management aims at professionalizing management in public sector organizations in order to boost efficiency. Certainly, elected officials play critical roles as nominal leaders of public organizations but given the focus on public management on service production and delivery those roles are not central to the theory. Indeed, in more extreme models of public management such as the 'public value' model, the elected officials are referred to as 'the authorizing environment' (Moore, 1995). Transferring control from politicians to managers is essential to the public management model. This is not least the case because it increases the similarities between public and private organizations and therefore makes the incorporation of corporate management models into the public sector easier.

If peer, collegial deliberation is an important part of leadership and control in the public administration model, the public management model draws mainly on external performance measurement and evaluation. Public managers are on the whole rather quiet on the role of organizational norms and values as guides for administrative behavior. Instead their focus is on the quality of public services and client (or customer) satisfaction with those services.

However, one of the key roles of organizational leaders is to create and nurture an organizational culture that reproduces the norms and values that make up the identity and mission of the organization. Altering organizational culture is one of the biggest challenges facing the leaders of any organization; it is, for instance, interesting to note the resilience of conventional public ethos in the British public service despite decades of public management reform (John and Johnson, 2008). The critical point here is that fostering an organizational culture is an essential managerial tool and public organizations do have a responsibility to pursue the public interest alongside managerial objectives.

Accountability

The public management objective to shift significant organizational control from elected officials to managers could potentially have major ramifications on the accountability of public service delivery. While the conventional leadership will be exercising less control over the mid- and lower levels of the organization, there will be an increased external evaluation of the organization's performance through performance measurement and feedback from its customers. Somewhat paradoxically, perhaps, the public management perspective thus claims to offer a more effective accountability than the conventional public administration can present. Performance measurement provides detailed data on how public resources were spent, and customer choice and feedback gives information on client satisfaction with the public services. Furthermore, these accountability mechanisms identify underperforming service providers more or less instantaneously and not, as the public administration model can offer, through a report a year or so after delivery (Bouckaert and Halligan, 2008).

In sum, the public management seeks to strengthen accountability by redefining it from a 'relationship between an actor and a forum' (Bovens, 2007: 450) where the actor's behavior is assessed, to a more indirect evaluation of performance and the degree to which recipients of services approve of the quality of those services. The relationship with the political environment, and with law, becomes somewhat attenuated within this conception of accountability.

Neo-Weberianism

We mentioned earlier that although public management and public administration focus on public organizations they highlight rather different aspects of those organizations. Both identify critically important aspects of the public bureaucracy in terms of how it relates to citizens and to the political level of government and how it operates and is organized. There are however also important differences between the two approaches, not least in their conceptualization of the state and the market and the broader discourse of market vs. collective action.

Administrative reform has been aptly described by the late Peter Aucoin as a pendulum movement where radically different ideas are implemented to solve problems while at the same time engendering new problems (Simon, 1947; Aucoin, 1990). If we apply that metaphor to the present discussion it would seem as if the New Public Management reform campaign addressed problems in the public bureaucracy related to inefficiency, organizational rigidity and a lack of customer orientation. In so doing, however, it also created or exacerbated problems of fragmentation, decreasing central and political control, and accountability.

Normative Theory

The past decade or so has seen a search for middle ground in many countries between ensuring the core values associated with the public administration perspective on the one hand while maintaining the gains in efficiency, fiscal and budgetary control, and client attention generated by public management control on the other (Christensen and Laegreid, 2011a; Pollitt and Bouckaert, 2011). In an assessment of administrative reform in Australia, John Halligan notes that 'management's place is relatively secure' (2010: 154), although there is increasing pressure towards aligning management with governance objectives (see below).

Finding the optimal balance between the two aspects of the public bureaucracy is certainly not an easy task. This section will highlight some of the key features of this convergence between the two approaches. As we go through these features we need to remind ourselves that there is extensive variation among different countries in terms of the extent of NPM reform. Much of this variation relates to administrative tradition and the legacy of a legalistic *Rechtsstaat* public administration emphasizing 'a public interest' and management model of administration (Knill, 1999; Painter and Peters, 2010; Pierre, 2011; Pollitt and Bouckaert, 2011). As a general pattern, the Anglo-American countries were the first to adopt market-based reform in different guises.

The continental European and Scandinavian countries and also several Asian countries have a public bureaucracy which is steeped in a legalistic tradition, and these countries were initially much less willing to consider such reform. Over time, however, we can see extensive public management reform also in these systems (Painter and Peters, 2010; Pollitt and Bouckaert, 2011).

Organizational structure

The main structural component of public management reform has been the split of conventional ministries into departments and autonomous executive agencies. This reform has been found to entail severe coordination problems; departments lack information about agencies' actions and have problems steering the agencies. This has in turn required strengthening coordination mechanisms within the center of government (Bouckaert, Peters and Verhoest, 2010) as the pendulum swings somewhat back toward control.

Organizational and institutional change tends to be slow, incremental processes and institutions have many times proven quite resilient. They do, however, change. In 2001, Nick Manning observed that 'most government functions remain performed by vertically integrated bureaucracies functioning pretty much as Weber might have intended' (2001: 300). This is still the case in some countries, although the vast majority of countries today have less vertically integrated bureaucracies, which is the problem that neo-Weberianism seeks to address by strengthening the political center and bring the executive agencies closer to the policy-making institutions.

Another component of neo-Weberian administrative reform is less concerned with organizational structure but more with the normative framework of the public bureaucracy. We mentioned earlier that the market-based normative foundation of public management as it emerged in the 1980s and 1990s puts it in contrast with the normative framework of the public administration perspective, which emphasizes legality, due process, equal treatment, meritocracy, transparency and accountability. How do you define a middle ground between these two different sets of norms? How do you weigh efficiency against legal security, or customer satisfaction against equal treatment? We find very little evidence that the neo-Weberian reform has explicitly addressed these complex tradeoffs. Instead, the pattern seems to be what Streeck and Thelen and their associates refer to as 'layering' (2009; see also Halligan, 2010); norms and rules associated with public management were simply placed in the same organizational context. As a result, it appears as if it has been largely up to the individual public servant to try to make sense of the apparent inconsistency between the conventional and the new norms and ideas about how to perform the role of a public servant.

Further along this theme, neo-Weberianism also includes a rearticulation of the unique features of the state: 'the public in public administration' (Kramer, 1999; Thomas 1999; Ramesh, Araral and Wu, 2010). In our analysis, this means bringing back some of the features and values of the conventional public administration model that were either explicitly downplayed during the NPM reform or simply ignored and replaced with (or 'layered' under) a norm derived from the public management framework. 'The public' in public administration relates to rules defining proper conduct in relationship to clients, to politicians and in internal deliberations such as transparency, legality, accountability and equal treatment. 'The public' also emphasizes that the bureaucracy's key role is to implement decisions made by elected politicians.

Leadership and control

We discussed earlier how public management reform, in the spirit of separating policy and operations, redefined leadership and control in the public bureaucracy by empowering the managers of the organization and leaving only goal-setting to the elected officials. This reform made sense from the point of view of injecting (more) professional management in the public sector to boost efficiency. Over time, however, it also became clear to the political leadership that this reform had serious downsides; by surrendering control to managers, the elected officials had effectively cut off the branch they were sitting on. As a result they found themselves left with few levers to control or lead the bureaucracy. At the same time, the growing lack of coordination made it increasingly difficult to address urgent issues that cut across sectoral and jurisdictional boundaries, such as climate change, domestic security and immigration.

Furthermore, public management reform also facilitated demand-driven organizational decision-making, whereby customer preferences and quality assessments should influence public service budget allocations. These reforms significantly weakened the position of elected officials in their relationship to the public bureaucracy. The reform also drove fragmentation in the public sector by creating agencies at some length from government departments and 'hybrid organizations' for service delivery that were even more challenging to control from the center.

Rearticulating hierarchy and political leadership is central to neo-Weberianism as a means of bringing back a clear chain of command and accountability (see below) and to increase vertical coordination (Dahlström, Peters and Pierre, 2011). This also meant a stronger emphasis on rules, again without necessarily downplaying performance targets. Thus, if the slogan of NPM reform was 'let the managers manage' (D. Osborne and Gaebler, 1993), neo-Weberian reform advocates prefer 'make the managers manage', that is, rearticulate the line command processes in public organizations (Norman, 2001).

Finally, neo-Weberianism emphasizes the growing importance of strategic leadership. The political center is challenged both domestically and internationally by strong political and economic developments. At the same time, coercive policies and regulations are today believed to be less efficient compared with a few decades ago; the preferred mode of shaping social behavior today is more to encourage the desired behavior than to punish less desired behavior. Thus, government today has less regulatory clout and fewer financial resources to back its regulation compared with a few decades ago. All of this suggests that political leadership has to be selective in which issues it decides to put on the agenda and to build coalitions with key societal partners to facilitate smooth implementation of its policies and service delivery.

Accountability

NPM reform has been criticized for complicating accountability. The problem is perhaps not first and foremost that there is no accountability, but rather that it is now to some extent the wrong actors who are accountable. As Johan P. Olsen notes, 'political leaders have (re)discovered that they are blamed even when authority is decentralized and that "technical issues" often have significant political implications' (2008: 24). This insight may well have spurred those political leaders to reclaim some of the control that had been decentralized to the managers of public organizations. As constitutional theory reminds us, power and responsibility must never be separated, but this has to some extent been the outcome of the empowerment of managers and the institutional split of ministries into departments and executive agencies.

At the same time, public management reform opened up a new channel of direct accountability through customer evaluation and choice which is not likely to be abolished. Combining that type of accountability with conventional, formal–legal accountability means blending upwards and downwards communication in the bureaucracy – indeed, blending two philosophies of public administration – which poses a major challenge (Kettl, 1997).

Concluding Discussion: Towards Convergence

We can now return to the question about what the new mix looks like. How salient are the ideals and norms emphasized by public administration and public management today? There are clear patterns of some degree of convergence or rediscovery of Weberian values (Olsen, 2006). In Norway, Christensen and Laegreid note 'traditional Weberian features, NPM features, and post-NPM features are blended in a complex combination' (2008: 20). Public management reform scholars acknowledge that the overall philosophy of management in the public sector is not likely to be replaced by the previous command and control systems, although management will become more embedded in governance than has previously been the case. This development is clearly underway in Australia and New Zealand (Halligan, 2010). In Sweden, a country that introduced NPM with some reluctance, there is now political movement to strengthen the professions in the public sector and to reduce performance management and marketization of public services. It is safe to say that many countries are currently struggling to integrate public management with the governance role of the public bureaucracy. The specific nature of such a convergence is probably related to the reform trajectory of the country. Jurisdictions with a strong legalistic tradition are likely to emphasize those aspects of public administration whereas national contexts where other values, such as efficiency and management are strong tend to prioritize those features of administration.

Embedding management in governance is important, not just for the sake of accountability or for ensuring that politicians are in control of the system they are elected to lead. Public administration is where citizens encounter the state on a daily basis and where their trust in government is either built or eroded, depending on the quality of the treatment they receive and the process through which those services are determined. The state, and indeed democracy, is a system of rules just as much as a forum for political discourse, and it is the bureaucracy that ensures that those rules are upheld. Public management, for all its virtues, is more concerned with other aspects of public service – its costs, its appropriateness and relevance to customers, and so on. These aspects of public service are certainly important but they are, or should be, embedded in the system of rules that define the framework for democratic government.

The reassertion of the center that has been happening in numerous countries across the world during the past decade (Dahlström, Peters and Pierre, 2011) should be seen as a strategy to reintegrate the bureaucracy with democratic governance. In that process we see some degree of convergence between the public administration and public management perspectives. We began this chapter by going over the many differences between those two perspectives. It is clear that convergence between the two may in some cases produce an outcome that is typical of neither. We may well be underway towards a new public administration that draws on public management objectives but in an organization embedded in governance.

3

Bureaucrats Versus Service Providers: Personnel in the Public Sector

In the study of public administration, organizations, or even government as a whole, are often anthropomorphized. Newspapers, media personalities, and even scholars, will talk about the 'Ministry of X making a decision', or say that 'the government undertook a new policy initiative'. That language is a convenient way to cope with the complexities of decision-making in the public sector, but ignores the important reality that it is individuals, or groups of individuals, who are making those decisions. To understand government, and the public bureaucracy within government, we need to understand the people who work in government. In particular, we need to understand how public employees define their jobs as parts of governing, and why they have chosen to work in the public sector.

We also need to understand that although public employees are often denigrated as 'shirkers' (Brehm and Gates, 1997) and as incompetent, or alternatively as power-mad empire builders, they are generally no more or less competent, or motivated, than their counterparts in the private sector. Unlike their counterparts in the private sector, however, they often express a strong desire for public service and seek opportunities to use their talents for developing and administering public services. Rather than being shirkers, many are highly motivated and find themselves frustrated by the structure and the rules of the 'bureaucracy' within which they perform their tasks.

People as The Actors in Public Administration

Public employees are the primary actors in governing. The public sector employs a wide range of actors to deliver its services and to help make public policy.

The upper echelons of public organizations are generally populated by individuals with university education and with substantial levels of experience, increasingly in both the public and private sectors. There are also numerous professionals – doctors, nurses, teachers, accountants, etc. – who work within government. And at the lower levels of government a number of white-collar (clerks, data technicians) and blue-collar (bus drivers, sanitation workers) employees provide essential services.

Although we talk rather easily about public employees, drawing the boundary of when someone is a public employee or not can be difficult. Some members of the public administration such as upper-echelon civil servants in a ministry or a school teacher in a public school are clearly part of the public sector. However, how do we count individuals who are working in a charter school, or some other type of school that is organized as a private entity but paid for by public money? And how do we count employees of defense contractors for whom government is a monopsonistic purchaser of their products? In the latter two cases, the position for the individual might not exist without the public budget but at the same time their organizations are generally considered to be in the private sector.

Several tests can be used to determine whom we should count as being a public employee. First, public employees tend to be hired and managed through a civil service system of some sort. That said, an increasing number of public employees are hired on individual contracts and are not controlled through a general set of formal rules. Second, we can determine where the funds to pay the salaries of these individuals come from, and to the extent that the money is public then perhaps they are public employees. Yet a third test is whether the actions of these individuals are controlled through instruments such as freedom of information laws and codes of ethics for the public sector.

Assuming that we can determine who is and who is not really a public employee, we need also to be careful not to assume that those public employees who are most important for both the government and society are those occupying the 'decision-making positions' at the top of public organizations. While those upper-echelon positions are indeed important, the people at the bottom of public organizations are also crucial actors in governing their societies. The policeman or policewoman on the beat, the school teacher, the clerk in the civil registry and all the other 'street-level bureaucrats' (Meyers and Nielsen, 2012) play major roles for the public sector. These are difficult positions that require decision-making just as do the positions at the apex of the administrative hierarchies (Tummers et al., 2015).

In some ways, street-level bureaucrats are the most important elements of public administration (see Hupe, Hill and Buffat, 2015), at least for the average citizen. They are the elements of the state with whom the average citizen interacts on an almost daily basis, and hence the decisions made by these lower-level officials are the ones that matter for the citizens. The actions of these lower-echelon officials are controlled in part by law and rules of the organization, however, they have a good deal of discretion (Lundqvist, 1980; Hupe, 2013) and there is a huge body of evidence that they exercise that discretion as they administer programs.

As well as the substantive decisions made by the lower echelons of public administration, the manner in which they treat the citizens is also important for shaping how citizens think of their government. Are these officials rude? Are they attentive to the needs of their clients? Do they demonstrate any empathy with the lives of ordinary citizens? The good news is that most available evidence is that citizens generally feel that they are treated at least as well by public employees as they are by the employees of large private organizations. The bad news, however, is that they tend to say that, in general, services provided by the public sector are not as good as those supplied by the private sector. Also, some interactions between the public sector and citizens the police and African-Americans for example – may be less positive.

Thus, the public sector should not be seen as being inhabited by a group of stereotypical 'paper pushers', but rather as being a complex set of organizations requiring a huge range of skills from an equally broad range of people. Those skills range from being a skilled surgeon in a public hospital to being a skilled sniper on a battlefield to being a janitor in a public building. What matters is that all of these public employees make their own contribution to the delivery of important public services.

To help understand how public employees do their jobs and contribute to the fulfillment of public policy goals, we are developing two alternative models of the roles of these officials. These are to some extent ideal type models of the roles that will be played by members of the public administration.[1] As such these two models are primarily intellectual tools to assist in understanding real-world cases, rather than descriptions of those realities.

In this chapter we will be focusing on the middle and lower levels of the public administration. We will reserve the discussion about the upper echelons of administration for Chapters (4 and 6), which cover the political and policy-making roles of administration. Some of the same dimensions of behavior discussed here are also relevant for those higher-level officials, but a number of other issues about their decision-making need to be discussed separately. This is especially so because higher-level officials rarely are involved in direct delivery of services to the public; rather they work in the center of government, making decisions about more general issues.

Bureaucrats as The Stereotype and as Reality

Just as bureaucracy can be a stereotype for the structure of public administration, the individuals who inhabit those structures may be stereotyped as 'bureaucrats'. Just as the term bureaucracy is often used as a pejorative for the structures, calling a public employee a bureaucrat is not usually intended to compliment that individual. That said, acting as a bureaucrat in the stricter denotative sense of the term does have a number of positive features that citizens

---

[1]The original model of bureaucracy developed by Weber was an ideal type, assuming that no real world administrative system would manifest all the criteria contained in the model. The model still constitutes a useful intellectual model against which to compare real-world administrative systems.

who come into contact with those bureaucrats should appreciate. Citizens may, in fact, consider some aspects of the bureaucratic model of behavior as essential for proper public administration.

The most central aspect of bureaucratic behavior in public office is that the bureaucrat applies the law to individual cases (see Derlien, 1999). Max Weber's model of bureaucracy was developed in response to the patrimonial administration of his time and the high levels of discretion that could be exercised by public employees. In that style of administration, citizens had few if any rights vis-à-vis the administration and could not even be sure of why and how decisions were being made, or indeed if a decision was going to be made. The bureaucratic model of administration is more transparent, with defined rights and obligations, and the use of files, so that the progress of a case through the administrative process can be tracked.

The use of law and rules also meant that universalistic criteria were applied to cases. The public administrator was deemed to act *sine irae ac studio* (without anger or bias) when making decisions and to treat all citizens equally. This standard is in marked contrast to administrative systems that even in the twenty-first century may make decisions based at least in part on ethnicity, religion, gender or political affiliations of the citizen.[2] Again, this equal treatment through the bureaucratic model of administrative behavior is expected by citizens in democratic societies as a fundamental right of citizenship.

A third important element of the bureaucratic model of public employment is that public employment should be a career and a full-time occupation. This professional model of public employment is in contrast to the more casual approach to these positions that characterized employment at the time that Weber wrote, and which also characterizes public employment in many contemporary political systems. In fact, part of the reform of personnel systems in the vein of the New Public Management (NPM) has been to deinstitutionalize public employment and to base it more on short-term contracts rather than on a more permanent civil service system (Laegreid and Christensen, 2013).

While the bureaucratic model had, and has, several virtues it also has some real difficulties for citizens and for the state. The first is that while rules can constrain the discretion of public employees, those laws and rules can also be used to protect the public employee. If an individual civil servant is expected to follow the rules, then those rules can also become a protection for those employees. If the employee follows the rules then he or she is by definition correct, no matter what may happen to the citizen. Only when the public employee exercises his or her discretion do they risk being sanctioned.

These rules also become the foundation for the (in)famous 'red tape' in bureaucracy (Kaufman, 1977; Bozeman, 2010). Government organizations develop rules not only to clarify procedures, and perhaps to protect the rights of citizens, but also to provide some protection for the members of the

---

[2]The behavior of Kim Davis, the county clerk of Rowan County, Kentucky, who applied her own principles in denying marriage licenses to same sex couples rather than the law is an obvious example.

organizations. If the member of the organization follows all the rules, as torturous as they may be at times, then he or she cannot be faulted as an administrator – as a bureaucrat. This means that in the view of many citizens decisions may be made slowly — but they will be made properly and legally (and safely for the individuals making the decision).

Even when all the rules are followed, however, the lower-echelon official may feel uncertain about his or her capacity to make a decision and may 'pass the buck' to a higher level of the officialdom.[3] Not making a decision is rarely threatening to an employee, whether public or private. The procedures can only specify the steps necessary to make the decision but they may not be sufficiently detailed to provide answers to all the questions that may arise. When those awkward cases arise, the decision is often transferred higher and higher within the organization.

Finally, the perhaps ultimate, and paradoxical, negative consequence of the legalism and formality inherent in the bureaucratic model is that the public sector will treat all cases as the same. While this universalism is in some ways a virtue (see above), it also can mean that government organizations appear unresponsive to their clients and to the citizenry as a whole. Citizens may not only want equality, but they may also want the special features of their own claims considered by government. Thus, responsibility to law as a virtue for government can be seen as trumping another important virtue in government – responsiveness.

Service Providers as Another Reality

Another way to think about the role of public personnel is as service providers for the public. In this conception of their role, public employees are less bound by legal constraints and more focused on the role of being a public *servant*. The primary responsibility of the public employee in this conception of their position in governing is to ensure that citizens receive the programs and benefits they are entitled to and do so as effectively as possible. More than pushing paper in an office, this conception of the public employee is a more active one, attempting to ensure that services are delivered.

The 'street-level bureaucrat' is perhaps the epitome of this conception of the public employee. The extensive literature on this group of employees emphasizes their direct contacts with citizens and their capacity to make decisions about eligibility for benefits, or the granting of licenses, or whether someone is arrested or not (see Smith, 2012). That direct contact with citizens enables them to exercise some discretion about individual cases and also to provide other forms of support for their clients. Indeed, in some of the literature on street-level bureaucrats the argument has been that these officials are too solicitous toward their client and do not impose the law in ways that would benefit their other clients – the public at large as taxpayers.

The role of service providers is especially apt for professionals who work within the public sector, such as doctors, nurses, and teachers. One standard

---

[3]The origins of this term are uncertain, but it is often associated with President Harry S. Truman, who had a sign 'The buck stops here' on his desk in the Oval Office.

sociological definition of a professional is that they will put the interests of their clients ahead of their own (Freidson, 1986). Thus, these professionals will tend to make decisions that advantage their clients rather than protecting the organization. That said, nonprofessional public employees may behave in the same way towards their clients. That behavior may be as simple as a bus driver stopping for a passenger who is obviously hurrying to get to the next bus stop.

While much of the literature on the service provider conception of the public servant emphasizes the positive aspects of this role for public employees, there can be a much darker side as well. In a classic study of social workers in the United States, Piven and Cloward (1993; see also Soss, Fording and Schram, 2011) argue that these employees 'regulate the poor' and impose rather harsh regimens on citizens seeking public assistance. Likewise, teachers may use their discretion to differentially punish students of color, and males more than females. And the police in any number of societies are accused of using excessive force in making arrests. The list might go on but if public employees are not to be bound closely by law or other means of enforcing accountability, there is the danger that the discretion will be abused (see Lipsky, 1980, on coping behavior).

This exercise of discretion raises a more general point that universalistic standards for treatment of citizens may not be applied to all citizens, and that some individuals may be advantaged and others disadvantaged by the discretion. Citizens always want themselves to be treated specially and to have all the details of their case considered carefully, while they may be happy to have everyone else treated in a legalistic, bureaucratic manner. The more personal style of providing services to the public may enhance the feelings of efficacy among some citizens but risks undermining uniformity for all citizens. The loss of uniformity and the increase in discretion may therefore provide distinct advantages for some segments of the population but not for others.

Finding a Balance Between Responsibility and Responsiveness

The two ideal type models of public employees developed above are both valuable ways of thinking about the role of public sector personnel, and some aspects of both also are found in the real world of government. The question is not necessarily choosing one or the other but rather finding some balance between the two. As already noted, both of these approaches to public personnel not only have important virtues, but they both also have significant deficiencies. Therefore, the task for designers of public programs and for managers within the public sector is to find the appropriate mix of attributes in order to be effective in governing. These two models can also be seen as representing two alternative approaches to the accountability of public administration. On the one hand, the bureaucratic model emphasizes accountability through legal responsibility. On the other hand, the service delivery model emphasizes accountability through responsibility to the clients of the programs.

The political and administrative culture of a country will influence the appropriate mix of bureaucratic and service delivery orientations in the public service (see Damaska, 1986). Legalistic political systems, such as those of Germany, are more supportive of the bureaucratic format for public employment than are others such as the Anglo-Saxon systems that focus more on management than law in defining appropriate bureaucratic behavior (Peters, forthcoming). Public administrators in the Anglo-Saxon systems must still comply with basic legal constraints on their behavior, but they may be more willing to focus on the performance of the system and the services being delivered than are public employees in the *Rechtsstaat* systems in Europe.

The nature of the policy being administered can also affect the extent to which bureaucratic models are being applied. Policy areas such as policing and revenue collection that have a strong legal foundation and which involve the basic rights and obligations of citizens, are more appropriately administered in a formal, bureaucratic manner. On the other hand, social, health and educational programs may be better administered using greater discretion on the part of the service providers. There is also some evidence that administered regulatory programs is more effective if the regulators are able to utilize their discretion in enforcing laws (Lundqvist, 1980; Christensen and Laegreid, 2006).

Managing Public Personnel: The Civil Service and its Alternatives

The conventional means of managing public personnel has been to use a merit system based on uniform pay and grading, tenure and firm hierarchies. These merit principles are typically enshrined in civil service systems that create and manage personnel systems that grade positions and individuals and attempt to match the two. That matching is based largely on performance on uniform tests, with program managers having limited discretion in choosing individuals for available positions. Furthermore, promotions and movement up an internal salary scale tends to be determined by seniority rather than by attempts to assess the performance levels of the individual employees.

While the civil service has been a standard instrument for managing personnel for some decades, it also can present significant challenges for managers. The standardization of rewards and the protections provided by the tenure system (and public sector unions in most cases) mean that managers have relatively few ways of motivating their employees. Although we will point out below that for many people in the public sector intrinsic motivations are more important than extrinsic motivations, for example money, the emphasis on uniformity does little or nothing to encourage more than adequate performance.

The constraints inherent in a civil service system have led to attempts to improve personnel management, or at least to make it more like personnel management in the private sector. Many countries have shifted away from civil service systems to personal contract, especially for upper-echelon employees. Performance management has also been introduced to provide clearer targets for the work of public employees and to make both sanctioning and rewarding performance easier. The latter changes have been reinforced by weakening the concept of tenure in public employment so that poor performers can be dismissed.

The other alternative to a civil service system for hiring and managing public employees is to use patronage and to permit elected political officials to hire their own partisan loyalists. We associate this pattern of employment with less-developed countries but advanced democracies also have significant numbers of appointees in public office (see Panizza et al., 2016). Furthermore, patronage provides political leaders with the opportunity to employ people committed to their political programs and to improve the probabilities that public employees will work to implement programs. This is yet another way in which governments must strike some balance between legal responsibility and political responsiveness.

Recruitment of Public Employees

We have discussed the behavior of public administrators in office, but an equally important question is why individuals choose to become a public employee. For the critics of government and public administration the facile answer might be that they are not qualified to do anything else, but the real answer is more complex. Indeed, if those critics were to meet their public employees, they would most often find a group of qualified and dedicated people who are working to solve complex problems in often difficult circumstances. As Graham Allison (1983) has argued, management in the public sector is substantially more difficult than in the private sector, given the absence of a bottom line such as profit, and having to govern 'in a goldfish bowl'.

In addition, some of the difficulties that managers in government face are also encountered by the lower-echelon workers in government. The demands of accountability and transparency in government make doing the job more demanding. And the legalism of the public sector, even in relatively nonbureaucratic systems, adds additional constraints on government officials. Public officials are also working without clear measures of their success or failure, unlike the availability of profit as a standard in the private sector. Performance management has provided more quantitative evidence of success, but even then the available measures are far from perfect, and often contentious (see Bouckaert and Halligan, 2008). And finally, civil servants do not earn huge compensation for their efforts. We know that many if not most public employees do not join government for financial rewards, and those rewards may be meager considering the responsibilities of their positions.

Incentives for Joining Government

To understand why people do choose to become public servants we can look at the incentives they may have for accepting a position in the public sector. Every organization can provide its prospective members some benefits, just as that organization may also impose some burdens on the individual. A classic argument for why people will participate in any organization, whether public or private, is that there are material, solidary and purposive incentives (Clark and Wilson, 1961) available to prospective members, and which shape their potential participation in the organization.

Material incentives

When we consider an individual joining an organization we usually think of the material incentives. What is the level of pay? Will they have a nice office? Or a company car? With a few notable exceptions such as Singapore (Quah, 2003), the material rewards available to public servants, as well as their nominal political masters, are quite modest. These limited rewards for public servants are especially noticeable at the top of the hierarchy in public organizations, with public servants having substantial responsibilities receiving extremely modest payments. For example, top public servants in the US Department of Defense (2015), managing the largest single organization in the world, have salaries of approximately US$183,000.

Table 3.1 compares the salary levels for top civil servants in a number of countries with the average level of pay in those countries. While these upper-echelon public servants may be earning a good deal more than the average pay, when compared with rewards for individuals in the private sector with comparable responsibilities the rewards are quite modest. The less visible rewards of public employment such as pensions also are rarely superior to those available in the private sector.

While rewards at the top of government are rarely outstanding, and often not competitive, pay and perquisites at the bottom of public organizations are often relatively good. The rewards for working at the street level, or in clerical positions are often good when compared with similar positions in the private sector. Likewise, some professional positions such as teachers are also reasonably well compensated, but other skilled positions such as computer engineers are extremely poorly paid in comparison with working privately.

Much of the above discussion has been about public sector employees in relatively affluent countries in Europe, North America and the Antipodes. In less affluent countries, however, jobs in the public sector are often considered to be very good positions. Even if the pay in these positions in the public sector is far from outstanding, it often is better and certainly more secure than most positions in the private sector. And unfortunately having these positions can also provide an opportunity to extract bribes and other informal rewards for office that can make the positions lucrative.

Although there is a good deal of evidence that material rewards are not particularly important for public employees, as part of the market ideology of the NPM, there has been an increasing use of pay for performance in the public sector.

Table 3.1 Average pay for higher civil service (as percentage of average wage in economy)

France	Italy	Japan	Germany	Singapore	Sweden	United Kingdom	United States
202	223	131	197	318	139	213	187

Calculated from Brans and Peters (2011), and Hood and Peters, with Lee (2002). These figures represent base salary only and do not include benefits such as pensions and cars, which may add significantly to total compensation.

The assumption is that if individuals are rewarded for good performance they will work harder and perform better. The evidence for that assumption is at best weak (see Moynihan, 2008). Public sector employees appear willing to accept additional pay, but do not appear to strive particularly hard to achieve those financial rewards. Indeed, in some societies when an individual receives additional pay from a performance-based system, the custom is for him or her to share that additional money among co-workers.[4]

Given the above, it is difficult to make generalizations about the material rewards available in the public sector. On the one hand, at the top of the hierarchy the pay tends to be poor, but the perquisites are often at least competitive. Pay at the bottom of the hierarchy, on the other hand, is often better than in the private sector, especially given the relative stability of the positions. Furthermore, in many civil service systems there is little flexibility in making those rewards. In general, however, material rewards in the public sector are rarely good enough by themselves to be able to attract the 'best and brightest' to it.

Solidary incentives

As well as joining organizations for material rewards, individuals may join simply because of the people involved in those organizations and the opportunity to be in a congenial environment. These so-called 'solidary incentives' are usually associated with social organizations, but they can be important in recruiting, and especially in retaining, members of organizations with other purposes. For example, although most people would consider political parties as concerned with winning elections, studies have demonstrated that many party members are there more so for the social aspects and friendships than for political reasons.

These solidary incentives are often important in retaining public employees. Surveys of employees demonstrate that they like the people they work with and generally are positive about the atmosphere of their organizations (Bertelli, 2007). In addition some organizations in the public sector, such as the military and civilian protective services generally develop an esprit de corps that is important for maintaining the performance of those organizations. There are, of course, major exceptions to this generalization about the public sector, organizations such as the post office in several countries have low morale and significant internal dissension. In addition, NPM and its emphasis on individual performance has tended to reduce morale (and perhaps even performance; see Diefenbach, 2009).

Purposive incentives

Finally, people may choose to join the public sector for purposive reasons. By this we mean that people join an organization because they want to accomplish something through membership in that organization. For example, people may

---

[4]Personal communication from several colleagues in Latin American countries.

join a political party because they want to influence public policy, or join a social service agency because they want to help the less-privileged members of the society. Whether it is in the public or the private sector, individuals will participate in order to make things happen.

Public employment can be a powerful means of attempting to shape the economy and society in which one lives. The purposes that motivate individuals to join the public sector may be general, such as providing public service, or they may be more focused in a particular policy area, or toward providing services to a particular segment of the population. Furthermore, there are some policy areas for which the public sector is the only viable alternative for influence – national security being the most obvious example.

The evidence for public employment is that purposive motivations are the most important reasons individuals join and remain in public sector employment (see Table 3.2). Purposive incentives appear to be important for motivating public employees in a wide variety of countries and policy areas. When asked in surveys, public employees tend to emphasize their capacity to serve the public and to make positive contributions in solving social problems, and much of their satisfaction in their jobs tends to derive from their opportunities to serve. These incentives tend to be much stronger than either material or solidary incentives in attracting and retaining public sector employees. This being said, the strength of incentives may vary significantly by the type of job held by the individual public servant. Individuals at the top of administrative hierarchies, and in so-called decision-making positions, are more likely to be motivated by service and the capacity to influence policy. Individuals occupying more routine jobs at the bottom of these hierarchies are more likely to be concerned with material rewards, although individuals providing direct services to clients may also be strongly motivated by service. And as noted above, individuals who are in uniformed services facing dangers may have strong solidary incentives.

Public service motivation

The strength of purposive motivations discussed above is the foundation for a more fully articulated model of the motivation of civil servants and other public employees. The idea of 'public service motivation' is that individuals in government are indeed motivated to accept and perform their jobs primarily through their capacity to provide public services. This very basic idea has been addressed through the development of a set of questions designed to tap into a number of dimensions concerning the attitudes of public employees about their jobs (see Vandenabeele, Brewer and Ritz, 2014). Public service motivation has been conceptualized to be composed of six dimensions (Perry, 1996):

- Attraction of policy-making
- Commitment to the public interest
- Social justice
- Civic duty
- Compassion
- Self-sacrifice

Several of these dimensions are closely related to the ideas of purposive incentives described above, however, they also contain several attributes that are about the substance of policies and the delivery of those policies. That is, as well as wanting to be involved in making policies this concept contains an idea that those policies should promote social justice, and should be delivered in a compassionate manner. Furthermore, this concept appears to contain some elements of professionalism, with inclusion of a dimension of self-sacrifice.[5]

These assumed dimensions of public service motivation did not demonstrate sufficient inter-correlation to comprise six unified scales. Rather, the responses of civil servants in the United States to the questions about public service motivation indicated that there was some underlying commitment to the purposive values mentioned above, although these commitments did not correspond neatly to the assumed dimensions of the concept. It appears that while the commitment to public service is rather pervasive, it manifests itself in a variety of ways.

Despite some of the problems with scaling, the components of the concept of public service motivation has been used extensively in the United States, where it originated, and in a wide variety of other settings. Leaving aside for the moment some of the finer points of methodology and scaling, it is important to note the extent to which a general commitment to public service and influence over public policies appears across cultures (see for example, Vandenabeele, 2008).

Representative Bureaucracy

As well as inquiring what may motivate individuals within public administration, we should also ask what kind of people actually join the government service. For example, how well educated are employees in the public sector? And do people come into the public sector and stay, or do they move in and out of the public sector? Perhaps most importantly, we need to ask to what extent employment in the public sector is representative of their society? These officials are responsible for administering policies for a society, but are they like the society and therefore more likely to reflect the values of that society?

The concept of representative bureaucracy was developed toward the end of World War II. At this time it was clear in the United Kingdom that the first postwar election would produce a Labour government committed to large-scale nationalization of industry and the creation of an extensive welfare state (Hennessey, 1993). The question raised by J. Donald Kingsley (1944) was whether a civil service composed primarily of individuals from an upper-class background and educated at elite institutions such as Oxford and Cambridge, would be willing to implement those socialist programs.[6]

---

[5]A standard sociological definition of professionalism, mentioned above, is that a professional is obliged to place the interest of his or her client ahead of personal interest. For public service motivation this may also mean putting the national interest ahead of any personal rewards.

[6]In the end the implementation went off with few if any problems, but at the time this was a very legitimate issue.

The term 'representative bureaucracy' was originally employed to address the possible negative effects of the composition of the civil service on their abilities to administer certain types of program. Although the original question of representativeness was phrased around issues of social class, in contemporary public administration questions of ethnicity and gender tend to be more central to discussions of representativeness than is class (see Tahvilzadeh, 2012). But social class does still matter, especially for the implementation of social programs that are directed primarily at the poor and the working class.

Representative bureaucracy can be used as both a normative and an empirical concept. Normatively, the argument is that the public sector should be a model employer and ensure that its employees are as representative of the society as possible, and indeed government have sometimes attempted to over-represent the less-advantaged segments of society. These principles of promoting greater equality of employment for the less-advantaged groups within society may be enshrined in law. For example, the constitution of India provides for special treatment of 'scheduled castes' to attempt to redress the inequalities experienced by some segments of society (De Zwart, 2000), and American affirmative action laws mandate that public sector employers take action to employ more members of minority groups.

Most of the research on representative bureaucracy has been empirical, assessing the extent to which public administration, and especially the upper echelons of public administration, are indeed representative of their societies (see Peters, Schröter and von Maravić, 2015). Some examples of these findings are included in Table 3.2. While there are certainly differences among the cases, the general finding is that the upper echelons of the civil service remain somewhat unrepresentative of their populations. In general the upper civil service is more representative in terms of gender than in terms of ethnic minorities, and a few cases are somewhat approaching equality.

Two additional points should be mentioned concerning representative bureaucracy. First, if we were to examine these data across time (see Peters, 2016) there have been significant improvements in the representativeness of public bureaucracies. Again, the differences among countries are significant, as are differences among the various minorities within individual countries. For example, African Americans have not been as successful in moving into the upper echelons of the civil service in the United States as have Latin Americans. And in general women have been more successful than minorities in reaching the upper reaches of public administration.

The second point is that most of the information we have on representativeness is for the upper echelons of public administration. If, however, we were to extend the data to lower echelons of the public sector then the findings would be somewhat different. First, for government as a whole, women tend to make up the majority of employment. This is in large part because several jobs in the public sector – teachers, nurses, secretaries – have traditionally been 'women's work'. Furthermore, these jobs make up a significant share of public employment in most countries: teachers are approximately 30 percent of total civilian employment in the United States.

Table 3.2 Representation of minority groups and women in public administration (numbers are percentages)

(a) Ethnic representation in public administration

United States (Higher Federal Civil Service)	
African American	8
Hispanic	6
Asian American	5
Canada	
Anglophone	67
Francophone	32
India	
Dominant group	95
Others	5

(b) Gender representation in higher-level public administration

Country	Percentage of women
Australia	19
Belgium	14
Canada	27
Israel	10
Norway	37
Sweden	38
United Kingdom	17
United States	19

Sources: Peters (2009); Peters et al. (2015). The comparison among these cases is difficult. These are derived from different sources and may cover different segments of public administration. Even with that, however, they do provide some understanding of variations in representativeness.

The representativeness of the lower levels of public administration can be especially beneficial for the delivery of public services (Maynard-Mooney and Musheno, 2012). Given that the recipients of social programs are disproportionately members of minority groups, having street-level bureaucrats who are also members of those groups may facilitate the delivery of those programs. In many cases, the capacity to speak the language of the program recipient, or to understand the values of that recipient, will be important contributions to effective service delivery.

Representative bureaucracy is also discussed in active and passive terms (Kennedy, 2013). Most of the discussion is about a simple sociological representation, without any clear assumptions about what difference the representativeness makes for decision-making by public employees. More active versions of representative bureaucracy (see Selden, 1997; Kennedy, 2014) assume that the individuals will indeed make decisions influenced by their gender or their minority status. The more active conceptions of representation tend also toward the normative argument that these employees should make decisions on this basis.

The Other Public Sector

To this point we have been discussing the members of the public administration who are formally employed in the public sector. We also need to consider the nature of the people employed by government indirectly. Governments have found it advantageous to utilize a variety of different market and non-market actors to deliver public services, or to provide goods and services required by government. These indirect employees, and the services they provide, are extremely diverse, ranging from religious groups providing social services to private security companies protecting government facilities in danger zones. These employees may be connected to government through contracts, through partnership arrangements or through their involvement in policy networks. Although it is difficult, if not impossible, to provide definitive information about these employees, or even to enumerate them (see Derlien and Peters, 2008), we do need to recognize their importance for the public sector. In some cases private employees may be more acceptable to clients than are direct public employees, for example, immigrants fearing being deported by government. And employment through the private sector can be more flexible than through civil service systems based on tenure and stability, allowing governments to add employees for peak demand times without needing to offer continued employment. Finally, using private contractors may permit government to mobilize talent that they might not be able to afford otherwise.[7]

However, while bringing in contractors may increase efficiency in public service delivery, it may also create problems. Leaving aside issues related to contracts as such, private contracts brought in to manage services where public law is exercised has proven to be a significant challenge. For instance, privately run prisons in the United States have been found to be poorly staffed by employees who were given only a minimum level of training for those challenging jobs (Bozeman, 2007). More broadly, Freeman (2003) discusses whether private contractors, as part of the contract specifications, should be obliged to put their staff through training programs specifically designed to give their staff some knowledge on public sector norms and ethics. Her conclusion is that this would make private businesses de facto components of the public sector and it would also mean that they would most likely not be very competitive in other markets (Freeman, 2003; see Pierre and Painter, 2010).

A consideration of the full range of employment that is funded by public money and/or is delivering public service provides a more complete perspective on public administration. If we think only about the formal members of the civil

---

[7]There are dangers in this strategy, however, as the experience of computer contractors involved with launching the exchanges in Obamacare demonstrated in the United States (Lipton, Austen and Lafreniere, 2013).

service and analogous organizations we can ignore a large, and apparently growing, segment of public activity. Furthermore, we need to question the extent to which these providers of public services are more or less representative of the public than is the civil service, and if they are as motivated by values of public service as are the officials employed in the public sector.

Summary and Conclusions

Although we think about the public bureaucracy as a set of organizations, or perhaps one big organization, organizations are empty vessels unless inhabited by people. This chapter has attempted to demonstrate the roles played by individual public employees in delivering public services, and the capacity those public employees have for making decisions that affect the lives of ordinary citizens. All positions in the public bureaucracy involve making decisions, and often extremely difficult decisions, that affect the lives of other people. We will discuss how best to understand that decision-making in a subsequent chapter, in this chapter we emphasized the decision-makers themselves.

This chapter has also emphasized the importance of getting the 'right' people to become public employees. There are two dimensions of recruitment that are especially important for the performance of public organizations. The first is the need to attract the 'best and brightest' to government. The public bureaucracy is often denigrated as a place to work for anyone with skills and talent, yet many extraordinary people do choose to spend their careers in public service. They make those career choices, often with significant financial sacrifices, in order to be able to work on important public policy issues and to serve their fellow citizens.

In addition to attracting highly qualified people, governments must be concerned about making the public sector as representative of the society as a whole as possible. Representativeness is an important attribute for the public bureaucracy, both for democratic reasons and to be able to enhance their effectiveness in delivering services to a diverse public. Few governments have achieved the high level of involvement of ethnic and religious minorities in government that they may like, in large part because education systems tend to be less welcoming for these citizens than for the dominant communities, but the employment of women has increased more rapidly.

Although the remainder of this book will focus on structure and process more than on the persons involved, we need always remember that it is the people involved who animate the actions of the public sector. Clever people may design elegant institutional structures and efficient processes for governing, but if the individuals involved (politicians as well as the public administrators being discussed here) are not equally adept then little good is likely to emerge from all the work of designing structures and processes.

4

Neutrality Versus Responsiveness

Public administration is a component of the political system. The managerialist approach to administration tends to consider the public bureaucracy in strictly instrumental terms and to assume that it is essentially the same as private management (see Chapter 2). But that managerialist conception tends to undervalue, or even ignore, the public nature of this institution. Especially in a democratic system, the public nature of the institution implies that public administrators should, up to a point, be responsive to political pressures. The questions, however, are how responsive should they be, and to whom? These are not easy questions and can be answered in several ways with equal validity.

This chapter will focus on public administrators and their individual political neutrality and responsiveness to political pressures. This is not only an important political question but it also has relevance for the accountability of public employees and public organizations (see Chapters 3 and 10). Should public administrators be responsible to their political 'masters', or to clients, or to more encompassing political values? Or should they be politically neutral, unaffected by political pressures, and more responsible to legal and moral principles, regardless of the pressures they may receive from within their own organizations? Individual public administrators therefore are situated in a complex field of conflicting demands and must make choices about the roles they will assume in governing.

The above discussion leads to two fundamental models of the role of the public administrator (see Fry and Nigro, 1996). The classic conception of the civil servant is one of neutral competence, that is, a civil servant should be capable of providing loyal service to any political master. At the same time, however, that civil servant does what he or she is instructed to do; they are not committed to the program of the government of the day but rather committed to the state, or to the public (Kaufman, 1956). The alternative conception is that the civil servant is indeed committed to the government of the day and is there to provide service that goes beyond merely obeying instructions. Both the models can be supported (see below) but they may be more viable in different contexts. For example, the model of strict political neutrality may be well suited for advanced industrial democracies, in which alternation of parties in government is expected and peaceful and the alternations of policy will be relatively minor. In contrast, the more responsive model is almost essential in more autocratic regimes. Also, some scholars have argued that developmental states require high levels of commitment from their civil servants in order to push through potentially contentious policies.

The Normative Model of Neutral Competence

Although there is some common model of neutral competence, there are at least two intellectual roots, one more commonly used in Europe and the other clearly based in the United States. They have a few common ideas about public administration but reflect different historical foundations and have somewhat different implications for the role of the public bureaucracy in governing. Although both models are over a century old, they continue as the normative models for public administration in much of the world.

The Weberian model

One of the principal models of the role of bureaucrats in the public sector is based on the work of the German sociologist Max Weber (Gerth and Mills, 1946). Weber developed a model of bureaucracy that an alternative to the cameralist and personalistic governance of the German empire at the time. This model of bureaucracy was designed as an ideal type,[1] rather than a description of any particular administrative system, and its model of the relationship between administrators and politicians is therefore somewhat idealized, as is that of Woodrow Wilson below.

We have discussed several dimensions of the Weberian model above (see Chapter 2) but here we will emphasize the argument on behalf of the political neutrality of the civil servant. That neutrality is related to the sense of the public administrator as a professional who treats all clients equally and implement laws without malice or consideration. Whereas Wilson's discussion of the role of the public administrator (see below) focused more directly on the interaction between politicians and administrators in the upper reaches of government, Weber's discussion focused more on the treatment of citizens. The conception of

---

[1]In this context 'ideal' does not mean perfect but rather that this is a conceptual model against which real-world cases are to be compared. It therefore represents one form of comparative analysis for the bureaucracies that exist in real countries (see Page, 1985).

the bureaucrat as a professional, however, leads to the necessity of political neutrality on the part of that bureaucrat. If being a civil servant is to be a career, then that civil servant is likely to see a variety of different governments and will be expected to serve governments that may have very different political complexions. Neutrality, along with professional competence, therefore is necessary for that career system to function. Furthermore, Weber emphasized recruitment by merit, so that patronage appointments and political commitments, would have little place in public administration. This conception of bureaucracy is indeed an ideal type, and cannot be encountered in any real-world administrative system. Even those administrative systems that might be thought most likely to conform to this model, for example Germany and Austria, have political civil servants (an oxymoron?). And indeed most senior public servants in Germany have a known party membership and are expected to serve primarily while their party is in office. They have the same training and educational backgrounds as any other civil servant but they are clearly political (Derlien, 1991).

Woodrow Wilson and the neutrality of public administration

For the United States, the ideas of Woodrow Wilson continue as an important model for the role of public administration. When Wilson (1887) wrote his famous essay arguing for the separation of politics and administration, the federal civil service was only in its beginning stages. The Pendelton Act had been passed just four years previously, with a small percentage of federal public employees actually covered by the merit system. The administrative system was somewhat removed from the Jacksonian spoils system, but not by very much. Wilson argued that there was a fundamental difference between politics and administration. On the one hand, politicians, especially in democratic systems, have the legitimacy to make policy decisions and also have the right to expect that those decisions will be implemented faithfully. Administrators, on the other hand, are responsible for 'mere administration', and should follow the directions of the political leaders to whom they report. Public administrators may advise politicians, but do so anonymously, with the politicians being responsible for the content.

Wilson had two intellectual connections for this model of administration. First, he was writing at the beginning of the 'scientific management' movement. Scholars such as Frederick Winslow Taylor and Henri Fayol (1917) argued that administration could be organized on scientific principles and that there was 'one best way' to perform tasks. Thus, Wilson appeared to assume that in reality administration was superior to politics given that it was a science while politics was only an art. That said, administration still was obliged to remain subservient to politics for democratic reasons. The other foundation of Wilson's thinking about administration was the progressive movement in the United States (McGerr, 2005). One of the fundamental arguments of this political movement was that government would perform better for citizens if it was more professionalized and depoliticized. These values were manifested in the creation of the independent regulatory agencies such as the Interstate Commerce Commission, the nonpartisan elections, especially in the upper Midwestern states, and the council–manager form of urban government. The same logic then applies to the development of a professional and depoliticized civil service system.

The Wilsonian dichotomy continues to influence thinking in American government. Even though the president can appoint several thousand officials at the top of the federal hierarchy (Hollibaugh, Horton and Lewis, 2014), the idea that the civil service should still be neutral and depoliticized remains widespread. This notion of neutrality was manifested in part in the Hatch Act, and its equivalents at the state level, which forbade civil servants from political activities that went much beyond voting.[2] And somewhat paradoxically this presumed separation from politics is often used as a criticism of the bureaucracy, with the critics complaining about decisions made by an 'unelected and unaccountable bureaucracy'.

Although the idea of neutrality is deeply engrained, it has been criticized from both the empirical and normative dimensions (Svara, 2001). One question about this dichotomy is the extent to which individuals involved in making and implementing policy can really be neutral. While they may attempt to provide good service to their political leaders they will still have political ideas, especially ideas about what constitutes good public policy in the areas within which they work. Civil servants may also perhaps have partisan identities – the suburbs of Washington DC in Maryland and Virginia are reliably Democratic because of the large number of federal employees living there. Another strand of criticism of the separation of politics and administration argues that administrators are indeed policymakers, and unless that fundamental fact is understood we risk misunderstanding how governments work and especially will have difficulties in understanding accountability: first, most rules made by government are not made by legislatures but are made through the bureaucracy through secondary legislation (see Page, 2003);[3] and second, when administrators implement policy they have discretion (see Chapter 6), and that discretion may determine what the laws really mean. The speed limit on highways is not what the legislature has declared it to be, it is what the police decide to enforce.

Building the merit system ...

The ideas of Weber and Wilson, as well as the experience of governments with the spoils system, created a strong normative bias in favor of the merit system. The process of building a career public bureaucracy that is divorced from politics has been a long struggle for most governments. Politicians who gain office may distrust the appointees they inherit from the previous government, and will therefore want to be able to appoint their own loyalists to office (see Geddes, 1994). The question for administrative reformers therefore is how to best move toward a more professionalized career public service. One of the more effective strategies has been a gradual 'blanketing in' of appointees as

---

[2]The courts have weakened these prohibitions, arguing that civil servants should have the same rights of free speech – at least when not in their offices – as do other citizens.

[3]For a more detailed description see Kerwin and Furlong (2011).

career positions. While this gives the party in government an advantage because of their appointees, it also converts positions from continuing patronage to the merit system, with long run benefits. Also, some governments have attempted to create 'islands of excellence', with individual organizations operating with merit systems in a sea of patronage (Grindle, 1997).

... and also a need for responsiveness

Even if one does not accept the rather extreme Wilsonian or Weberian versions of the separation of politics and administration, there must still be some working relationship between these two crucial actors in governance. Politicians need the expertise held by many civil servants, and they also require the commitment of those civil servants in implementing public programs, even if the civil servants do not necessarily agree with those programs. And civil servants need the legitimacy of politicians as well as protection from public scrutiny given that they usually have anonymity.

There is also a clear political relationship between the sets of actors, both in democratic and nondemocratic systems. As Wilson argued, political leaders have legitimacy and citizens should expect the unelected members of the bureaucracy to be responsive to the preferences of those legitimate actors. While political leaders in less democratic systems may not have legitimacy in the same sense, they should also expect their civil servants to be responsive. They will also have more powerful ways of enforcing that responsiveness than will leaders in democratic regimes. But bureaucrats can find it difficult to be total ciphers and only follow orders. They too may have ideas and want to get things done in government. This relationship therefore is one of the crucial connections within the governing process and needs to be understood in some detail if we are to understand governance.

Attitudes and roles

The relationships between politicians and bureaucrats can be understood in several ways. One means is through the attitudes held by politicians and administrators about their roles in governing. Aberbach, Putnam and Rockman's (1981) research, and a number of others who have used their basic model, has provided a great deal of comparative evidence about the perceived roles of politicians and administrators. This model of the roles of the two sets of actors is based on a dichotomy between traditional bureaucrats and political bureaucrats. The former group of bureaucrats accepted a relatively passive role, following the lead of their political leaders and would be quite comfortable with the Weberian conception of the bureaucrat. The other group of public administrators conceptualize their tasks more in policy and political terms, although political in this context may mean organizational politics as much as partisan politics.

Although the original dichotomous conception of the roles dominates much of the discussion, it is important to note that (just as it was discussed about the Wilsonian separation model) in reality individuals may not fall into those neat categories. And indeed the nature of the tasks of upper-echelon public servants is such that they can rarely be entirely one or the other. Thus, many public servants are in practice hybrids (Lee and Raadschelders, 2008), playing both roles in response to different situational pressures. Likewise, we may think of them as 'amphibians' (Campbell and Peters, 1988), going back and forth between the two environments of politics and administration, and functioning with equal ease in both.

De Graaf (2010) has also used attitudinal and role information to examine the roles of civil servants and their relationships with politicians. In particular, he has examined the loyalties of civil servants whether to political leaders or to their organizations or to personal values. This provided a more complex understanding of how public administrators think of their jobs, and how they balance a variety of competing demands on their loyalties. This study was conducted on higher-level public servants but some preliminary research on lower levels in the organizations found other important loyalties, especially loyalty to clients.

Structures of Interaction

Although attitudes of public employees can tell us a good deal, we can also attempt to examine the structural and behavioral characteristics of the relationships between bureaucrats and politicians. One of the present authors (Peters, 1987) has argued that these relationships can be described on a continuum that ranges from the Wilsonian/Weberian domination by politicians to the dominance of governance by bureaucrats. We have already argued that domination by politicians may be an ideal type, and domination by bureaucrats may be even more so. That said, the asymmetries in information and the permanence of bureaucrats may give them some advantages over more amateurish politicians (see Workman, 2015). In between these two extremes, we can think of three other patterns of relationships between bureaucrats and their political masters. The first is 'village life'. Hugh Heclo and Aaron Wildavsky (1974; see also Parry, 2003) described working in the British treasury as living in a village. The 'inhabitants' had relatively similar social backgrounds, they had lived and worked together for years and even decades, and they had a common interest in governing. There was limited conflict within the village because of common values. While that comfortable village might have, in most instances, been destroyed by the reforms of NPM and modernization more generally (see Halligan, 2001), there are still instances in which the political and the bureaucratic classes function comfortably together (see 't Hart, 2006).

An alternative model of the relationship between politicians and bureaucrats is described as 'functional village life'. In this case, the villages are not located horizontally at the top of government but rather they are vertical, and are described by functional policy areas – health, agriculture, the environment, etc. These vertical divisions within the public sector have also been described as 'silos' or 'whirlpools' and by several other colorful phrases, but the basic point is that each policy area within government wants to control the policies in its domain, and politicians and their bureaucrats work together to protect their autonomy from the incursion of other interests. In many instances, career bureaucrats will have to attempt to draw their ministers and other politicians into accepting the views on policy held by the permanent members of the organization, and ministers tend to gain their own political power by defending and promoting their ministries. There is therefore a symbiotic relationship among the actors within these vertical structures.[4]

Finally, there is a relationship pattern characterized by conflict between politicians and administrators. It is perhaps natural that there is some tension between these actors: they come into their offices in government in different ways, have different career paths, and may have different policy priorities. This conflict may occur especially when there is a change in the political party in control of an organization, and that organization has a clear commitment to a particular policy stance. For example, when conservative governments take charge of environmental ministries they often face committed environmentalists who will not be receptive to changing policy priorities. This conflict may not be partisan in a strict sense but rather more over the policies being pursued.

Public Service Bargains

A third way to understand the interactions of politicians and bureaucrats is as bargains between the two sets of actors. Bernard Schaffer (1973) first advanced this perspective, and Christopher Hood and Martin Lodge (2006) developed the argument about bargains much further. Their study of public service bargains in a number of settings analyzed the nature of the bargains – often more tacit than explicit – that may exist between those actors. On the one hand, politicians seek, and depend on, the expertise, loyalty and support of their civil servants. On the other hand, civil servants are generally willing to provide their support to the politicians provided they are also supported and given anonymity and protection from external sanctions for their policy advice.[5]

Although the general notion of the public service bargain is useful for understanding the relationships between public servants and politicians, finer grained versions of the concept can provide more insights. For example, Hood and Lodge distinguish between trustee type bargains and agency type bargains. In the former the civil servants in question have some independent source of their authority from the constitution,[6] whereas the more familiar agency model involves some more explicit delegation from a minister or another political official. The concept of the public service bargain emerged from the British experience, but it has been used to explore the relationships between politicians and bureaucrats in a range of other countries. For example, the changing nature of

---

[4]These vertical structures also connect to policy networks and epistemic communities in the environment of these organizations. See Chapter 6.

[5]Of course, they do not expect protection against actions against them based on malfeasance in office.

[6]This bargain results from the perceptions of the civil servants involved. Even if there are no formal powers ascribed to them, they may believe themselves to be first the servants of the crown or the public, rather than their ministers. This perception is often ingrained in the ethos of a public service. See, for example, Bourgault and Van Dorp (2013).

government in Hong Kong has produced a significant shift in the public service bargains existing there (Burns, Wei and Peters, 2013), with the role of the civil service becoming significantly reduced in a more politicized government. Also, in Denmark there has been a gradual transformation of the bargains toward being increasingly tacit (Salomonsen and Knudsen, 2011).

Growing Politicization

Another important pattern noted in the public sector that is affecting the relationship between politicians and civil servants is the increasing politicization of the public sector, even in countries that have had strongly merit-based recruitment (see Peters and Pierre, 2004; Neuhold, vanhoonacker and Verhey, 2013). There is evidence that an increasing number of positions in the public sector are being filled by means other than merit examinations, and that political loyalty is being increasingly valued by ministers and other politicians.

But why have political systems that have emphasized merit recruitment become more interested in political appointments? One of the principal reasons has been the emphasis on organizational and managerial autonomy associated with NPM. One can easily argue that NPM both made politicization of the bureaucracy more necessary (at least in the eyes of political leaders) and more possible. First, the creation of agencies and other types of autonomous bodies within the public sector (Pollitt and Talbot, 2004) placed political leaders in the position of being responsible for policies (at least in the minds of their constituents) while having relatively little influence over those policies. Adding more political civil servants to these organizations may provide one means of addressing that gap between responsibility and control. Second, the NPM reforms also provide the means through which political leaders may justify increasing the level of politicization of the administrative system. One central argument of NPM is that management is management, whether in the public or the private sector. The advocacy of generic management in turn makes it more acceptable, and even desirable, to break the closed career structure of the civil service and allow more outsiders to take posts in government. While this may be justified on the basis of hiring more qualified managers for the public sector, it can also be used to recruit political loyalists into positions that had been held by career civil servants.

Types of Politicization

To this point we have been discussing politicization and all political appointments as if they were the same. We should, however, differentiate types of politicized appointment and attempt to understand their different implications. In a study of patronage appointments in Latin American governments, Francisco Panizza and his colleagues (2016) argue that there are three basic types of political appointee in those systems,; these categories also appear applicable to other parts of the world (see Meyer-Sahling and Veen, 2010). Some of these patterns of politicization and patronage in fact persist in regimes that are usually thought to be fully functioning merit systems (Grindle, 2012).

In the classification developed by Panizza and colleagues, *clients* is the variety of patronage that is generally considered the most egregious diversion from the merit system. This term is used to mean hiring a large number of political loyalists to fill jobs in government that are not policy oriented or that do not require any particular commitment to the goals of the governing party other than the fundamental goal of re-election and maintaining the strength of the party as an organization. This pattern of politicization as 'jobs for the boys (and girls)' is common in many countries in Latin America and in Africa (see Grindle, 2012; Hyden, 2013), and may lead to significant levels of over-staffing of the public sector.

A second type of patronage appointment has been termed *cadres*. These officials are utilized as the link between the political party in power and the government, and may perform a variety of functions. One is to ensure that the government is indeed following the program of the party, especially when the party is strongly programmatic. Cadres may also work further down within the bureaucracy to attempt to enforce the program of the party and the government. As already noted, these patterns are not confined to Latin America or other transitional regimes. Paul Light (2005) has noted a similar use of partisan appointments deeper down within the American federal bureaucracy.

Finally, some patronage appointments are *counselors*. This is the type of patronage that most people would consider acceptable or at least less destructive of merit system principles than the other two varieties. Counselors are advisors to political leaders, whether on policy or management, and exist in all political systems, albeit in varying numbers. For example, ministers in France, Belgium and a number of other European governments have *cabinets* to provide advice and to help enforce their policies within the organization (Eymeri-Douzanes, Boix and Mouton, 2015). And many other countries use the equivalent of 'SPADS', or special advisors, in the United Kingdom (Shaw and Eichbaum, 2014).

Consequences

Politicization of the public service has a number of consequences for the public bureaucracy itself, as well as for the capacity of governments to make and implement good policy decisions, and not all these consequences are necessarily negative. The general normative appeal of the merit system has institutionalized an assumption that any politicization is negative. But a more analytic stance reveals that a more politicized administration is not necessarily inherently evil or inefficient. As with many other aspects of the choice of administrative system, the best choice depends on a number of contingencies. Perhaps the most important negative consequence of widespread politicization has been the demise of the institution, or perhaps the failure to create the institution, of the civil service. While we tend to discuss the legislature, the executive and the courts as the major institutions of government, the bureaucracy is by far the largest institution in the public sector. The permanence and stability of that institution is to some extent crucial for its success. That stability provides an organizational memory for policymaking and also creates some level of 'credible commitment' for the clients of the organization. Giving that up in favor of political responsiveness is not necessarily the best value for government and citizens.

In additional to the consequences for the institution, there may be important consequences for recruitment. It may be difficult for governments to hire 'the best and brightest' when individuals know that they may be dismissed for political reasons, or may have a political appointee placed over them in the organizational hierarchy. If prospective bureaucrats do want to have a career, and do seek some level of predictability about their careers, they may find the potential political influence on their career less than desirable. These prospective employees may also feel more committed to the State and the public than to any particular political party (see J. R. Thompson, 2006). In contrast, however, the prospects of being able to move in and out of a more politicized administrative system may attract other individuals who want to be able to influence government but do not want to make the public sector their career. The political executives recruited into the American federal government, for example, are often highly talented individuals who may be committed to a political leader or to a particular policy issue but who do not want to spend their entire career in government. From this perspective, governments may be able to attain the services of better employees, albeit for short periods.

Finally, we need to ask if the level of politicization of the bureaucracy makes any difference to the performance of government. The assumption of the advocates of the merit system tends to be that individuals recruited from outside government are inherently 'political hacks' who do not understand government or have the appropriate set of norms to be involved in the process.[7] The evidence from the United States has been that as program managers, political appointees tend to be less successful than their career counterparts (Gallo and Lewis, 2012). That may be, however, a function of the particular pattern of patronage in the United States, with some appointments coming from presidential campaigns (Hollibaugh, 2015). This does mean that appointees functioning as policy advisors or appointed managers to whom the president is not beholden for campaign activities will necessarily be less successful.

Responsiveness to the Public

As well as being responsive upward to the political leaders of their organizations, public administrators are expected to have some degree of responsiveness outward to the stakeholders of their programs and downward to the public whom they serve. This responsiveness is important for the capacity of government to serve the public, but a commitment to responsiveness may also raise questions about the extent to which the organizations are being captured by special interests, or perhaps being excessively responsible to the needs of their clients – to the detriment of taxpayers and 'the public interest'.

All public programs have groups in society that are concerned with the content and implementation of those programs. For example, farmers and food

---

[7]And this is true of some appointees, as in the infamous case of Michael D. Brown, who ran the Federal Emergency Management Agency (FEMA) during the administration of President George W. Bush. Brown headed FEMA during is disastrous response (or lack thereof) to Hurricane Katrina in New Orleans.

processors both have a stake in the operations of ministries of agriculture, albeit with different interests, and their component agencies, and retirees are interested in the decisions of social programs providing pensions. Public organizations are meant to be responsible to the laws they administer, but they also exist in a political environment in which they require support for their budgets and the legislation they may want to introduce. Thus, these organizations in the public sector have to somewhat walk a tightrope in responding to their programs stake-holders at the same time as administering the law as it was intended to be administered when it was written. There is a significant literature on the capture of organizations by stakeholders (see Bo, 2006) and with that the use of public power for private purposes. Those stakeholders may want to influence the deci-sions of the organizations that affect them and are willing to utilize their political influence with legislatures and voters to provide that influence.

Public administration is also in direct contact with the clients of public pro-grams, and may be expected to be responsive to those clients. The study of 'street-level bureaucracy' (Meyers and Nielsen, 2012) is based in part on that expectation of responsiveness. Again, the organization and the individual administrators have to somewhat walk a tightrope in balancing that respon-siveness with the other demands on their behavior. On the one hand, these administrators are meant to follow the law and treat their clients *sine irae ac studio* as good Weberian bureaucrats. On the other hand, those interactions with clients may lead them to be responsive to the needs of those clients, and perhaps too responsive. In the extreme they may be captured by clients in much the same way as they are by stakeholders.[8]

Balancing Neutrality and Responsiveness

The above discussion has demonstrated the utility of the concepts of neutrality and responsiveness in understanding public administration. All governments must make choices about how to manage their public personnel, and to what extent merit recruitment should extend throughout the public sector (Jacobsen, 2006). Although everyone sings hymns of praise to the merit system, all political systems also have some political appointments, and the question therefore becomes at what level and for what purposes are those politicized officials to be utilized within government. The long-standing administrative traditions in coun-tries affect the relationship between politicians and bureaucrats (see Peters, forthcoming). There were, for example, marked differences in the countries included in the original book *Bureaucrats and Politicians in Western Democracies* by Aberbach, Putnam and Rockman (1981). Furthermore, the Anglo-American administrative tradition emphasizes the separation of politics and administration much more than does, for example, the Napoleonic tradition, in which these two sets of actors tend to be more closely aligned (Ongaro, 2010). Likewise, the tradi-tion of patronage in Latin America and other developing and transitional regimes leads to minimal separation of these actors (Panizza, Ramos and Schleris, 2016).

---

[8]Some literature argues quite the opposite, and sees civil servants as using their power to regulate their clients (see Piven and Cloward, 1993).

The manner in which bureaucrats and politicians interact, and their relative powers in the policy process, may also be influenced by various contingencies encountered in the structures and processes of governing. For example, crises tend to push power upward to politicians, who must make crucial policy decisions (Peters, Pierre and Randma-Liiv, 2011) albeit with the advice of their civil servants. That said, politicians may also seek to offload difficult policy decisions on to their civil servants to avoid blame for failure or unpopular decisions (Hood, 2011). And some policy areas, especially those with a significant technical content, tend to allow greater latitude for decision-making by expert bureaucrats than would be true for most policy domains. Finally, different individuals will 'perform' their roles as politician and bureaucrat differently, and those individual differences will influence the patterns of interaction. For example, some American presidents and senior cabinet officers may attempt to have detailed control over policy, while others are willing to delegate to other politicians or to career public servants.[9] Some civil servants may be more expert at, or simply more aggressive, and therefore be able to gain greater influence over policy. These patterns might depend on the matching of politicians with bureaucrats who may share their views on policy and on the appropriate level of delegation. All of these individuals may work within institutions with established expectations about behavior, but they will still bring their own views of how best to govern with them when they work within those systems.

Summary and Conclusions

This chapter has addressed one of the fundamental issues in public administration – the extent to which individuals occupying administrative positions in government should be politically neutral or politically committed. This issue has been discussed for decades, and has been associated with two of the most important figures in the field – Max Weber and Woodrow Wilson. Although there have been numerous waves of change in patterns of public administration, the discussion concerning personnel policies and the political recruitment of public employees persists. This is true both in countries with institutionalized merit systems and in those with high levels of political patronage.

Although there tends to be a strong normative preference for neutral bureaucracies, there are also reasons to favor more politicized administrators, at least at some times and in some contexts. All political systems tend to have some political appointees, especially as policy advisors, for example, the counselors discussed above. The question then becomes how far down into the bureaucracy do these appointments extend? Furthermore, how do those political appointees interact with the career civil servants who also occupy government? These issues point to additional questions about the autonomy and responsiveness of public administrators. While the neutral bureaucrat tends to be praised widely, they can also be seen as detached from political control and excessively autonomous.

---

[9] For example, one of the more interesting findings of the dump of emails from Hillary Clinton's time as secretary of state was the extent to which she was willing to delegate to career staff in the US State Department.

That autonomy is extremely valuable for positions in which legalistic decisions must be made, or in fact when allocations must be made to individual citizens. But that autonomy may be anathema to politicians who want their bureaucracy to conform to the demands of their (presumed) political masters. This conflict between autonomy and control, neutrality and responsiveness, will be a continuing feature of public administration.

5

Fragmentation Versus Strategy

Another of the fundamental dilemmas for governing is how to cope with specialization and integration of organizations and policies. Like the other dichotomies we have discussed already, this dimension is as old as government itself. On the one hand, governments are composed of specialized organizations, and they are specialized in order to focus attention on one particular set of issues and to utilize expertise to address policy problems arising in that domain. We can see that specialization in the names of government organizations – the ministry of agriculture, the environmental agency, etc. On the other hand, most of the important problems confronting contemporary governments do not fall within the usual domain of a specialized agency. For example, every country wants to improve the health of its population, and the ministry of health has primary responsibility for health. But a population will not be healthy unless it has adequate nutrition, adequate recreation and adequate housing, and can live in safe communities. Also, specific groups within the population – the elderly and children, for example – may require more specialized attention if healthcare is to be effective. Therefore, improving the quality of health for the population requires the involvement of a number of different organizations, each bringing its specialized knowledge to bear on the common problem.

What is Coordination?

The word coordination is used rather freely in both ordinary and scholarly discourses on government, but what exactly do we mean by the term? A formal definition of coordination would be:

> a set of decisions is coordinated if adjustments have been made in it such that the adverse consequences of any one decision for other decisions in the set are to a degree and in some frequency avoided, reduced, counterbalanced, or outweighed. (Lindblom, 1965)

To further elaborate the nature of coordination, Fritz Scharpf (1997) distinguished between negative and positive coordination. The former is easier to achieve, meaning primarily that the actors involved know what the other is doing in policy terms and make attempts not to conflict. Positive coordination, on the other hand, implies that not only do the actors involved – usually organizations – know what the other is doing but they make some effort to cooperate around the goals that they may share. This does not mean that all elements of the policies will be coordinated, but that where they agree, there will be some joint action. This same basic idea of different levels of coordination is contained in Les Metcalfe's (1994) scale of coordination. Although written in the context of the European Union, the same levels appear applicable to almost any setting in the public sector. This scale begins with organizations essentially ignoring one another doing nothing to help one another. At the other end of the scale several different programs are integrated and run virtually as one. In reality this level of coordination is rarely achieved, but it can serve as a goal for the would-be coordinator.

Although the term coordination is commonly used, many other terms can be used to describe attempts to make programs in government work together more effectively. One term is horizontal management (Peters, 2015a), expressing the idea that although most management is conceived within a single program and working vertically from the top of the organization through to implementation in the field (see Chapter 6), some management also works across programs and attempts to build more coherent delivery of a range of services. Policy integration is another term that is also used to describe the process of building greater coherence among policies and programs in the public sector (Jordan and Lenschow, 2010). While coordination and horizontal management tend to emphasize administration and ex post building of coherence, policy integration tends to emphasize ex ante designs for policy. This approach to coherence in the public sector therefore must be more political, and will involve policymakers confronting differences as they construct solutions to problems, rather than having public administrators attempt to make them work together during implementation.

Public Sector Inherently Fragmented

Coordination is needed because the public sector, and indeed all organizations, will have some level of segmentation and fragmentation. Specialization is important as a means of focusing attention on particular issues and of mobilizing expertise to solve policy problems. This fragmentation is also important politically as it provides structures that interest groups and ordinary citizens can focus on in order to get what they want from government. And finally segmentation is important for accountability. When something goes wrong there is at least a clearly identified place to begin the inquiry, if not perhaps always the place to end that investigation.

Political and Policy Foundations of Divisions

Although all governments are to some extent fragmented, there are several reasons for that fragmentation. Gulick and Urwick (1937) argued that government organizations were based on one of four bases – purpose, people, place or process. Each of these foundations for organization has its advantages and disadvantages, but most governments have some organizations that are based on each. Furthermore, these foundations for organization in the public sector have consequences, and causes, that are political as well as administrative.

Purpose

Most government organizations are based on purpose. Common examples of these organizations are ministries of defense and departments for social services. The titles of these and similar organizations convey their purposes and the policy areas in which government is intervening. Organization on the basis of purpose enables governments to amass expertise in order to address policy problems. And that expertise in turn allows the organization to develop a strong internal culture that can be used not only in political battles over the budget and over policy but also to facilitate internal management. The commitment to particular policy goals is the foundation of the political strength for these organizations. But it also may be a source of weakness as it narrows the vision of the organization and focuses it perhaps too single-mindedly on its purpose. Furthermore, it may attract professional employees – doctors, nurses, etc. in a health organization – who are members of a particular epistemic community (Dunlop, 2014), which makes it difficult for them to accept other perspectives on a problem and to consider alternative solutions.

People

The second major basis of organization in the public sector is by the people who are being served by government. Common examples of organizations of this type are organizations serving veterans, women and children, and labor. These types of organization are becoming increasingly common in the public sector as more and more groups in society become mobilized politically and seek to have their demands institutionalized into an organization within this sector. Even within organizations based on purpose, there are often components that attempt to service particular clientele.

Whereas the principal reason for specializing by purpose is to marshal expertise to address policy problems, politics is more at the root of organizing by clientele groups. Having an organization with the name of the group attached to it emphasizes that the group has an obvious locus within government for lobbying and for service delivery. Also, this form of organization is a recognition that client groups often need a variety of services that might be divided among a number of different organizations that are based on purpose. For example, children will need a range of services, such as education, healthcare, recreation, transportation, and others, covering almost all the departments in most governments.

Place

The public sector can also be organized on the basis of place, recognizing that just as groups in society may require some special attention so too might different parts of the country. There are often ministries or agencies to deal with the problems of cities as well as rural areas. Moreover, disadvantaged parts of a country – for example, the Mezzogiorno in Italy and Appalachia in the United States – may be given their own organization to promote development. Furthermore, the federal structure of a country, or other forms of regionalism, may be seen as another way of organizing government to deal with issues of place.

Process

Finally, some organizations in the public sector are organized on the basis of the processes that they manage. For example, budgeting, accounting and human resource management organizations are found in almost every government. In countries influenced by the French tradition, there may also be organizations responsible for accountability and oversight; the number of these organizations, such as inspectorates, are increasing in many other countries as auditing and performance become more central to managing the public sector (Pollitt, 2003). These organizations are often much segmented from other organizations in government, as the classic distinction between line and staff organizations continues to be played out. On the one hand, organizations responsible for actually delivering services to citizens tend to resent the 'central agencies' that only appear to meddle with and slow the processes of implementation. On the other hand, the process-based organizations may consider the line agencies as too willing to skirt important requirements in their pursuit of fulfilling their own missions and as not understanding the importance of the control functions within government.

Analysis

Although there are some clear examples of each of the above types of organization, many examples are ambiguous. For example, we can argue that a ministry of agriculture is based on purpose, but it could also be argued to be serving a particular clientele – farmers – or a place – rural areas. And the probable answer is that ministries of agriculture in reality are doing some of all of the above functions. In different settings, ministries may emphasize one function more than others, given the political and economic pressures on the ministry. For example, in settings in which there is significant rural depopulation, there may be more emphasis on how to help farmers and rural communities than on the economics of agriculture.

In addition, most departments organized on one principle will have components that are organized on other principles. For example, the above department of agriculture may have one bureau that is concerned with rural development (place) and another that provides loans to farmers (people) and yet another that does its budgeting and accounting (process). While these internal structures are useful for meeting the policy and management needs of the organization, they may also create internal conflicts, given that the different units will have different priorities and political constituencies. Finally, although these distinctions are far from watertight, they do matter and perhaps they matter more politically than in any other way. Interest groups and groups in society will fight to maintain their own organization as a focus for their activities. And the organizations themselves will fight to protect their own conceptions of policy and to protect their 'heartlands' (Weible and Jenkins-Smith, 2016).

Other barriers to coordination[1]

Although to some extent specialization is the foundation of coordination problems within the public sector, there may be other sources of these problems. Perhaps most importantly, organizations and their leaders will fight to defend their organizational 'turf' regardless of any specific policy conflicts or lack thereof. That is, organizations want to protect their budgets and their personnel allocations against perceived threats from other organizations or from central agencies (see below) attempting to impose cuts. If an organization believes that cooperation will threaten those resources, they are less likely to do so.

One of the most important resources organizations have is information. In any organization such as those in the public sector that depend on information as a fundamental policy instrument, information is power. If person A knows something that person B does not, then A has some power over B. And the same logic applies to whole organizations. But information is also crucial for coordination and collaboration, as the events of both 11 September 2001 in the United States and 11 November 2015 in Paris have demonstrated (Breeden, 2016). Time also imposes constraints on effective coordination. This is true in part simply because negotiating arrangements for coordination is time-consuming, and not all organizations will want to invest that time and effort. In addition, in many policy areas coordination must occur over time. For example, to ensure food safety, products must be inspected on the farm, in transit, during processing and then in distribution. If any link in this chain of coordination fails, then the entire system may fail.

Finally, some of the mechanisms associated with NPM tend to reduce the willingness of individuals and organizations to coordinate with others. Perhaps most importantly, performance management (Bouckaert and Halligan, 2008) emphasizes the ability of individual administrators and their organizations to reach certain targets, and potentially punishes those who are not successful. If any of those actors perceive that investing in coordination with other organizations will in any way diminish their ability to reach their goals, they are less likely to invest, even if doing so might assist in reaching broader social goals.

Why Coordinate?

Although we have been arguing in favor of coordination in public administration, why is this so important? In addition to simple tidiness and the appearance

---

[1]For a more complete discussion of barriers to coordination see Peters (2015a).

of a well-organized governing apparatus, there are several other good reasons for improving coordination. Perhaps the most important of these is that it can create better services for citizens. For example, if a citizen is receiving social benefits, it would be useful to coordinate those benefits with education and training services, perhaps with health, and perhaps with housing programs. Dealing with the 'whole client' might be a cliché in social services but it is an important means of providing better services to the public.

As well as improving the services provided to citizens, improving coordination can improve the internal functioning of government. Government programs can at times contradict one another, or duplicate one another, and addressing these issues can reduce the total cost of government and make it appear better managed to citizens. Eliminating duplications and contradictions will also save money and provide more resources for other policy purposes. All of these factors can contribute to greater public confidence and legitimacy for government.

Although coordination has always been a concern for government, its importance has been increased by the NPM reforms of the past decades. These reforms have tended to fragment further already fragmented governments, and to emphasize performance in individual programs and organizations over more collective goals. Such changes in public administration have produced more autonomy for organizations and individuals, with the consequent need to create 'joined up government' (Pollitt and Bouckaert, 2011) out of the extremely segmented and fragmented public sectors that have been created.

We have also seen a growing need for coordination alongside the increasing salience of issues that cut across jurisdictional borders in government, such as immigration, climate change, safety and security and social policy issues such as homelessness and housing. A single department or agency cannot devise a program on any of these issues that is likely to succeed. Instead, several organizations, coordinated horizontally and vertically, need to find a collaborative framework within which all actors can offer a contribution based on their expertise toward a coherent, collective effort.

Mechanisms for Coordination

Even if there is a commitment to coordination among the actors in government, actually achieving greater coherence in policy and administration may be difficult. There are at least four approaches to coordination in government, all of which have some validity and utility. All of these approaches can be seen both as intellectual explanations for the processes and as means through which real-world administrators can pursue coordination. However, all of these approaches to coordination also have their own problems and their own sources of failure.

Markets

The neo-classical model of the market is essentially that of a coordination device. It coordinates buyers and sellers using a price mechanism. While that model of coordination may work well for markets, at least in theory, it appears less readily applicable to coordination within the public sector. To a great extent the logic of the public sector is contrary to that of the market, and decisions are meant to be made on criteria that go well beyond simple efficiency or the search for the lowest price.[2] That said, there are market-type mechanisms that can be used for coordination and policy-making in the public sector. Perhaps the clearest example is the use of internal markets in healthcare and social services (Jerome-Forget, White and Weiner, 1995). Although all the bargaining is done with public money, internal markets separate purchasers from providers of services and have those actors bargain over price and quality. The same mechanisms can be used to purchase services from other policy sectors, for example, social care for individuals discharged from hospitals.

Networks

Networks are almost inherently coordination devices, being composed of actors who have some common interest in a policy area or areas and who interact on a more or less regular basis concerning that policy. Whether they are explicitly discussing coordination or not, these interactions are likely to facilitate coordination and to demonstrate possible areas of cooperation among them. Furthermore, if there is a coordination problem, being a member of a network provides a public servant or politician with the connections needed to address the issue.

The career civil service is a natural network that can, and generally does, facilitate coordination. Civil servants who have worked in government for some years have interacted with their counterparts in other organizations and tend to know whom to call if there is an issue. This is especially true if, as is the case in the British and Canadian civil services, an individual is likely to have moved around among different organizations and to be acquainted with a range of people (and policy issues). Unfortunately for the coordination process (and perhaps policy-making more generally), the opening of the public service to outsiders as another component of NPM has eliminated some of the possibilities for networking within government.[3]

The public sector can also institutionalize networks of public and private sector actors to address specific policy problems, especially those that tend to persist across time. For example, after a spate of child abuse scandals in the United Kingdom that went undetected for some years because of coordination failures among the police, schools, social workers and hospitals, the Children's Act of 2004 mandated local safeguarding children boards to attempt to provide more integrated protection for vulnerable children. In addition to the networks within the public sector, other forms of networks can also be beneficial to efforts at coordination and policy integration. The large literature on network governance (Koppenjan and Klijn, 2004; Sørensen and Torfing, 2007a) has emphasized the capacity of actors – even those with divergent interests – to work together to

---

[2]This is not to say that efficiency is not desirable, but only that it is one of numerous criteria that any public organization must consider in its decision making.

[3]Yet another example of the excessively narrow concept of efficiency that has been at the heart of NPM reforms.

solve policy problems. While some of this literature may paint an excessively rosy picture of the capacity of networks, there is little doubt that the interactions characteristic of these structures, and their interactions with multiple actors within government, can contribute to coordination.

The above said, the network literature tends to assume that once actors join a network structure, they suddenly become less self-interested. In reality, they may want to be involved in networks because they need to defend that self-interest. Furthermore, given a number of actors are involved and the frequent absence of clear decision rules, networks may be able only to produce decisions by the lowest common denominator rather than through more innovative solutions to coordination, or public policy more generally (Scharpf, 1988).

Collaboration

The third approach to coordination involves the use of ideas and framing issues as opposed to more structural and process methods. All policies are, whether explicitly or implicitly, based on ideas about the nature of the problem being addressed as well as about the instruments that are available to 'solve' the problem. The different possible ideas about policy, often based on professional as well as organizational commitments, then serve as effective barriers to coordination (Payan, 2006). Eugene Bardach (1998) has discussed 'collaboration' as a mechanism for coordination, which means having individuals in different agencies discuss the ideas underlying coordination difficulties and to find some common ground. Schön and Rein (1994; see also van Hulst and Yanow, 2016) have discussed this process as 'reframing' and as a means of solving difficult policy disputes. The fundamental idea in this approach is that coordination can be best achieved through developing some common frame for the policy. This process is often difficult, given both organizational interests and commitments to particular conceptions of policy, but if it is successful it can be more enduring than other forms of coordination.

Hierarchy

Hierarchy is by far the most common means for attempting to create coordination and integration in the public sector. When faced with problems of fragmentation and policy coherence governments usually revert to the usual top-down mechanisms (but see Chisholm, 1989). Although they all involve hierarchy to some extent, governments have a wide array of mechanisms to produce the desired coordination. A country's cabinet is the clearest example of a hierarchical coordination device. The ministers responsible for the major organizations and policies of a government meet together in cabinet to decide on the collective policies of the government, and this provides an extremely useful locus for coordination. That can happen, however, only if the members of the cabinet are aware of the policies being advocated by their colleagues and have sufficient time to consult with one another. It also requires that the cabinet is an effective decision-making body and not just a rubber stamp for the prime minister or president.

Cabinets also function through committee systems designed to bring together ministers working in relatively similar policy areas and to provide them a forum for discussion and collective decision-making (Vercesi, 2012). These committees at the ministerial level tend to be supported by committees of senior public servants from the same ministries that are also are engaged in coordination activities. Again the effectiveness of these structures will depend on the level of information of the members and their capacity to make decisions that have some impact on final decisions of government.

The use of so-called central agencies is perhaps the most common mechanism for producing coordination. By central agencies we mean those organizations that control other organizations within the public sector – such as ministries of finance, personnel agencies, budget organizations (Campbell and Szablowski, 1979; Craft and Peters, 2015b). These organizations do not provide services to other organizations but they do function within the public sector. One of their tasks is to serve their political masters and create greater policy integration. They use their hierarchical power, and especially their control of finances, to 'encourage' other organizations to cooperate. The most important of these central agencies is the office of the prime minister or the office of the president (see Dahlström, Peters and Pierre, 2011). As even parliamentary governments become more 'presidential', with prime ministers acquiring increased powers (Poguntke and Webb, 2007; Eymeri-Douzanes, Boix and Mouton, 2015) these offices have increased in power and have the capacity to create greater coordination among the ministries and agencies of government. But even those powerful offices may encounter substantial difficulties in overcoming the commitment of individual ministries to their programs and to their clientele.

Some of the capacity for the offices of presidents and prime ministers will depend, however, on their own organization. For example, the *Bundeskanlersamt* in Germany is organized primarily on a 'mirror principle'. This means that it mirrors the structure of government, which gives the Federal Chancellor a good deal of control over the individual ministries; however, it tends to segment the manner in which this office deals with policy issues. The Executive Office of the President in the United States, in contrast, has three councils that coordinate policy within broad policy areas.[4] These councils, perhaps especially the National Security Council, are faced with organizations with fundamentally different policy perspectives and attempt to provide a more integrated approach.

Central agencies

While central agencies are important sources of coordination, governments sometimes encounter the problem of 'coordinating the coordinators'. That is, although they all may have coordination functions, central agencies may themselves have organizational goals that are not compatible and which

---

[4]The problem of coordinating across these three areas does remain, of course, and more problems than one might initially imagine do cut across national security, economic policy and domestic policy.

cause conflicts. For example, offices serving a prime minister with ambitious policy goals may conflict with ministries of finance committed to fiscal rectitude. Or personnel organizations may be committed to the pay and benefits of the public service and find any austerity measures imposed by finance to be unacceptable.

Junior ministers and ministers without portfolio

A second strategy for coordinating fragmented programs within the public sector is to assign a minister who may not have departmental responsibilities to attempt to bring together the necessary services and to coordinate the programs. In some cases, ministers without portfolio are close allies of the Prime Minster and serve as his or her deputies for these and other tasks. Junior ministers may be given the tasks of coordinating services for a particular client group, such as women, children or immigrants. These junior ministers may also have a geographical orientation, as they have had in Canada in some instances. While these coordinating ministers have the virtue of not having to defend a ministry and its budget in cabinet, they have the associated difficulty that because of having no organizational base, they have relatively less power and fewer resources than do departmental ministers.[5] Therefore, unless the minister without portfolio enjoys the strong support of the prime minister or the central agencies, they may not be effective in generating the type of cooperation that would be required.

Superministries

Creating large ministries that contain a number of organizations, which in principle should be coordinated, is another hierarchical strategy for coping with fragmentation. For example, Employment and Social Development Canada comprises a wide array of labor market and social programs that consume a large proportion of the total federal budget. All these programs contribute to broad social goals and would have to be coordinated if they were implemented by different departments.

But, putting organizations into a single ministry does not guarantee coordination, but may only make the coordination issues intramural. For example, the US Department of Defense was created in 1947, but the various armed forces continue to have their own policy perspectives and priorities, and procurement continues to present problems. The army wants heavy main battle tanks, while the marines prefer lighter tanks that can be more easily delivered by airplanes. And in practice, internal coordination difficulties may be greater than those across departments simply because the lack of coherence may be less obvious.

---

[5]When one of us interviewed such a minister and asked what powers he had, the answer was 'The power to beg'.

Czars

While the junior ministers mentioned above are functioning within the ordinary hierarchy of cabinet, other officials may be appointed outside that usual hierarchy to address issues that are of special importance and which may cut across usual departmental lines. These officials have come to be called czars. The idea is to make a single individual accountable for performance in a particular narrowly defined policy area and give him or her the backing of the chief executive to achieve those goals. The first recent example of this strategy was the appointment of the 'drug czar' in the United States, but during the economic crisis after 2008, a number of such positions were appointed to coordinate action in particular areas (Vaughn and Villalobos, 2015). The problem with coordination through czars is that these individuals themselves often have tightly defined spheres of power, so that there is again some need to coordinate the coordinators. In addition, much of their power is symbolic, and like junior ministers, they have more responsibility than they have power and resources. Still, even with those limitations, identifying important policy problems and giving individuals the responsibility for them does send important signals to the rest of government and to society.

Moving from Coordination to Strategy

Although coordination is an important goal for governments, even the positive version of coordination described above may be insufficient. Positive coordination assumes that the organizations involved will find means of cooperating on existing programs. But that approach may not emphasize the need for more strategic approach to governing. Not only is there a need to coordinate in the present, but there is also a need to consider longer-term goals and programs. The question may be best phrased as how to integrate policies and implementation in order to reach broader social goals. Achieving and maintaining a strategic perspective is difficult for governments (see A. M. Jacobs, 2011), especially for democratic governments. Each government will want to implement its own priorities and not be bound by earlier decisions; however, continuity is important for providing effective governance. While most of the enthusiasm about public planning has vanished from politics, there remains a need for some strategic sense of governing for the future, and a capacity to invest both real resources and political commitment toward strategic goals.

Somewhat paradoxically, although we are discussing strategy as a higher level of coordination among organizations, it may be easier for individual organizations within the public sector to create and maintain a sense of mission and a strategic vision of the future. A single organization will have a more integrated set of values and may be able to insulate itself more from contradictory political pressures. A single organization may also find it easier to create a 'credible commitment' (North, 1993) to its long-term goals so that its members and clients can plan effectively for their own behavior. But with that we may simply return to a longer-term version of the fragmentation that besets government.

The Limits of Coordination

Much of this chapter has praised increasing policy coordination, but despite claims by some that coordination is the 'philosopher's stone' of public administration, there are some limits to its capacity to solve administrative problems. Not all administrative problems are coordination problems, and perhaps more importantly, an emphasis on coordination may in some cases limit the capacity to solve problems. The managerialist assumptions (see Chapter 2) of neat, efficient public administration must sometimes confront the messier real world of administration.

The rationality of redundancy

One of the usual tenets of efficient administration is that there should be no redundancy. There should be one office or one official responsible for an activity and anything more is wasteful. But some systems, such as spacecraft or nuclear power plants, are designed on the principle of having at least one level of redundancy of crucial components, if not more – moreover, these seemingly over-designed systems may also fail. And even if the possibility of policy failure is not paramount, at times redundant organizations may provide different perspectives on a problem and improve the overall quality of public programs.

Redundancy is obviously most important when the costs of failure are the highest. For example, warning systems for military attacks or for extreme weather events will be safer if there are multiple sensors, perhaps using different types of information. Health organizations at several levels of government monitor disease patterns, and although they exchange information, their different perspectives may also be valuable for obtaining a full picture of the dangers of communicable and especially pandemic diseases.

Where to draw the line?

Although we may want to create higher levels of coordination within the public sector, there is no clear answer of how much coordination is enough, or perhaps too much? To some extent all programs impact each other, if only in minor ways. So when are the right programs included in coordination, and when do we need to add more? For example, in the United States, the Department of Homeland Security was created to coordinate responses to terrorism, and other threats to national security. As it was created, it included 22 organizations that were drawn from six cabinet departments, but it did not include other organizations, such as those responsible for intelligence gathering and processing, which might well have been done so.

Accountability

Maintaining accountability is the second major reason for questioning the importance of coordination in all settings. Accounting and legal organizations at the center of government (see above) want to be able to track money and legal authority in the implementation of public programs. If programs are well coordinated then those resources may be too intertwined to monitor as effectively as some officials might like to do. The extent to which this tracking of resources is central to governing will differ across administrative cultures, with more legalistic systems tending to encounter greater difficulties in accepting highly integrated public services.

Managing creative and scientific activities

Contemporary governments are involved in a number of scientific and creative activities, ranging from hiring their own scientists to develop higher-yield nuclear weapons to providing grants to ballet companies. What may bind such disparate activities is that they may be extremely difficult to coordinate, and indeed coordination may be undesirable and counter-productive. For example, Vice-President Biden in the United States initiated a 'Moon Shot' to deal with cancer treatment, but it remains to be seen if this approach to biomedical research is superior to the typical pattern of multiple avenues of research with many failures.

Specialization

Finally, we return to the fundamental virtue of specialization in public sector organizations. While coordination can produce benefits through cooperation and collaboration, specialization produces real benefits through expertise and a focus on single policy areas. The question for institutional designers, and for government more generally, is how to balance these two important values in governing? The balance may be struck differently depending on the values of the government in question, the costs of coordination and the nature of the policy areas involved.

Summary and Conclusions

As we have argued in each of the preceding chapters, the study of public administration has been constructed on a number of contradictory principles. This chapter has addressed the contradiction between fragmentation, or more politely specialization, and coordination in governing. Both of these concepts are important for good governance, so the question clearly becomes how to balance them when confronting real-world policy problems. And as is true for the other principles we have discussed, there is little theoretical or analytic guidance for choosing the right mix of the two. Even with the conflict between the principles of coordination and specialization, the need to coordinate is often present, and unfulfilled. Perhaps even more important is the desirability of developing more strategic approaches to governing and public policy. Public policies and administration are often fragmented and designed to cope with short-term issues rather than longer-term problems. With the increasing complexity of public policies and their connections both within the national government and the international environment, the need to coordinate will only increase. However, the increasing technical content of many policy areas means that specialization may also be more important, and that the debate over these two concepts will continue.

6

Simplicity Versus Complexity: Programs and Implementation

Of all the dichotomies that describe public administration, one of the most basic is the distinction between simplicity and complexity. While to some extent all of governing and policymaking is complex and involves a number of actors and organizations, some problems – the proverbial wicked problems – are more complex than are others (but see Peters, 2015b). Likewise, some administrative systems build in greater complexity in their structures and processes than do others. That said, in almost all cases administration has become more complex in response to the ideas of New Public Management (NPM) and participatory reforms in public administration.

Even if we recognize that a policy problem is complex, how do we address that problem with the greatest likelihood of success? The general response of policymakers and public administrators has been to match the complexity of issues with equally complex solutions, as well as with complex structures for implementation. Moreover, even for more mundane policy problems the solutions are becoming more complex and attenuated. Interestingly, these changes in administration often are done in the name of efficiency and good management, whereas they may complicate administration and obscure accountability.

Matching Problems and Solutions

Public administration is about solving public policy problems. While most citizens think that the design of interventions is, and should be, done by the legislature and by ministers, the role of public bureaucracy in advising those political officials is important for the final design of policies. Furthermore, the implementation of any programs designed to 'solve' policy problems depends heavily on public administration, and the capacity of bureaucracies to translate great policy intentions into action.[1]

The tendency in most analyses of public policy and public administration is to discuss policy problems using the names of functional policy areas – health, defense, or whatever. Alternatively, policymakers and scholars describe the problems in terms of the instruments that are usually employed to address them: 'This is a regulatory problem'. Both of these characterizations of policies are useful, but tend to ignore the significant degree of variation within those categories, for example, the differences between kindergartens and research universities in education; the differences between anti-trust regulation and regulating food safety are just as large. Therefore, we should begin to think about policy problems in more analytic terms if we want to make good matches between those problems and the putative solutions that may be chosen.

The available literature provides a variety of means of classifying public policy problems (Peters and Hoornbeek, 2005). For example, some policy problems such as defense involve creating public goods, while others such as social services create more private benefits.[2] Likewise, some policy problems – building a bridge as a simple example – are large-scale and require policy interventions that will address the problem in its totality, while others can be addressed more incrementally (Schulman, 1980). Also, some problems can be addressed simply by providing money – old-age pensions – while others involve deprivations of rights and human dignity that may be more difficult to remedy.

One of the most important ways to think about the problems faced by government is to think in terms of their complexity (Klijn, 2008; Room, 2012). That term is used frequently to describe the problems encountered by governments, but we should be careful to distinguish problems that are complex from those that are merely complicated. The latter type of problem may involve several actors and have a number of moving parts, but the relationships are largely linear, is predictable, and there is a relatively accepted methodology for dealing with the problem. For example, conventional public sector functions such as water treatment or building streets involve well-established and readily manageable technologies, whereas policies for climate change have neither of those characteristics. An increasing number of major problems in the public sector, however, are complex in the more precise meaning of the term (Room, 2012). Complexity is not, however, new in government. Indeed, some old functions of the public sector involve technologies that are contested, not least of which is education. And the emergence of issues such as climate change, which are almost classic cases of 'wicked problems' (Rittel and Webber, 1973), makes the tasks of

---

[1] The word 'solve' is in quotation marks because very few policy problems are ever really solved. The conditions may be ameliorated, but most policymaking is actually returning to old problems with new policies and with renewed high hopes.

[2] These examples are not watertight at all. Defense spending creates substantial private benefit for defense contractors, while social services may create some public goods through reducing crime and violence, as well as the public benefit of living in a more humane society.

governing more difficult. These types of problem do not have ready solutions and involve numerous unpredictable relationships among variables that will be difficult to manage.

One of the several questions that arise about the real and probably increasingly complex problems facing the public sector is the extent to which the solutions offered by the public sector need to mirror the complexity of the problems (Galaz, forthcoming). The usual assumption is that complexity requires as much complexity in the answers, but if there are numerous unknowns about the dynamics of the policy area then arguably simple answers may be preferable. If a complex attempt at a solution fails it may be difficult to determine what aspects of the solutions were at fault. However, if simpler modes of intervention are selected, it may be possible to understand better how the possible elements of a more complex solution may function.

The experimental logic of selecting interventions expressed above is in contrast to the usual political logic of making policy. Given the competition for scarce resources, politicians and bureaucrats usually must make excessive claims about their certainty about the intervention, its likelihood of success, and the social benefits of that success. Yet, learning from an intervention is important and may sound reasonable to policy analysts, but it is unlikely to please citizens who neither want to be experimented on nor want to pay for that experiment. That said, to some extent any policy is an experiment. There are relatively few certainties in policy designs. Furthermore, the implementation process itself is to some extent experimental, given that although there are some well-established patterns, predicting the outcomes of implementation is not easy. The environment of policy may change, and even slight changes in a policy may reduce or enhance the possibilities of success. Therefore, as we examine implementation, with both its simple and more complex of forms of intervention, we will understand the difficulties involved in making the good ideas of policy actually work for citizens. And we may also think about forms of implementation as experiments themselves.

Simplicity as the Default Solution

Implementation is the process of putting public programs into effect. Legislatures may pass laws, or the executive can issue decrees, but these are virtually meaningless unless they are put into effect. This is the classic role of public administration which we generally call implementation (Pressman and Wildavsky, 1974). Governments have been engaged in implementation since their inception, but the term is a more recent creation and has become a significant component of the study of public administration.

Over the course of development of implementation research, there have been at least four major periods of analysis, each building to some extent on the previous ones.[3] The first, as mentioned above, was the initial definition of the term by

---

[3]Malcolm Goggin (1990) argued for the existence of three stages in implementation research, but we have elaborated this somewhat. See also Saetren (2005; 2014).

Pressman and Wildavsky and their identification of 'clearance points' as a means of understanding the complexity of the process. The idea of a clearance point is that there is a location, and with that a decision-maker, where a positive decision must be made if the program is to be implemented as intended, or not. This perspective on implementation is analogous to the more general model of 'veto points' posited by George Tsebelis (2002) in comparative politics. The Pressman-Wildavsky idea of clearance points is a simple but powerful model of how public administration functions when putting programs into effect, but it has not been without its critics. Elinor Bowen (1982) argues that the model essentially lacks agency and the clever administrator or politician can devise means of evading or overcoming the obstacles appearing at 'clearance points'. For example, a dedicated implementer does not give up if he or she fails at one of the clearance points, they may try to gain acceptance several times or find ways of evading the obstruction. Likewise, Ernst Alexander (1989) argued that the serial implementation model of Pressman and Wildavsky is only a special case of a more general model of the policy process and one that is most likely to fail.

The second stage of development of implementation research emphasized the debate between 'top-down' and 'bottom-up' approaches to implementation (see Linder and Peters, 1989). The Pressman–Wildavsky approach was in these terms 'top-down'. It assumed a law that had to be implemented and then deviations from the intention of the law were in essence implementation failures. The contrasting argument was that the design of implementation, and even of the legislation itself, should begin from 'bottom-up', with consideration of the types of program that would be most easily implemented (Elmore, 1979). Thus, the bottom-up approach emphasized feasibility in the design of legislation as well as in the selection of means of implementing programs.

The critiques of both approaches to implementation contained normative as well as practical elements.[4] On the one hand, the top-down approach is argued to be excessively legalistic and to involve perhaps unrealistic assumptions about the hierarchical nature of the way in which government functions. Furthermore, the top-down approach does not take sufficiently into account democratic politics and negotiations with stakeholders. On the other hand, the bottom-up approach may place excessive emphasis on feasibility, and lead to making policies based on what is easiest to do, rather than on policies that may have the greatest benefit. In addition, working from the bottom to up does not provide a clear sense of how implementation performs as it conflates implementation and policy formulation.

The third stage of implementation research consists of a number of more empirical analyses of implementation processes. These have not tended to break new theoretical ground but they have focused more on measurement, hypothesis development and the application of the usual canon of social science methodology to the study of implementation. There has also been an increase in the number of studies comparing implementation efforts, as opposed to the numerous single case studies that characterized the earlier work. This corpus of

---

[4]For a review, see Hill and Hupe (2015).

research has brought implementation more into the mainstream of the social sciences, but in the process it has revealed some important weakness in the literature. One of these problems is the presence of too many variables to explain success, or more commonly failure, of implementation (see below, pp. 79–80). That multiplicity of variables reflects the absence of any unifying theoretical approach in the literature that has been characterized more in identifying issues within individual cases (see Bozeman, 2013). And, as we will argue in more detail below, much of implementation research remains focused on the core public sector rather than on the numerous interactions with private sector actors that are important for implementation.

The fourth stage of implementation research, which has been emphasized during the past several years, focuses on the exercise of discretion by public administrators (Hupe, 2013), especially public administrators in direct contact with the public. Discretion has always been available for 'street-level' bureaucrats,[5] and that discretion is crucial for the implementation process (see Tummers and Bekkers, 2014). Implementation research has become more focused on the manner in which this discretion is exercised, and controlled, and the implications of the uses of discretion for the public sector. This shift in focus also emphasizes the agency of the individual implementer as opposed to more structural features of organizations that are involved in implementation.

Although some of these approaches to implementation, such as the original Pressman and Wildavsky model, do point to the number of actors involved in the process of implementation the orientation was that the process was relatively linear and governmental. These conceptions of implementation therefore provided relatively simple solutions for the problem of making government programs work. As well as emphasizing the role of state actors in implementation, these approaches to implementation assume that the outcome of the process should be uniform. While that assumption is important from the perspective of equality, it may not reflect the desires of individuals to have some choices in the programs they consume. Although those implementation strategies may produce benefits for citizens, they also will introduce increased managerial complexity into the implementation process.

Instruments and Implementation

Although the four strands of research on implementation discussed above represent an important chronology for the development of this field, there is another strand of thinking that has been involved in all four. Implementation can be seen as being carried out through policy instruments, ranging from very simple instruments such as direct provision of government services through to more complex contracting and partnership arrangements (see below).

The instruments or 'tools' literature (see Hood, 1974) itself has interesting dimensions of simplicity and complexity. Christopher Hood's initial discussion

---

[5]Political anthropologists tend to refer to these officials as 'interface bureaucrats', a more apt term in many ways. These officials represent the interface between state and society. See Olivier de Sardan (2014).

of instruments listed four basic instruments – nodality, authority, treasure and organization. Nodality refers to the role of government as an information node, and its ability to use that information both to monitor society and to control the economy and society.[6] Authority and law are fundamental instruments available to government, as is treasure – the ability to spend and to tax. And finally governments are composed of organizations that have personnel and procedures for implementing public policies. Other scholars have advanced even more basic lists of two or three fundamental instruments – carrots, sticks and sermons, for example (Bemelmans-Videc, Rist and Vedung, 1998), and Gormley (1989) argued that there are basically two – muscles and prayers. The numerous other instruments that are discussed, these scholars argue, are all variations on these few underlying instruments. For Gormley, for example, all policy interventions are based either on some form of coercion or on some form of persuasion, or perhaps a combination of those two underlying instruments.

The alternative approach in tools research is to develop large catalogs of instruments and to examine the characteristics of each. An early use of tools to examine economic policy discussed 64 possible tools (Kirschen et al., 1964) and more recent catalogs have contained at least several dozen alternatives. These individual instruments – for example, subsidies, grants, monitoring, regulation – are, however, hybrids involving most if not all of the more basic instruments discussed by other authors. A tax subsidy, for example, obviously involves treasure but it also involves legal authority and the organization that administers the law. While tools are often discussed by policy designers as if there were merely technical and managerial, they should also be considered more politically. Each of these instruments for delivering public services has a political meaning just as does the content of the legislation being implemented. For example, a tool that uses the authority of the state, such as direct student loan, will involve a different constellation of political forces than will one that involves actors from the private sector through partnerships or loan guarantees. And the choice of tools may be a political strategy for building support for a program that might otherwise be difficult to enact.

The use of tools that involve coalitions, and with that the use of multiple tools to address a problem, also increases the complexity of the implementation process. However, as noted below, somewhat paradoxically the advocates of efficiency also tend to advocate the use of implementation schemes with multiple actors involved in partnerships and contracts. The dominant assumption is that direct government implementation is less efficient than the use of nongovernmental actors – especially market actors – in implementing public programs. The importance of coalitions in understanding policy tools is reflected in the hybrid nature of most policy programs. Few programs attempt to achieve their targets with a single tool but tend to utilize a variety of different instruments that can provide a range of incentives and disincentives for behavior. These combinations arise in part because of political necessity, while also reflecting

---

[6]Building on that thought, Hood (1976) argued that each of the basic types of instrument could be conceptualized as a 'detector' and as an 'effector'.

the complex and variegated nature of policy problems. For example, a basic public program such as taxation involves law, organization, treasure and to some extent nodality in order to collect taxes and detect noncompliance.

Finally, implementation practice has moved away to some extent from reliance on law and treasure to develop more mechanisms for self-enforcement – nodality or sermons, albeit sermons that are said very much sotto voce. The use of 'nudges' (Thalen and Sunstein, 2008) reflects a movement toward providing subtle behavioral cues to induce citizens to do what governments want them to do. For example, simply parking an empty police car on a road can reduce speeding, without the costs of enforcement (at least until speeders catch on).[7]

Barriers to Implementation

Although implementation is a classic function of government, even in its simplest forms it is not easy, and any number of factors can prevent effective and timely implementation. Therefore, we need to understand the classic implementation model and the barriers to putting programs into effect. And, in turn we need to examine the alternative instruments for implementation and consider the challenges which those patterns of implementation pose for effective governance. Some of these barriers are inherent in the nature of governing, while others are products of the particular design of the policy being implemented, and the process of implementation. Christopher Hood (1976) discussed the barriers to perfect implementation some decades ago, but the same barriers to implementation arise today.

The nature of the policy problems themselves is the most important barrier to effective, much less perfect, implementation. As already noted policy problems come in a variety of forms, but an increasing number are characterized as 'wicked' or even 'super-wicked' (Levin et al., 2012). Herbert Simon (1973b) had referred to these problems as 'ill-structured'. These policy problems pose particular problems for policy formulation, but they also impose substantial problems for implementation (see Head and Alford, 2015). The uncertain nature of these problems and their very scale may make devising effective implementation schemes substantially more difficult than for more well-structured problems.

In addition to the nature of the problems, one of the most fundamental barriers to effective implementation is the legislation that is being implemented. Because legislation is created through a political process, it often reflects compromises that produce internal contradictions or virtually impossible demands on the implementers. Similarly, the legislation may have been written with little regard to the tasks of implementation, so that even if the policy logic is valid the constraints on implementation may prevent a program from being effectively put into practice. Legislators are not administrators and often do not think in terms of the actions that will be required to make a program function effectively, much less efficiently. Even if the legislation to be implemented is designed well,

---

[7]These 'nudges' are cheap and often effective, but they do raise ethical questions about the extent to which citizens are being manipulated.

it often will still constitute a departure from the established programs,[8] and hence require some change in routines within the implementing organization. Generally there will not be overt resistance to a new program, but it still represents new rules to learn and procedures to implement. Change becomes all the more difficult when, as in many areas of social policy, change follows change and the individuals responsible for implementation become somewhat jaded about the potential wonders of the 'new' program.

As well as the implementation problems arising through weaknesses, or innovations, in the legislation, implementation can also face barriers because of inadequate resources. Even if a program is well-designed and has a good implementation plan, if the resources are inadequate then it is not likely to be effective. For example, the plans for combating the Ebola virus in West Africa were based on the best available knowledge of the World Health Organization and other advisors, but simply not having enough doctors and quarantined hospital beds and outreach workers permitted the epidemic to persist longer than it might have done.

In addition to the fundamental problems of providing financial and personnel resources for the implementation of programs, implementation can fail through the failure to provide essential elements of the program – what has been referred to as horse-shoe-nail problems (Hood, 1976). If crucial elements are not included in the program and the implementation plan, then the program is doomed to failure. For example, the Department of Homeland Security in the United States wanted to make the national borders more secure after 9/11, and therefore required everyone crossing the borders with Canada and the Bahamas to have a passport. That crossing previously had been possible only with proof of identity. The organization failed to note that millions of Americans worked in Canada but did not have passports and had made no provision for issuing passports quickly to those workers.[9]

Implementation problems also arise from the multiple organizations that may be involved in making a program work effectively. The original Pressman and Wildavsky book, *Implementation*, looked at this problem vertically, given the number of levels of government that were involved in making the economic development program that was the subject of the book function effectively. But horizontal coordination issues can also undermine the successful implementation of programs. For example, healthcare costs may be increased because of inadequate cooperation between social services organizations and health organizations for providing services for elderly patients who could be discharged from the hospital but have nowhere to go for supportive care.

Finally, organizations may fail at implementation because of their failure to adapt. Rigidity is often mentioned as a failing in organizations, and especially for public organizations. While to some extent rigidity in following

---

[8]Most 'new' programs represent reworking of existing programs so the departure may not be as great is it is sometimes made out to be, especially by the political advocates of the program (Hogwood and Peters, 1984; Carter, 2012).

[9]This can also be seen as a coordination problem (see below) because passports are issued by the US Department of State.

legal mandates is admirable in a public organization, that rigidity can also reduce the capacity to cope with changing the circumstances in the relevant environment. To be effective in dealing with any complex policy problems, organizations need to learn and adapt.

Organizing for Implementation

The simplest organizational format for implementation is a ministry or agency with its own field staff that takes the laws that the organization is charged with implementing and puts them into effect on their own. In this pattern of implementation, government organizations have an increased, if far from perfect, capacity to control what is happening in their names. There are, however, relatively few cases of this direct style of implementation remaining in the public sector. As we point out below, the tendency of government has been to develop more complex modes of implementation, which involve actors from the private sector.

The 'agency model' for implementation has a long history in Scandinavia, but has been adopted as a part of the NPM remedy for the ills of public administration (Pierre, 1995a). In its original form, as still largely practiced in Scandinavia, implementation is delegated to independent or quasi-independent agencies that are largely governed by their own boards or Director General. As it has been diffused to other administrative systems (see Pollitt and Talbot, 2004), that independence has been largely lost in favor of executives who are held more directly responsible to their ministers.[10] In any of the versions, however, the underlying principle is to separate policy and administration, with agencies having substantial latitude to make implementation decisions, and therefore, effectively, policy decisions on their own.

Another structural arrangement for implementation relies on subnational governments. Especially in federal governments, a good deal of policy that is made in the central government is implemented by the states or provinces. This pattern of implementation also, first, allows the implementing organization to make a number of its own decisions, and in federalism can be used to reduce the power of central government,[11] and second, enables central government to limit its own need to hire personnel, thus allowing it to appear smaller and less intrusive to voters than it might otherwise seem to be. Although discussed here as involving state or provincial governments, the same pattern could be, and often is, developed using local governments.

---

[10]The original copying of the model, through the 'Next Steps' agencies in the United Kingdom, appeared to attempt to tailor the model to fit the concepts of ministerial responsibility in the system. That, however, may have diminished some of the utility of this style of implementation that was premised on very high levels of autonomy for the agencies.

[11]For example, in Germany, the federal government implements few of its own policies, a conscious choice of institutional designers to limit the powers of the center after the experience of the Third Reich.

All of the above structural solutions to the implementation problem depend on government actors, with various forms of connection to the center. As we explore implementation issues further, we will also point to solutions for implementation problems that go beyond government and involve a variety of private sector actors. Such implementation patterns have become common and although they address some of the issues raised within the public sector, they also present problems of their own.

Complexity as Solution

The above discussion of implementation has to this point discussed the process in relatively simple and legalistic terms. There is a law and public organizations and their members are obliged to make that law work in practice. The assumptions of uniformity, legal certainty and hierarchy all emphasize the linear and *relatively* simple nature of the process. But in practice, implementation has become increasingly complex and we need to understand how that complexity plays out. The complexity is a function not only of an increasing number of actors involved, but also the political values involved in these processes.

The academic discussion of complexity in administration began some decades ago with the identification of 'implementation structures' as the alternative to the typical hierarchical model of implementation. David Porter and Benny Hjern (1981) argued that 'the single, lonely organization was dead' and that scholars (and practitioners) need to understand the increasingly complex interactions within these structures. Furthermore, Lawrence O'Toole (2000) has written extensively on multi-actor implementation. We can conceptualize those implementation structures involving multiple actors as institutions, given that they often represent stable patterns of interaction of organizations and individuals that are involved in implementing particular programs (Peters, 2015a). The increased complexity of implementation reflects important changes in politics and in ideas about how government should administer programs. These ideas have been components of NPM, as well as more participatory ideas about governance (Peters, 2010b). One of the now familiar adages of NPM was 'steer, don't row'. This implied that governments should set policies but not be involved in their direct implementation. The assumption was that implementation could be done more effectively and efficiently by nongovernmental (usually meaning market) actors. More democratic approaches to reforming the public sector also argued for using nongovernmental actors for implementation, justifying the interventions through participation.

Changing Ideas of Administration

The changing nature of administration can be justified through several values that have become enshrined in thinking about administration. These all reflect significant departures from the Weberian or Wilsonian foundations of public administration. We have briefly discussed some of the aspects of changing values in public administration in previous chapters, but the changes in institutional design, and the consequent impacts on implementation, are no less profound and no less important.

Delegation is perhaps the major change in contemporary public administration, which also reflects a change in the complexity of administration, representing moving a good deal of the 'rowing' out of the public sector itself. This delegation corresponds to the principal–agent model, which has informed recent thinking about administration in NPM, as well as in other economic models of governing (Miller, 2005). Delegation is an enduring problem in governing (see McCubbins, Noll and Weingast, 1989; Le Grand, 2013) but has become a dominant pattern in contemporary administration. Much of this delegation has been within the public sector itself, with the agency model for administration described above becoming widely dispersed (Laegreid and Verhoest, 2010). Decentralization can be conceptualized as simply another form of delegation, as administrative tasks, and perhaps policymaking, are passed down to subnational governments. Even in unitary states such as the United Kingdom many functions have been devolved to the constituent parts of the country to provide greater opportunity to produce different policies and different forms of implementation. The emphasis on decentralization has been in part for democratic reasons, and in part for pursuit of efficiency through less hierarchical management systems, and has been instituted in any number of places in which that strategy may be inappropriate (Falleti, 2010).

Another characteristic of newer forms of implementation is the greater use of nongovernmental actors in implementation. It is easy to forget that governments have always used nongovernmental actors of implementation. For example, laws about the practice of medicine and law have almost always been administered by those professions, and policies in areas such as agriculture, fishing and technical standards have often been administered by the parties involved. Whether this is termed 'micro-corporatism' or 'self-regulation' (Steurer, 2013) the effect is the same, with the state delegating to nongovernmental actors.

A variety of mechanisms are used to implement programs through delegated means. The principal means of delegating implementation is through contracting. Governments have long purchased goods through contracting, but the level of contracting for government services has been increased significantly (see Kettl, 2015). Although contracting has numerous virtues for government, it also poses a number of problems. The first is simply that contracts attenuate the implementation process by involving that many more actors and makes accountability more difficult. Second, the problems of accountability in contracting are especially so because it is difficult to write contracts for service provision that are sufficiently clear to be enforceable. Legally contracts depend on specific performance, and defining when adequate social services have been provided can be difficult, and contracting may not be nearly as efficient as having public employees who are committed to their programs. Without the capacity to specify performance there is a strong possibility of shirking and inadequate provision of services. The advocates of contracting and partnerships appear to assume that public employees are lazy and inept (for a critical discussion of the 'shirking' hypothesis see Pierre and Peters, 2017) but the evidence is generally that they are at least as committed to service provision as contractors.

As well as contracting, a variety of partnership arrangements between the public and private sectors have been used to implement public programs.

Many of the partnerships have been in developing physical infrastructure, and they also have been used as instruments for implementing public services such as education or social services. The idea of a partnership is that two relatively equal actors can agree on mechanisms for collaboration around some common goals. The assumption, sometimes explicit but more often implicit, is that the public sector actors would be committed to the service values while private sector actors would be more committed to efficiency and to the use of their managerial expertise to improve the quality of the programs. Like contracting, the use of partnerships involves some heroic assumptions about the capacity of these arrangements to specify what is to be provided and to find ways of bleeding public sector and private sector values in making them work. The tendency appears to be for private sector values to dominate, especially given that public sector actors committed to using these instruments tend themselves to be strongly affected by private sector, managerialist values. And as with contracting, the more attenuated chains involved in service delivery mean that enforcing accountability becomes more difficult. The public sector actors should be the watchdogs for the public interest in these arrangements but the intertwining of the public and private may make them implicit in any misuse of funds or authority (Bozeman, 2007).

The final element of changes in implementation in the contemporary state is that there is an emphasis on choice. The traditional forms of government provision tend to be take it or leave it, with education, public housing or other services being provided by government. Reforms in implementation, and in public policy more generally, have emphasized the ability of individual citizens to choose for themselves what type of policy provision they will consume. In more market-oriented forms this has involved the use of vouchers for a range of services, while in other instances it has involved greater voice by the consumers of programs in shaping the manner in which they are provided. In either case, the citizen or client is not the passive recipient of services but rather a more active partner in the process.

'Soft Governance' and Policy Instruments

If we expand on the notions of choice mentioned above, as well as on the use of partnerships and other collaborative instruments for service delivery (Sandfort and Milward, 2009), we can conceptualize an emerging form of 'soft governance' that is becoming common in implementation. This form of governing, also called 'new governance', involves moving away from traditional command and control instruments toward less directive means of implementation (see Heritier and Lehmkuhl, 2008). Instead of saying 'Thou shalt' or 'Thou shalt not' governments are increasingly saying 'Why don't you?' Instruments such as guidelines, partnerships and benchmarks all enable governments to steer, but to steer at a distance. In this form of governing the client or perhaps the target for regulation, becomes a party to the process of defining the policy and implementing the policy. Co-production, in which the clients become producers, for example neighborhood watch, is perhaps the softest of these forms of governing.

Of course, this style of governance is not entirely new. Governments have permitted self-regulation of actors – perhaps particularly the professions – for centuries, and the delegation of responsibility for governance to private actors often has also led to the misuse of public power for private gain (see Lowi, 1969; Andres, 2009). But permitting greater levels of self-governance need not be invidious, and with appropriate design of mechanisms and appropriate forms of accountability, the softer forms of governance and administration can provide benefits for citizens and for government itself. For citizens, the softer forms of governance may provide greater choice over the types of policy they will consume, and the manner in which they will receive those benefits. The hierarchical model of governance, and of implementation, emphasizes uniformity and minimizes the opportunity of citizens to shape the packages of services they want to receive from government. At the extreme, market-oriented mechanisms such as vouchers (see Bellfield and Levin, 2005) would permit citizens to choose the type of education or housing they might receive. Less extreme versions of this style of governing permit individuals or communities to have direct influence on the policy choices affecting them.

For individuals working within the public sector, the softer style of governing also provides greater opportunities. While NPM has been associated with some forms of delegation, primarily to autonomous and quasi-autonomous organizations, softer and more participatory forms of internal management permit lower echelons of public organizations to make more of their own choices about service delivery. While discretion for street-level bureaucrats (Meyers and Nielsen, 2012) is almost inherent in governing, the softer forms of governing tend to amplify and to laud greater autonomy for these actors, who have regular contact with citizens.

Finally, these mechanisms of softer and more collaborative governing provide benefits for government as a whole, not least because of the capacity to leverage the involvement and resources of nongovernmental actors. At the most basic level the use of nongovernmental actors in collaborative arrangements can reduce the cost of providing services. At another level, collaboration between the public and private sectors can improve the quality of the services delivered, and produce synergies among the organizations. And finally, providing services in this manner can present a less hierarchical perspective of government to citizens who encounter public services on a regular basis. These various forms of collaboration and soft governance will all, everything else being equal, be related to greater diversity in the outcomes of policy and implementation. This diversity appears to provide some greater popular impact on governing, but it may reduce equality in fundamental policy outcomes of government. Thus, like so many choices that must be made about public administration and policy, there are important tradeoffs in the extent to which implementation is more legalistic or softer and more collaborative. Furthermore, the success of softer instruments and citizen choice may be less effective when citizens must choose among rather complicated options, for example health insurance plans in the Affordable Care Act in the United States (Haeder and Weimer, 2013). When confronted with difficult choices or inadequate information some of the most vulnerable members of society may not take up the benefit, exacerbating the inequalities in the system.

Like other mechanisms of private governance, these collaborative arrangements can also pose significant problems for government, and the public. As was argued above concerning self-governance, there is the continuing danger of the purposes of public programs being compromised for private gain. At a minimum there is the danger of public goals becoming tainted by private sector thinking, especially given that NPM and other aspects of the market approach to governing have been accepted by members of the public bureaucracy, or indeed members of private sector organizations have been recruited into open public sector positions. And even legitimated forms of collaboration encounter the risk of being diverted for the benefits of the participants.

Summary and Conclusions

Much of the discussion of implementation above has focused on academic models of implementing public policies. As well as being intellectual exercises, these academic models reflect patterns of implementation in the real world of governing. The different patterns of implementation, especially difference between top-down and bottom-up approaches, and between simpler and more complex implementation, also influence policies and their ability to produce desired outcomes for citizens. In addition, the nature of implementation processes also has political consequences just as do debates over the substantive aspects of policy.

The other major choice that must be made in the design of programs and their implementation is simplicity versus complexity. This entire chapter was framed around that distinction and it is important to understand the potential consequences of each choice. On the one hand, simple strategies for implementation tend to involve instruments that are primarily governmental and organizational structures that depend very strongly on direct implementation by government itself. That strategy allows greater control and also allows learning more readily about the success or failure of the intervention strategy. On the other hand, however, complex problems may be better served with equally complex solutions, especially solutions that involve multiple actors from the private sector. By involving multiple actors and utilizing mixtures of policy instruments an intervention may be able to produce more results. That said, complex solutions – like any activity involving multiple actors – will have multiple opportunities for failure. And the complexity itself may be a source of failure, analogous to the multiple clearance points in the original Pressman and Wildavsky analysis. If nothing else, employing complex solutions makes it more difficult to determine the sources of policy failure.

As well as balancing simplicity and complexity, the choice of implementation strategy also involves balancing equality and equity of outcomes for clients. The legal foundations of much of implementation analysis emphasizes equality – if policies are being implemented well then everyone who is receiving those services will receive the same level and type of service. On the other hand, more complex forms of implementation, and especially those involving nongovernmental actors, may emphasize choice and equity for the individual citizens as opposed to uniformity. Both of these values are important in the public sector, but they involve rather different outcomes for the citizens and mean very different things about the nature of the state.

Implementation, whether conducted through the public sector itself or through complex arrangements involving private sector actors, is crucial for the effectiveness of governance. For most scholars and citizens this is the central role for public administration in the governance process. While that is almost certainly true, public administrators cannot perform this crucial task on their own. Even in administrative systems that rely on direct administration through public employees, these employees do not work for a 'single, lonely organization' but rather are embedded in a web of interactions with other public organizations, their own clients, and stakeholders of the program. Some complexity in administration may be inevitable, but the questions posed here are how much complexity should we design into the implementation structures, and how can we manage that complexity.

7

Rationality Versus Routine: How Do Public Organizations Make Decisions?

We have been discussing the role of public sector organizations in making and implementing public policy, but to this point we have not discussed how those organizations make their decisions. Public organizations make thousands of decisions every day, and those decisions essentially define their performance. The decisions are being made at all levels of public organizations, with individuals at the top of the organization making policy decisions while individuals toward the bottom of organizations apply policies to individual cases. We should think of this decision-making as problem solving. When confronted with a problem, whether it is a major policy issue such as climate change or an individual claimant who thinks that he or she is eligible for a public benefit, an individual or group of individuals in government is confronted with a problem. And that problem appears to require a decision. The assumed decision-maker may be able to avoid the issue, whether by passing the buck to a superior or simply by ignoring it, but even that apparent nondecision is in fact a decision. Doing nothing means that the policies currently in place will prevail and that is certainly a substantive policy choice with real consequences.

This chapter will discuss and evaluate a variety of approaches to understanding policy choices. Each of these approaches to decision-making has its virtues and also has it limits. Understanding these various alternatives therefore provides a set of alternative lenses that can together provide important insights into decision-making. Furthermore, some of the approaches are more applicable at different levels of an organization than at others. For example, more rational forms of decision-making may be applicable for questions like building a road, while less applicable for more complex decisions in foreign policy or health policy.[1]

One of the major limitations of any approach to organizational decision-making is the tendency to anthropomorphize the organizations involved. Although we commonly say the organization makes a decision, in reality it is the individuals within the organization who make those decisions. That role for the individual does not mean that the nature of the organization is irrelevant. The structure of the organization will shape the flow of information and authority among the individuals who occupy it (Thompson, 1961), and hence the nature of an institution is hardly irrelevant for the decisions that are being made in its name. Furthermore, organizations may have collective values that are inculcated into their members and that influence the types of decision that will be made (Goodsell, 2011).

Although individuals must be the actual decision-makers within an organization, it is also crucial to understand that individual and organizational decision-making are different. First, as Herbert Simon (1947) pointed out, individuals are serial processors of decisions. An individual will consider one issue and either reach a decision, or decide to defer that decision, before going on to the next issue. Organizations, in contrast, can parallel process and consider several different issues at the same time. That parallel processing within an organization can obviously be a benefit, but also may pose some problems for it. The various components of an institution may not make decisions that are entirely compatible with each other, producing coordination problems within the organization as well as across organizations within the public sector. Organizations are also different from individual decision-makers in that they may have more consistent preferences than do individuals. Organizations and institutions tend to develop a set of preferences and to inculcate those values into their members.[2] Those preferences may be written down in a book of procedures, or they may be spread informally within the organization, but they do exist and are intended to shape behavior. While those values may be imperfectly institutionalized with the organization, there will still likely be greater intertemporal stability of preferences than for individuals. That consistency of preferences and decision-making is important for public organizations implementing laws, especially when they are implementing laws that affect the basic rights of citizens.

From the perspective of the political leadership responsible for a public organization, however, the stability of preferences and decision-making that is built into public organizations may be a liability rather than a benefit. When there is a change in the leadership of an organization, for example after an election, the new political leaders often want to be able to change the decisions made

---

[1]Scholars such as Thompson and Tuden (1959) and Perrow have discussed different types of policy problems and the possible linkages to styles of decision-making. On policy problems in general, see Peters and Hoornbeek (2005).

[2]In some versions of institutional theory and organization theory, the structure is largely shaped by its values and symbols (see March and Olsen, 1989).

within organizations. But the members of the organization may find it difficult to change their fundamental beliefs and policy preferences, and the political leaders will be faced with a major governance challenge within their own ministry or agency. This discussion of decision-making within public organizations is obviously related to the role of public administration in governing, but it is obviously also about public policy. The decision-making within a public organization is almost entirely about policy, whether it is concerned with advising the political leadership or actually making policy (see Page, 2010) or whether it is implementing a public policy. Therefore, the preferences and values that are institutionalized within the organization are important not only for the internal processing of the organization but also for what actually happens for citizens.

At the extreme, the institutionalization of values and decision premises within organizations may lead to the domination of 'standard operating procedures' within public organizations. Decision-making is difficult and time-consuming, so if the internal procedures of the organization are sufficiently well institutionalized, then active decision-making will be less necessary. The procedures may be successful in many situations and also may produce inappropriate responses in other situations, perhaps in the most important circumstances facing an organization (see Rainey, 2009). The problem may be that the commitment to the procedure may suppress any significant review of the success or failure of those decisions.

It is important to recognize that the lower levels of organizations – often characterized as street-level bureaucrats – are also making a large number of decisions. Indeed most of the decisions made in the public sector are made at that lower level. Those decisions may approximate the rational model more closely than do the decisions made at higher level of the organization. At the lower echelon, there is a relatively clear set of decision premises in the form of law and organizational rules. Furthermore, the needs for information may be more constrained at this level than for policy decisions made at the upper levels of the organizations. The information required at the street level may be contained in the case file of the individual, rather than broader sources and types of information required for making broader policy choices.

The discussion that follows will begin with the assumption of rationality in decision-making that dominates much of the contemporary social sciences. As noted, this approach has some virtues, not least of which is that it provides a clear set of predictions about the behavior of individuals and their organizations. In public administration there has been a long tradition of utilizing bounded rationality as an alternative to the assumption of full rationality. The predictions from this approach are somewhat less clear than those of the approach of full rationality, but it does provide interesting insights into the way in which governments function. Finally, there are several alternative ways of thinking about decisions that are concerned less about rationality and more about interactions and evolution.

The fundamental question in this chapter, therefore, revolves around whether decisions in the public sector are made rationally, or whether they are made in less-demanding ways. The dichotomy between rationality and more routinized forms of making policy, or ways of limiting the demands of rationality for decision-makers, has been a persistent question in the study of public administration and public policy. This chapter assesses the empirical and normative cases for different styles of decision-making, as well as examining the role that political pressures play in those decisions.

Rationality as the Normal Assumption

A common assumption of humans in general and social scientists more particularly is that decision-making should be, can be, and even is rational. The a priori assumption that most people have about decision-making, whether individual or collective, is that the process is rational. The rational process, in turn, assumes that there is a stable set of preferences among decision-makers, that the decision-makers can rank those preferences, and that he or she has sufficient information to understand the likely consequences of their decisions and the impacts of those decisions on their preferences. In other words, the decision-maker must know what he or she wants and can assess how the alternative choices available to them can help them reach their goals. This assumption about decision-making in the public sector has been institutionalized in contemporary political science and public administration. In public administration, one of the fundamental applications of rational choice theory has been in analyzing the behavior of organizations and their leadership. Rather famously, William Niskanen (1971) has argued that bureau chiefs are utility maximizers, and that the object of that maximization is the size of the bureau's budget. The larger budget is assumed to provide the bureau chief with more resources that he or she can use for their own purposes.[3]

Niskanen's conception of budget maximization was somewhat simplistic, but subsequent research has attempted to refine the concept and to point to more subtle strategies that the bureaucrat and the organization can pursue. For example, Patrick Dunleavy (1985) has argued that not all budgetary resources for an organization are equal. Money intended as transfers or grants, for example, cannot be retained by the organization for the benefits assumed by Niskanen to accrue to the organization, while other types of funds can be. Therefore, the rational bureaucrat will attempt to shape his or her budget in particular ways to maximize the retained funds rather than the total budget.[4]

Another, and somewhat contradictory, assumption about the behavior of public bureaucrats is that instead of being budget maximizers, they are leisure maximizers (Hanusch, 1980) or 'shirkers' (Brehm and Gates, 1997). In this perspective public employees attempt to avoid work, and especially attempt to avoid decisions for which they may be held accountable. This rather negative conception of the public employee has a long history in the popular press and in academic literature (see for example Crozier, 1964) but has reached its apotheosis in the conceptions of public employees in rational choice approaches.

---

[3]Unfortunately for the advocates of this approach, there is little or no evidence supporting these assumptions (see Blais and Dion, 1991).

[4]Just as was true for the Niskanen approach, there is little evidence to support this contention (see, for example, Marsh, Smith and Richards, 2000).

Rational choice approaches have also been applied to career choices and strategies of individual civil servants. Even before Niskanen's statement about budget maximization, Anthony Downs (1967) discussed the behavior of bureaucrats and their career choices from a rational perspective. More recently, Teodoro (2011; see also Gailmard and Patty, 2007) has examined the career strategies of bureaucrats through examining their policy entrepreneurship. These accounts assume that rather than some sincere commitment to policy and public management these civil servants are interested primarily in their own advancement. Much classical theory in public administration tends to assume rationality, although not explicitly stating that the decisions are rational in any meaningful sense of the term. For example, the principles of administration associated with Gulick and Urwick (1937) and with the Brownlow Committee (see Hammond, 1990) argue that if these principles of organization are followed then good decisions will be the result. While these classic models of administration do not address the concept of rationality per se, they do make assumptions about the capacity of administrators to make decisions that can directly link policy choices with the premises of those policies.

The classic model of administration therefore adopts in essence a procedural approach to rationality in public administration. The implicit assumption is that following the rules and the procedures within an organization will produce acceptable decisions, and those that are implicitly rational. This concept of procedural rationality also appears in the classic Weberian conceptions of bureaucracy, with the assumption that if the rules and procedures within an institution are obeyed then *Zweckrationalität,* or instrumental rationality, can be achieved (Albrow, 1987).

Strategic management has been another rational approach to public administration. Strategic management argues that managers in public organizations should develop medium and/or long-range plans for their organizations and then link shorter-term goals and behaviors to the more strategic goals (see Bryson, 2012). This longer-term strategic planning is rather standard practice for the private sector and the notion of public organizations having business plans (*sic*) has become common in the public sector. The problem for the public sector, however, is that developing and implementing such strategic plans is substantially more difficult than it is for private sector organizations. Although public organizations do have their own ideas about, and commitments to, policies maintaining a long-term strategy may be difficult given changes in the political leadership of the organization. In addition, the environment of the policy may change. For example, an economic policymaking organization may have a wonderful strategy in place only to be confronted with a recession or with high levels of inflation. Finally, while the goal of a private sector organization is relatively straightforward – profit – but for public sector organizations there are multiple and perhaps competing goals.

Limits on Rationality

While the model of decision-making based on comprehensive rationality is appealing, if for no other reason but that we tend to applaud the notion of rationality, there are a number of barriers to achieving that goal. The model of rationality that is at the heart of much economic theory, and to some extent also in contemporary theories of public management, imposes a number of requirements that may be largely unachievable.

Perfect information and the cost of information

The first barrier to the model of comprehensive rationality is the need for perfect information. A decision-maker should be able to make adequate estimates about the decision-situation he or she is facing, and about the probable consequences of any decisions that will be made. For many, if not most, decisions of any consequence being made in the public sector, those demands for information are difficult to meet. James G. March (1994) points to four constraints on having perfect, or even adequate, information for rational decision-making:

- *Problems of attention* – Decision-makers are busy and are faced with many simultaneous demands of their time. Can they pay enough attention to the information needed for any decision?
- *Problems of memory* – Rational decisions will require linkages to prior decisions and previous events, but individuals and organizations are often inadequate retainers of information.
- *Problems of comprehension* – Decision-makers may have difficulties in understanding complex information and seeing the relevance of information that is readily available. They may not be skilled in making inferences from available information.
- *Problems of communication* – Information may not be shared adequately within the organization, and not all relevant actors will be using the same information.

Even if all the relevant information were available, obtaining that information is costly. Even in the age of the internet and widely available information, collecting information and analyzing it requires time and talent. Indeed, given the availability of information the challenge to public sector organizations attempting to make 'rational' decisions is processing information rather than simply collecting that information.

Clear preferences

To be able to make rational decisions an actor must be able to identify and rank order preferences. Individuals have to make decisions using preference orderings on a daily basis – we choose how to spend our money or what to have for dinner – but making those decisions about complex policy problems in government may be more difficult. To be able to make fully rational decisions preferences should be consistent and transitive, and also should be well understood by those making the decisions.

The problem of preferences is exacerbated in organizational decision-making when there are multiple actors involved. Even if all the actors involved in a decision can know their own preferences, they likely will not be the same. Kenneth Arrow (1974), for example, pointed out the difficulties of making choices within groups of people, without using some form of hierarchical imposition. These inherent difficulties can be exacerbated by the problem of intensity of preferences (Binmore, 2009). While methods such as log-rolling are possible when there are multiple decisions to be made by the same group, any one decision may not produce the greatest collective benefit, given that intensity of preferences is difficult to include in the decision. The preferences of decision-makers can also be influenced by psychology and the perception of risks and benefits. There is, for example, a good deal of evidence that people mistakenly estimate the risks of some events as too high (death in airplane crashes) and others too low (death in automobile accidents).[5] Similar discrepancies exist between estimates of the likely deaths from nuclear power plants and from coal-fired plants. This lack of information, or misinterpretation of available information, will alter preferences and reduce the rationality of any decision process.

Time constraints

Decision-making in the public sector is conducted under time constraints. Especially when dealing with issues in foreign affairs and defense, decisions may need to happen very quickly. Even in other policy areas there may be important time constraints on the decision-making behavior of public administrators. Furthermore, if an attempt at a comprehensively rational decision were to attain the goal, the degree of analysis involved would surpass that available to most if not all public organizations. A comprehensively rational analysis would also have to consider the future and the longer-term consequences of action taken in the short run. Forecasting those longer-term consequences is difficult, and perhaps impossible, and leaves open the possibilities for numerous unintended consequences (see Merton, 1936). But failures to forecast the future accurately have undermined any number of programs. Perhaps the largest failure of this sort is the failure of public sector pension planners to take into account significant increases in the longevity of their clients, and with that the significant increases in funds required.

Bounded Rationality as an Alternative

Given the difficulties in sustaining the argument for rational decision-making in public administration, are there alternative models for making decisions? The most commonly utilized alternative has been 'bounded rationality', proposed first by Herbert Simon (1947) and then developed by him and a number of

---

[5]One common estimate is that there is one death per 100,000,000 miles of flying, while there are 57 deaths in automobile accidents for the same mileage.

significant scholars following in his intellectual footsteps. This model not only assumes some rationality on the part of decision-makers, but also assumes that significant bounds must be placed on their attempts to make rational decisions if organizations are to function effectively. Simon argued that instead of optimizing, decision-makers should 'satisfice'. That is, decision-makers should attempt to reach decisions that are 'good enough' for the time being and then continue to make decisions after evaluating the consequences of those initial satisficing decisions. The strategy of satisficing is justified largely through the constraints on information and information processing discussed above, with Simon arguing that if decision-makers waited to make fully rational decisions they would never make decisions. There is always more information to be gathered and more alternatives to be considered so a decision would never happen.

Further Developments of Bounded Rationality

The basic model of bounded rationality developed by Simon and colleagues was extremely important in the development of public administration, but there have been other analogous developments that also have helped shape thinking about administration. These alternatives all question any rational conception of decision-making and indeed approach being anti-rationalist, assuming that decision-making in the public sector may be as much accidental as rational. Furthermore, for organizations these models of decision-making may be more open to influences outside the formal structure than would be true for other models. One of the most interesting of these models of decision-making is the 'garbage can model', which assumes that decisions are reached when several elements that are swimming around in a metaphorical garbage can come together (Cohen, March and Olsen, 1971) to produce a decision. These elements that are present in that garbage can are problems, policies, participants and choice opportunities. Decisions result when these elements combine, and hence the decisions made are neither predictable nor strategic.

The random nature of the confluence of the elements of a decision is in itself a denial of rational assumptions about decision-making in which actors pursue specific goals. However, this model of decision-making makes a further assumption, that at times solutions pursue problems. That is, both individual policy entrepreneurs and organizations with standard solutions for issues will search out problems to which they can apply their favored remedies. Even when those entrepreneurs do find the appropriate problem, however, they may still need to find a suitable policy window in order to be able to make policy. John Kingdon (2003) posited another version of the multiple streams approach (see Zahardis, 2014). His model contained many of the same elements of the garbage can model, but emphasized the role of actors more than pure randomness. In particular Kingdon emphasized the importance of policy entrepreneurs who develop, or who harbor, policy alternatives waiting for a 'window of opportunity' to open. When that metaphorical window does open, the entrepreneur is ready to push for a decision.

Neither of the approaches to decision-making in organizations is particularly useful for the day-to-day decisions that lower-level bureaucrats must make. These decisions are more routinized and more based on law or formal rules within the organization, while the decisions arising from the multiple-streams approach may represent more significant policy choices. Both of these types of decisions, however, are important for public organizations, as well as for the citizens whose lives are influenced by those decisions.

Incrementalism as another version of bounded rationality

Bounded rationality is usually associated with the work of Herbert Simon, and as demonstrated above has been developed by Simon and other scholars elaborating the basic arguments and demonstrating the applicability of the approach. Another strand of thinking about the limits of rationality in making choices – labeled incrementalism – also has roots in the United States (see Hayes, 2006). The incrementalist logic, however, makes somewhat clearer predictions about the behavior of individuals and organizations, and has been used in a variety of settings to describe the behavior of individuals and organizations. Furthermore, incrementalism has both empirical and normative strands of literature, both of which have been important for developing an understanding of the public sector.

Normative incrementalism

The normative strand of incrementalism argues, very much like bounded rationality, that comprehensive, rational decision-making is not as desirable as might be assumed for the public sector. However, whereas the bounded rationality literature tends to argue for the impracticality of full rationality, incrementalism tends to argue for the superiority of incremental choices, even if more synoptic decisions were possible. Dahl and Lindblom (1953) for example, consider incrementalism an aid to rational policymaking rather than as an alternative.

The basic argument for the superiority of incrementalism as a mechanism for making decisions is that when a decision-maker in the public sector makes comprehensive, presumably rational, decisions the chances for error are significant. In the public sector the problems that are being addressed are difficult, and 'wicked' (Rittel and Webber, 1973), or even 'super-wicked' (Levin et al., 2012). Therefore even with a great deal of information and analysis the chances of making mistakes, and making big mistakes, are high. And when an organization makes a big mistake that mistake may be more difficult to reverse or to overcome. A great amount of resources will have been invested that cannot be recouped, and commitments to citizens and employees may be made that will be difficult for government to reverse, if major policy changes are made.[6]

---

[6]For a thorough discussion of the potential advantages of incrementalism, see Dahl and Lindblom (1953, 82–4).

While incrementalism may have substantial benefits for decision-making, there are also some significant problems inherent in this approach. Perhaps the most important is that incremental decision-making may be excessively conservative, making responses to real problems facing society only incrementally when more decisive action may be necessary. Some problems may be large scale (Schulman, 1980), or may be extremely urgent, so that any small response will be inadequate and will perhaps only waste time. Indeed politically adopting the incremental style of response may be a means of appearing to address an issue without doing anything significant (see also Maor, 2014).[7] As well as the problem of proportionality of the responses, and the possible slowness in addressing problems, the assumption of the reversibility of interventions, even small interventions, is problematic. Most attempts by government to address problems involve creating organizations that have employees, clients and budgets. Once those vested interests are created, they become difficult to eliminate or alter. While most of the actions of governments are modifying existing policies (Carter, 2012), relatively few of those modifications represent direct reversals of commitments that have been made.

Just as the bounded rationality approach to decision-making discussed above has linkages to the normative version of institutional theory, incrementalism can be seen to be linked to historical institutionalism (Steinmo, Thelen and Longstreth, 1992). This version of institutionalism emphasized 'path dependence' of the actions being taken. In the original version of historical institutionalism change was conceptualized as occurring through a 'punctuated equilibrium', meaning large-scale and essentially paradigmatic change in the policies or the organization. While this rather dramatic form of change was useful for describing (but not really explaining) some major changes in policy within an organization, less-dramatic changes in policy also need to be understood. Therefore, subsequent developments in this literature (Streeck and Thelen, 2005; Mahoney and Thelen, 2010) have discussed alternative forms of change, such as layering, conversion and displacement, to describe less dramatic changes within institutions and within policies. All of these alternative forms of transformation permit change without a radical restructuring of the existing paradigm (see Hall, 1993) for policy within the organization.

The empirical strand of incremental research

As well as the normative strand of incrementalism stressing the virtues of this approach, there has been an empirical strand, which has concentrated on public spending and was initiated by Aaron Wildavsky and colleagues. In his more descriptive studies of budgeting at the federal level in the United States, Wildavsky (1975) argued that budgeting was not comprehensively rational but rather represented the product of experience and the use of relatively simple rules of thumb that enable decision-makers to cope with the task of allocating

---

[7] Of course, if the problem being addressed is 'ill structured' (Simon, 1973), then not investing heavily in the response may ultimately be a more desirable response.

massive amounts of money each year. Those decisions about spending public money did not begin with first principles about what would be the most efficient and effective use of the funds but rather began with existing patterns of spending and made marginal adjustments in them. The system of budgeting thus was more rational in the use of time than in the allocation of funds. These stable patterns of spending were also a function of the stability of the personnel involved in both the executive and legislative branches, so that trust and past experiences working with one another mattered. This incremental pattern of budgeting was confirmed in the statistical analysis of federal spending across a number of years (Davis, Dempster and Wildavsky, 1966). These scholars demonstrated that expenditures for federal organization in any one year could be predicted with high degrees of consistency by the previous year's expenditures plus a fixed percentage increase. While some organizations had more variable budgetary outcomes, the majority of decisions appeared to have been made through simple rules of thumb rather than any rational calculations of the relative benefits of allocations among competing purposes.[8]

The quantitative analysis of incrementalism in budgeting was supported by qualitative studies that demonstrated the importance of institutional patterns in shaping budget outcomes (Wildavsky, 1984). As with the arguments for bounded rationality discussed above, the task that confronted budget-makers (see Padgett, 1980) was simply too large and complex for comprehensive rational analysis; therefore decision-makers developed rules of thumb and shortcuts for decisions that made it possible for them to cope with the immensity of their tasks. Their rationality tended to be more in reducing decision-making costs and less in the actual allocation of the funds.

Although this research on the public budget has been driven by empirical questions it also has raised some analytic and theoretical questions. One of the more important of these is the rather fundamental question of how big is an increment? (Dempster and Wildavsky, 1979). That is, if making decisions about policies, and especially budgets, is indeed primarily incremental, how can we determine what is incremental and what represents a more fundamental policy change – a 'punctuation' of the equilibrium in the terms of the historical institutionalists (see below). A second more analytic question about incrementalism is at what level in government can this phenomenon most readily be observed, and conversely changes in what aspects of government may not be so readily predictable? For example, most of the incrementalist studies of budgeting have concentrated on the level of the agency or some intermediate or higher level of government. If, however, we examine policymaking for individual programs or budget categories there is a great deal more turbulence (Gist, 1977). The greater variability in expenditures across time at lower levels of aggregation reflects political forces that would produce wide swings in spending in small programs.

---

[8]A rational, Pigovian allocation would mean that the last marginal dollar or euro allocated to each agency would have the same marginal utility. Even if we were able to measure those marginal utilities accurately, making the allocations would require remarkable political and administrative commitment to rationality.

Issues in Bounded Rationality

Although bounded rationality provides an interesting perspective on the manner in which decisions are made in public organizations, several questions arise when this model of decisions is considered. While this model is less demanding for decision-makers than more comprehensive forms of rationality, it still requires some explication of the linkages between the organization within which the decision is being made and the nature of the decisions.

Sources of bounds

The first question that arises concerning bounded rationality is where do the bounds come from? To some extent the bounds on rationality arise because we are all merely human, and therefore do not have infinite capacities to collect and process information. Organizations, through parallel processing (see Simon, 1991), can help to alleviate some of that inherent weakness in decision-making, but only up to a point. If a comprehensively rational decision is to be made then all information must be processed and all possible alternatives considered and that is, as Simon argued so forcefully, merely impossible.

Organizations are themselves a major source of the bounds on rationality. Decision-makers face, in Simon's words, the 'blooming, buzzing confusion of the world' and therefore must find ways of narrowing attention to what is relevant to their principal concerns, and what is not relevant for their decisions. The policy priorities of the organization, its commitments to particular clients, and its legal responsibilities will define what is important for the organization, and for decision-makers acting in the name of the organization. Those priorities for the organization are also associated with a limited range of possible policy responses to change their environments. Thus, the bounds affect the focus of attention within the organization as well as the range of possible solutions that will be considered.

Is this not still rationality?

While this approach to decision-making is referred to as bounded *rationality*, we could question the extent to which it is actually a model of rationality. On the one hand, it is clear this model conceives of actors as having goals and engaged in some sort of purposive action. A policy can only be 'good enough' if there is some underlying conception of the goals being pursued, and some value system in place for assessing the quality of the outcomes. That an actor may pursue those goals in a more disjointed and opportunistic manner does not necessarily mean that he or she is less rational. Indeed, some of the arguments presented above imply that this disjointed strategy might be more rational, given that it allows for greater agility and continuing adaptation to changing circumstances. On the other hand, these models do permit means to determine to some extent the ends being pursued by the organization. This may mean that actors decide to do something they can easily do, rather than doing what they might actually prefer, which, in turn, also means that their preferences are not as clearly defined as might be required for fully rational decision-making. The logic of backward mapping in implementation studies (Elmore, 1985) to some extent has followed the same logic, using what can be done most readily at the implementation stage to determine what should be done. That logic can ensure smoother implementation, however, it may put means well before ends in shaping policy.

Links to the new institutionalism

The line of thinking about bounded rationality begun by Simon has culminated (at least at this time) in the normative strand of the new institutionalism (March and Olsen, 1989). On the one hand, in particular, this version of institutionalism has emphasized the role of a 'logic of appropriateness' as opposed to a logic of consequentiality in shaping the behavior of members of an organization or institution. The concept of appropriateness is shaped by values, routines, symbols, myths and a host of other bounds on the exercise of rationality. The logic of consequentiality, on the other hand, implies means-ends style of making decisions, and with that a more rational approach to making decisions. As well as defining the nature of an institution, this version of the new institutionalism also contains a clear argument about the behavior of individuals within an institution or organization. The assumption is that the preferences of individuals are shaped by their membership in the institution, and again that the endogenous shaping of individual preferences will place bounds on their pursuit of goals. There may be a number of bounds on the rationality of individual actors, but clearly membership in an organization is one, and one that is perhaps particularly relevant for public administration.

Other Models of Decision-Making in the Public Sector

In addition to the more central models of decision-making discussed above, a number of other approaches also have relevance for the study of decision-making in public administration. These alternative approaches to making decisions have some similarities with those already discussed, especially bounded rationality. But they also bring their own distinctive perspectives to bear on this crucial activity within the public sector.

Mixed scanning

Amitai Etzioni (1967, 1986) argued that the debate between synoptic rationality and bounded rationality and its ally incrementalism was to some extent arguing over a false dichotomy. Or if it is not a false dichotomy it is certainly overstated. He argued on behalf of a 'mixed scanning' approach that combined some aspects of both the comprehensive planning model and incrementalism. At one level there is a need for strategic decisions that set broad parameters for policy interventions. Those initial strategic choices then can narrow the range of options considered for intervention and enable decision-makers to engage in more comprehensive analysis of a narrow range of options. This approach to some extent represents the same logic as bounded rationality. The initial choices of strategy and priorities can be seen as establishing the boundaries for a more constrained search than would have been possible without those initial decisions. The approach also appears similar to the logic of 'strategic agility' that has been advanced in private sector management (Lewis, Andriopoulos and Smith, 2014). This approach to making decisions also advocates maintaining a strategic vision while at the same time making lower order decisions in a more adaptive and incremental manner.

Both of these 'blended' approaches to making decisions may be easier in private sector management than in the public sector. Maintaining a clear strategic position in the public sector may be difficult given changes in political office-holders, and the inevitable needs for compromise when making policy. While that compromise may be valuable politically, it may create vague policy positions that provide insufficient guidance for administrators (Chun and Rainey, 2005). Those administrators may, in turn, maintain their own positions or interpret policies in a way they find most comfortable.[9]

Collaboration

Most decision-making focuses on the 'single lonely organization'[10] or perhaps even more on the single lonely individual. In contemporary government, however, there is an increased awareness of the need for, and utility of, collaboration among actors. Few, if any, policy problems confronting governments can be contained neatly within the domain of a single organization within the public sector, despite the importance of specialization in managing within government (see Chapter 5).

As well as coordination and collaboration within government, the emphasis on collaborative decision-making in the public sector is also extended to involving the public – whether as individuals or as groups – in the process (Agranoff and McGuire, 2004). As such, collaborative decision-making can be seen as an extension of the network approach (Sørensen and Torfing, 2007b) and even some aspects of corporatism and corporate pluralism. In all of these approaches it is assumed that decision-making in the public sector can be improved by involving market or nonmarket actors from the outside. In the extreme, this pattern of

---

[9]Somewhat paradoxically, this may invert the usual positions of strategy and incrementalism in Etzioni's model. If the goals with which administrators are operating are vague and ambiguous, then the strategic level becomes more incremental and reflects political adjustment, while the administrative level maintains its own approach and strategy through implementation.

[10]This term was used by Hjern and Porter (1980) in their study of implementation to argue that these solo actors are rare in the contemporary public sector, even if they may have existed historically. They argued instead for the importance of 'implementation structures' composed of many actors.

collaborating with the private sector has been discussed as the 'hollow state' (Porter and Hjern, 1981, or 'governance without government' (Rhodes, 1997) in which the real work of government is being done by nongovernmental actors. Even in less-extreme versions, however, the monopoly of governance is often attributed to the public sector (see Peters and Pierre, 2017).

While the collaborative models of decision-making are certainly useful for describing and possibly even explaining some aspects of behavior within the public sector, they present their own difficulties as models of decision-making. Perhaps most important is the implicit assumption that the actors involved in a potential collaborative decision are all willing and cooperative. While that would be wonderful if true, the literature on coordination (see Peters, 2015a), as well as numerous vignettes from administrators and politicians about working in government organizations, reveals that this assumption is perhaps too felicitous. A second potential with collaborative models of decision-making is that the results of such processes may not be what anyone wanted in the first instance. A decision that can be approved by multiple actors, often with competing goals, is not likely to be an innovative and well-designed intervention. As Fritz Scharpf (1988; see also Heritier, 2013) has pointed out at a higher level of generalization such decisions are more likely to represent the lowest common denominator rather than a firm solution to the problem at hand. In some ways these decisions may approximate those reached through multiple streams, with the opportunities presented in essence being the points of agreement among disparate actors.

Organizational culture and programmed decisions

We have already discussed organizational culture as a general means of understanding the behavior of organizations in the public sector. Organizational culture can also be seen as a means of understanding decision-making in those organizations, with the internal values of the organization assigning values to both process and outcomes. Organizational culture is usually discussed more in terms of the management of personnel within organizations (see Hofstede, Hofstede and Minkov, 2010) but it can influence the manner in which decisions are made about public policy. For example, time is one of the dimensions of culture that Hofstede mentions for societies and organizations, meaning the extent to which traditions are honored and change is difficult. A commitment to the preservation of administrative and policy traditions will mean that organizations will not be innovative and will tend to dismiss information and ideas that do not conform to its internal values. This resistance to change and a narrow range of values corresponds to the stereotypical conception of bureaucracy and its rigidity. While it may produce rigidity, the commitment to a stable set of values will also produce predictability for clients, and for employees.

The dependence on organizational culture as the foundation for making decisions is analogous to the logic of normative institutionalism discussed above, and hence can be linked to bounded rationality as a means of making decisions. In this case the cultural values held by the organization constitute the limits on rationality and provide the simplifying assumptions that permit decision-making to occur more readily even when faced with the external complexity of the world of public policy.

Elinor Ostrom and the institutional analysis and design framework

Finally, although it is usually discussed as a model of policymaking or of institutional analysis more generally (see House and Araral, 2014) the institutional analysis and design (IAD) framework developed by Elinor Ostrom and colleagues (Kiser and Ostrom, 2000; Ostrom, 2007) can also be seen as a model of making decisions in public administration. As already noted, decisions in public administration, except perhaps those concerning the most mundane internal matters, should be considered as policy relevant, and therefore this model of decision-making is relevant for understanding how public administration functions. The model considers decision-making occurring at three levels of generality. At the most general, there is the set of exogenous conditions, including rules that define the possibilities for action within the institution. There are then action arenas in which actors combine factors from the broader environment to make decisions, and those decisions are reflected in interactions between the institution (in this case a bureaucratic agency perhaps) and its environment. These interactions based on decisions then produce feedbacks and evaluations, and subsequent rounds of decision-making.

While broader than most of the other models of decision-making already discussed, this framework does provide a way of looking at decision-making in public organizations in a more systemic framework than most of the other approaches. It links the environment of decisions, including the central position of rules, to the choices being made. It further emphasizes that each decision may be only one component of a chain of decisions that reflect the continuing elaboration of policies.

Summary and Conclusions

The above discussion of decision-making in public organizations has presented a number of alternative perspectives on this fundamental task within the public sector. These are based on various levels, and various definitions, of rationality, but they all raise some common questions. One of the most important of these issues is how information is processed within the organization. Any high-quality decision depends on adequate information, but developing and processing that information is difficult and expensive. Furthermore, how do we know how much information is enough?

Making decisions also depends on understanding clearly the preferences of the actors involved. The nature of human preferences, especially when operating individually or in organizations and other groups, poses significant difficulties in making decisions. Even if individuals knew their own preferences perfectly, they would still have to interact with other individuals within the organization who may not have the same preferences, or at least the same ordering of those preferences. And then any one organization will have to interact with others who may have very different preferences. Thus, any decision that emerges will represent compromises and a decision that everyone will consider suboptimal.

The notion of rationality has been something of a straw man in this discussion. The fully rational model of pursuit of goals is a useful ideal against which to compare the actions of real-world decision-makers. In reality most decision-making falls somewhere between a rational conception of the process and the more chaotic approach implied in the garbage can. Decision-makers may have general ideas about their goals and the means to achieve them but are functioning in a complex environment in which information and opportunities are often scarce. Opportunities to pursue what might appear to be less-significant goals may be available, and accepted, when seemingly more significant goals cannot be pursued successfully. In that complex world of public policymaking, and even implementation, muddling through may be a rational means of trying to accomplish something.

The above statement is another means of saying that public administration and public policy are pursued in a political environment that may privilege certain types of actions and not others. There may be a political logic that dominates the substantive means-ends logic of policymaking. For many political leaders, and for many leaders of individual organizations, doing something positive may be better than inaction. And opportunities that do appear may provide means of enhancing the image of the organization. Students of public administration may become enchanted with models of decision-making, but on the ground within government there is a more immediate and pressing political reality.

8

Autonomy Versus Integration

Public bureaucracies are embedded in a societal context, but the more specific nature of that embeddedness is a contested issue. One of the emerging patterns of administration has been to link it with networks of social actors, although this pattern was preceded by corporatist patterns of intermediation. In some administrative systems, however, there is a continuing separation of the public sector from society, and perhaps a hierarchical relationship with society. The embeddedness of the public bureaucracy is a complex issue, both in terms of whether it increases or decreases the regulatory efficiency of the bureaucracy and the quality of the services it delivers, as well as in terms of whether such embeddedness is desirable or should be avoided.

The public administration literature offers two conflicting accounts of how a bureaucracy should best organize its exchanges with its environment in service delivery and enforcement of rules. One perspective argues that a public administrative institution should maintain its autonomy in relationship to clients and targets of regulation. Such autonomy helps protect the integrity of the institution and may reduce the risk of capture, patronage and corruption. Furthermore, the movement toward the use of agencies for the delivery of public services has increased autonomy within government. According to the other view, public institutions need to actively engage society and its organizations in order to ensure efficient and appropriate public service. Much of the expertise on the needs of clients in targeted groups is not found within the bureaucracy, the argument goes, but is rather found among nongovernmental organizations (NGOs) and, indeed, the clients themselves. Therefore, service should be given its final design and implemented in close collaboration between the bureaucracy and key societal actors. Such close collaboration could include delegation of public authority, for instance on how to allocate public resources committed to specific programs, to private actors and NGOs. While critics may agree that this strategy could improve the quality of public service, they caution that this form of collaboration will confuse accountability and may compromise the intent of political decisions.

There is an interesting timeline underpinning this debate. Collaboration gained popularity in the public sector in the 1980s and 1990s along with budget cutbacks, marketization of many public services and increasing specialization of those services, for instance in the social welfare and healthcare sectors. Equally important, the growing interest in 'governance', as opposed to 'government' in the 1980s and 1990s implied that networks, partnerships and other forms of collaboration between public and societal actors were now the appropriate problem-solving strategy and such collaboration almost had a positive value in itself. There is also, to some extent, a distinction between law and regulatory enforcement on the one hand, and service delivery on the other. Previously, services tended to have a more standardized design or could be a matter of law enforcement with even less adaption to the clients' circumstances. Today, service delivery frequently includes customer choice and other mechanisms to adapt a service to client needs and demands. Along with advances in medicine, healthcare, including primary care, is also more complex. In addition, there is today often an understanding that the bureaucracy needs to work across sectors to devise appropriate programs and strategies to address societal problems. All these developments suggest that delivering public services today is a more complex task than just a few decades ago, and this has made collaboration with actors in society more attractive to the public sector.

This chapter will discuss the tension between the public administration's autonomy and its integration with the rest of society. The issue is more complex than might appear at first glance. It is not merely a matter of choosing which strategy will lead to the best implementation or delivery of service. The autonomy of the bureaucracy is a prerequisite for the pursuit of the public interest and the bureaucracy's capacity to fend off parochial or corporate or even individual interests if they are in conflict with broader societal concerns, for instance in planning or environmental protection. Legality and equal treatment are also important in strengthening the public's trust in the public administration. On the other hand, bureaucracies that become perceived as inefficient or arrogant or incapable of delivering meaningful public service may lose much of their legitimacy. Thus, there are significant values at stake in this discussion. We first compare the role of the public administration in two stylized models: a conventional government model and a governance model. From there, we will analyze in detail the issues that follow from a more socially integrated and embedded public service. We conduct this discussion against the backdrop of a scholarly debate over the past couple of decades on 'new public governance' and the role of the public bureaucracy in the post-industrial society. The final section of the chapter asks what all this means for the bureaucracy in terms of challenges of adapting its performance to different societal contexts.

Public Administration in Government

Previous chapters have discussed the role of public administration in government from different analytical angles. In the present analysis, we apply an institutional focus to help understand the contribution of the public administration to effective government. This approach suggests that the core mission of the public bureaucracy is to implement the programs it has been charged to deliver; to uphold a legally defined process of decision-making; and to ensure that administrative matters are addressed equally among its clients. The common denominator among these organizational tasks is that they are all devoid of political and social context. In fact, the institutional and procedural setup of a conventional bureaucracy is designed specifically to minimize the impact of external, contextual factors; this organizational structure and modus operandi were designed to secure equal treatment and legality and were less concerned with ideas about tailoring services to clients' varying needs.

The organizational design of the bureaucracy in this perspective emphasizes hierarchical control and accountability with limited discretion at individual work stations. Dating back to the 1800s or even earlier, this organizational design made sense in a context when public servants had only limited training and corruption was a potential problem. By perceiving bureaucrats merely as cogs in an administrative machinery, politicians and senior bureaucrats minimized the risks of any deviations, for whatever reasons, from the programs and rules that the bureaucracy was charged to implement. This model of public administration also has other advantages. A tightly vertically integrated bureaucracy probably works better with other elements of government of similar design, and allows for specialization and the development of expertise within the bureaucracy. It is customary to criticize these vertically integrated 'silos' for preventing horizontal coordination when addressing issues that cut across jurisdictional boundaries, but on reflection these 'silos' remain an unsurpassed institutional arrangement for the development of expertise and specialization in the public sector.

There are also downsides to this organizational design. Perhaps the most obvious problem is, as mentioned, that it greatly complicates horizontal coordination and collaboration between bureaucracies. The main problem here is that more and more issues facing the public sector, such as environmental issues and climate change, national security and migration, involve several policy sectors and can best be addressed by coordinated, inter-sectoral programs. States are not unfamiliar with this mismatch between the problems facing the country and its institutional setup – we need only think of wars, famine and pandemics – but apparently there was some conviction that vertically integrated hierarchies were the unsurpassed model of organizing the public sector.

The relationship between organizational structure on the one hand and the organization's preferred way of acting on the other is quite clear in this analysis. Organizations that emphasize autonomy in relationship to their clients combined with loyalty to their masters (see below) will typically have a hierarchical structure and management. The bureaucracy's cues in this perspective do not come from below but from the top, hence there is little need to delegate authority to the middle or lower levels of the organization. Conversely, as we will see later in this chapter, a bureaucracy that seeks to forge partnerships or 'hybrids' with NGOs and other societal organizations tends to delegate authority to the lower levels of the organization where such alliances are formed and where the actual collaboration takes place.

Relationship with ministries

The key mission of a public bureaucracy is to serve the political leadership by executing its programs and implementing its policies. We discuss this relationship between the political and administrative spheres of government from different perspectives throughout this book. For the present analysis, we note that the autonomy of the public service is present in the exchanges with elected officials, too. This may sound paradoxical, given that the bureaucracy is accountable to politicians and basically serves as their executive arm. As we saw in Chapter 4, the bureaucracy is expected to be neutral in its relationship with the elected government, that is, it serves elected leaders of all ideological orientations equally and to the best of its ability. How is this key constitutional rule compatible with notions about administrative autonomy?

The paradox is resolved by the distinction between *what* the bureaucracy is expected to do on the one hand and *how* it should do it on the other. This distinction is at the heart of classic public administration theory from Max Weber and Woodrow Wilson onwards, arguing that politics and administration are two separate spheres of government. Politicians are expected to give the bureaucracy firm instructions on policy objectives, that is, what to do, while being much less specific in terms of the strategy that should be employed to solve the task. The bureaucracy is charged with upholding an administrative process characterized by legality, equal treatment and a transparent and accountable process of decision-making. This arrangement hinges on mutual respect between politicians and public servants. Too strong political involvement in the administrative process would raise serious concerns about the integrity of the bureaucracy and lead to decreasing legitimacy of the bureaucracy and decreasing trust among citizens in administrative institutions. If elected officials fail to set goals for the public bureaucracy the polity may find itself de facto governed by a self-serving and arrogant public service beyond accountability.

Thus, the autonomy of the public bureaucracy, not just from societal and parochial interests but also in relationship to the elected level of government, is essential to the quality of administration and the upholding of legal requirements of public administrative office. The bureaucracy is a key executive component of the policy process but its conduct is defined not by political decisions but by administrative law. This constitutional arrangement ensures that politicians cannot interfere with the details of the administrative process and also that bureaucratic power over citizens is held to administrative and ultimately political account.

Why is autonomy still important?

These aspects of the strict institutional focus of a public bureaucracy emphasize the significance of finding an institutional balance that ensures a high degree of administrative autonomy without creating a state effectively governed by the bureaucracy. Contemporary observers might argue that this is a quaint and obsolete model of organizing a public service, but the loss of bureaucratic autonomy in relation to societal or parochial interests may have far-reaching consequences. Consider, for example, Aksel Sundström's (2016) recent account of South African public servants who choose to 'stay in their office' rather than conducting inspections and enforcing rules of fear of retribution by gangs to themselves or their families. The bureaucrat in this situation does not enjoy the autonomy and security required to do what they are assigned to do. This might seem a rare and extreme account of what happens when administrative autonomy is compromised, but there are other examples – less dramatic, perhaps, and also more common – of similar types of problems.

Much of domestic policy has a strong regulatory component as an instrument to shape societal behavior. Regulation requires that those who regulate can maintain some distance and autonomy vis-à-vis the targets of regulation, so that the regulation is not influenced by those who are being regulated. However, regulators often recruit staff from the organizations and businesses they regulate, leading to what Makkai and Braithwaite (1992) refer to as the 'revolving door' problem, where skilled staff moves either from regulator to regulate or back and forth between the two. This can lead to 'regulatory capture' where the targets of the regulation through various channels can influence the design of the regulation to which they are subjected (Draca, 2014). These two examples show how easily administrative autonomy can be compromised and the consequences of such development, both for administrative practice and the external perception of the public administration. Bureaucratic autonomy is critical both to good public administration and also to the capacity of the bureaucracy to pursue the public interest.

Public Administration in Governance

As we now turn to the role of the bureaucracy in different forms of governance, we immediately see that we need to change focus, from institutions to processes. This change of perspective, as we will see, solves some problems at the same time as it creates others. The governance approach to public administration, as discussed in several chapters of this book, highlights the role of formal and informal interaction between public institutions and actors and organizations in society. All else being equal, such a process paradigm for public administration would appear more accessible to societal interests compared with the institutional paradigm which, by definition, precludes such interaction. In other words, it would appear easier for societal actors to get access to government in an open, contextually defined process than in the conventional, highly regulated process of deliberation and decision-making that is a trademark of traditional public administration.

Interaction and collaboration between the public bureaucracy and societal actors has become a routine element in public service delivery in most countries.

Perhaps the most common form of such interaction is the contracting out of public services to for-profit organizations. Such contracting out and the creation of internal markets have been at the heart of New Public Management (NPM) reform and is today an established practice in essentially all advanced countries. Thus, there are several different blends of governmental and societal involvement in service delivery and governance, ranging from the ad hoc, short-term collaboration via the creation of hybrid organizations where public and private actors jointly deliver public service, conduct infrastructural development, run research parks or similar projects, to full-scale collaborative governance. Tanya Börzel and Thomas Risse (2010) outline a ladder describing incremental changes in the role of government and societal actors in governance (see Table 8.1). Such governance occurs when the public bureaucracy and societal actors, for instance NGOs, share all significant elements of the process including decision-making.

One might suspect that the sector-based 'silos' nature of the public administration could have facilitated efficient exchanges with narrowly defined segments of society. Indeed, much of the empirical evidence we have seen seems to corroborate this pattern; when government departments and agencies create or join networks with societal actors they are overwhelmingly found in the policy sector in which those institutions are embedded (see Rhodes, 1997; Pierre and Sundström, 2009).

Table 8.1 Governance with(out) government: the non-hierarchical involvement of nongovernmental actors.

Public regulation
No involvement of private actors
Consultation/cooptation of private actors
Participation of private actors in public decisionmaking
(for example private actors as members of state; delegation; outsourcing)
Co-regulation/co-production of public and private actors
Joint decisionmaking of public and private actors
(for example social partners in tripartite concertation; public-private partnerships)
Delegation to private actors
Participation of public actors
(for example contracting-out; standard-setting)
Private self-regulation in the shadow of hierarchy
Involvement of public actors
(for example voluntary agreements)
Public adoption of private regulation
Output control by public actors
Private self-regulation
No public involvement
(for example private regimes; social partner autonomy)

Source: Börzel and Risse, 2010

For example, a ministry of foreign affairs and foreign aid agencies will typically forge networks with domestic and international NGOs and consultancies in the foreign aid sector, just as a ministry for economic development and its agencies will want to team up with business organizations, trade associations and chambers of commerce. Interestingly, however, the notion that public institutions and actors should engage actors in society in order to collaborate in service delivery and governance coincided with the increasing emphasis on strengthening horizontal coordination within government. This has been a significant problem for government in all times; specialization leads to vertical coordination and top-down flows of information and control, and these patterns have become part of the institutional setup in most public organizations. Increasing horizontal coordination has become increasingly important along with the growing salience of issues that cut across delineations between policy sectors, such as climate change, migration, social exclusion, and safety and security. Little surprise, therefore, that supplementing the institutionalized patterns of vertical organizational control and behavior with horizontal coordination has proven to be a major challenge (Peters, 2015a; see also Chapter 5 in this volume). Thus, the increasing emphasis on governance and collaborative arrangements represents a challenge to the public bureaucracy and its autonomy in relationship to actors and interests in its environment. Contemporary bureaucracies are expected to respond to, or initiate, several potentially conflicting strategies of engaging actors and institutions in their environment at once: maintaining some degree of vertical, intra-organizational chain of command and management; opening up for collaborative arrangement with societal actors in the agencies' field of jurisdiction; and to work across sectoral boundaries in order to address cross-cutting issues. And, in the midst of these challenges, the public administration has to maintain its autonomy and integrity in order not to be 'captured' (see below) by other institutions or by societal actors.

The demands for developing new, informal and contextualized patterns of interactions with other actors inside and outside government do not suggest that the institutions of the bureaucracy do not matter as institutions even in the most interactive governance arrangements. They do, probably more so than we tend to understand, and here lies at least part of the answer as to how public bureaucracies tend to respond to these challenges. Studies suggest that societal actors entering some form of collaborative governance or hybrid arrangement with government actors expect them to deliver high-quality service swiftly and reliably and to uphold a due process of decision-making. To put this in a slightly different language they expect government actors to deliver good old government and not a hybridized version of a public institution. Instead, hybridization is the outcome of the interaction (see Pierre and Schütt, 2005; Pierre, 2012, 2013a). Thus, a core element of the governance approach remains, somewhat paradoxically, institutions. We should think of the public administration as a core element of democratic governance connecting citizens to the state. In that context, we should note that scholars disagree on the extent to which collaborative governance in general and the presence of interest groups in political and administrative processes in particular alters the quality of democracy. Some argue that such involvement can address the 'democratic deficit' in public institutions and help legitimize public collective action. This argument has been advanced mainly in the context of the European Union (EU) (Scharpf, 1997, 2009; Kohler-Koch and Finke, 2007; Sanchez-Delgado, 2014).

A related issue is to what extent a shift from conventional government to governance alters the public administration's legitimacy among its clients. Scharpf (1999) and others have argued that the legitimacy of an institution can stem from either its democratic nature ('input legitimacy') or its performance as a service provider ('output legitimacy'). If a governance approach increases the performance of the public bureaucracy as a provider of public service, then engaging societal actors would help boost the legitimacy of the public administration. Recent studies argue that output legitimacy is at least as important as input legitimacy (Pierre, Röiseland and Gustavsen, 2013, 2015; Röiseland, Pierre and Gustavsen, 2014; Pierre et al., 2015), a pattern which would suggest that adopting a governance-oriented strategy is not merely a way to cut costs or tailor services more efficiently but also a means of increasing the legitimacy of the bureaucracy among its clients. We should also note that input- and output-based legitimacy are not mutually exclusive; in the EU context, as Lindgren and Persson show (2010), the best predictor of output legitimacy is, in fact, a high level of input legitimacy.

These observations also hold a part of the answer to how public administration systems maintain their autonomy at the same time as they develop new ways of engaging strategic actors in their external environment. In these contexts, the public bureaucracy is not, for the most part, expected to perform in radically new ways or engage in new types of issue; they are mainly expected to deliver on conventional government and public administrative tasks. The important point here is that autonomy and embeddedness are both essential for good governance and the contribution of public administration towards that objective. By opening up for collaboration with societal actors the public bureaucracy can make a stronger and more diversified contribution to the governance of society. At the same time, this strategy seems to serve to boost the legitimacy of the public bureaucracy itself. It achieves these objectives not by compromising on its integrity but rather by delivering the conventional functions of government.

Societal embeddedness in empirical context

The public administration can play an essential role in integrating state with society, building legitimacy and support. Public bureaucracies around the world give high priority to finding new channels to reach out to the surrounding societies. Interestingly, however, the manner in which they do so tends to reflect historical and cultural patterns, or 'administrative traditions' (see Painter and Peters, 2010). Thus, for instance, bureaucracies with a strong legalistic culture find it more difficult to implement reforms to boost efficiency, something which systems with a more managerial culture find less challenging. Good examples of the legalistic tradition include Germany, the Scandinavian countries and Japan.

These countries are well familiar with the societal embeddedness of public institutions, but that embeddedness has primarily been in terms of interest representation. Teaming up with societal actors in service delivery or contracting out services to private businesses, in contrast, has meant entering unchartered waters for public servants in these countries. These administrative systems cherish ideas of equal treatment and legality, and delivering services in partnership with external actors may potentially jeopardize the bureaucracy's capacity to uphold those values. Indeed, the very idea of bringing for-profit organizations into the process of delivering public service has been hard to accept for many of these bureaucrats. Over time, however, we now see extensive collaboration between state, market and society in these countries.

The United States, the United Kingdom, Australia and New Zealand are good illustrations of a different administrative tradition. Here, the emphasis has been on efficiency, management and client relationships. Legal aspects certainly matter here, too, but they are less prominent in daily administration. Indeed, attempts to rearticulate foundational norms and values in order to align reform strategies with constitutional norms have proven difficult for precisely these reasons (Rosenbloom, 2000). However, given that the basic tenor of administrative reform across the Western world has included efficiency and 'customer satisfaction' – incidentally a concept which public servants in legalistic systems often see as alien to public administration – the Anglo-American countries have had less problem adapting to that zeitgeist than have, for instance, continental European bureaucracies. The New Zealand public service is keen to experiment with new organizational and managerial models to develop its service. A forerunner in NPM reform, New Zealand has also explored new ways of aligning the public service with society, for instance in attempting to adapt government to society rather than the other way around. However, attempts to build government around social structures, or what was known as 'governing towards outcomes', have proven extremely difficult. A different set of problems can be found in more state-centric societies such as the Latin American countries. Here, perhaps the main problem has not been that the public service has not been sufficiently embedded in society in order to contribute to governance and to partner with societal actors, but rather that it has been *too* embedded (see Peters and Pierre, 2017 and relevant literature cited therein).

These scattered examples show how governments around the world, facing different types of challenges and operating under different constraints, seek to bolster their interaction with the surrounding society and to develop new points of contact with key societal actors. These interactions may start out as concerted action to deliver public service to specific groups but they may also be, or evolve into, arenas for collaborative governance delivering service but also deliberating on policy design and funding (Ansell and Gash, 2007; Donahue and Zeckhauser, 2011). Indeed, the general idea of collaboration, specified in co-production (Alford, 2009) or co-design, has gained massive attention among practitioners and scholars recently. Some of these collaborative arrangements clearly indicate shared decision-making and governance whereas others are mainly concerned with service delivery.

Why is collaboration important?

Public sector strategies to enhance points of contact with strategic actors in their environments raise a couple of interesting questions. What are the costs and benefits of this form of collaboration? What does such collaboration mean to the values that we associate with administrative autonomy?

Collaboration seems to be driven by several factors. One is quite simply that the bureaucracy believes it can save resources by teaming up with societal actors. That may well be the case, but those external actors are likely to ask for something in return for their commitment to public service delivery; they may want to have input on program design or be duly compensated for their work. Indeed, many NGOs today have contract revenues from public institutions accounting for the bulk of their budgets, so much so that they are debating whether this situation is consistent with the original mission of the organization. Another important reason why the public administration approaches actors in the surrounding society is that it allows the bureaucracy to tap into the knowledge and expertise of these actors. Designing appropriate programs to assist people in the HIV/AIDS community or disabled people, for instance, requires extensive expertise in the needs of these patients, and that expertise is often found in NGOs and not in public sector organizations. Collaboration thus helps the bureaucracy design programs that target those needs more efficiently.

Models of Embeddedness in Emergent Theories of Public Administration

In the wake of NPM and the market 'turn' in public service delivery, a number of approaches have emerged exploring alternative scenarios for the public service. These approaches share a perspective that in many ways rejects not only the conventional model of public bureaucracy but also the tendency in NPM to introduce a market-based discourse in the public administration. They tend to depart from a rather similar analysis according to which both conventional public administration and NPM are inefficient in tackling current policy issues. Furthermore, there is a consensus that the complexities of contemporary society necessitate major rethinking about how we want the public service to operate. As we will see, these new approaches agree that the future public service will be less autonomous and more embedded in society than the public service we see today. We briefly introduce four of these emerging approaches.

New public governance

One emergent approach has been outlined by Stephen Osborne and his followers (see Osborne, S. P., 2006, 2010). Proposed under the banner of 'new public governance', Osborne (2010: 7) argues that this approach 'is not integral to PA or to the NPM but is rather an alternative discourse in its own right'. The basic argument here is that both conventional public administration and NPM 'fail to capture the complex reality of the design, delivery and management of pub-lic services in the twenty-first century'. Against that backdrop, Osborne and associates explore 'whether there is a pressing need now for a more sophisti-cated understanding of public policy implementation and public services delivery ... that moves beyond the sterile dichotomy of "administration versus management"' (Osborne, S. P., 2010: 5).

Thus, the argument in brief is that the state and the policies and programs it delivers are not appropriately designed to match the needs of contemporary society. New public governance signifies improved policy design to make policy better geared to address the issues of society today; as S. P. Osborne (2010: 9) puts it, 'New public governance is both a product and a response to the increas-ingly complex, plural and fragmented nature of public policy implementation and public service delivery in the twenty-first century'. The new public govern-ance approach sees networks and other collaborative arrangements as integral to the modus operandi of the future public service. Collaboration will help the public service design more appropriate and targeted services while facilitating learning and sharing of knowledge and other resources. At the same time, the new public governance approach leaves issues related to democracy and accountability undertheorized (Torfing and Triantafillou, 2013).

Collaborative governance

New Public Governance is far from alone in promoting collaboration with societal actors as key to the future of the public service. Collaboration between the public service and actors in society is believed to enhance service quality, improve knowledge and expertise in the public service; and to help legitimize the public service (Donahue and Zeckhauser, 2011). Collaborative governance in various forms and including different actors is today seen among both scholars and practitioners as key to solving problems of societal complexity, accelerated costs and the dispersion of expertise across society (Kooiman, 1993).

Recent work in the field of collaborative governance is perhaps less promot-ing and unreservedly positive in its assessments than the initial accounts. Today, scholars are more aware of not just the potential of collaboration but also of its perils and pitfalls. Some point out that even when participants see strong potential gains from collaborating, conflicts (or even a history of con-flict) within the collaborative arrangement can lead to failure (Ansell and Gash, 2007). Others look at the symmetry in the collaboration and emphasize that in order to work both parties should be involved in decision-making as well as implementation: 'shared discretion is the defining feature of collabora-tive governance. If one side makes all the decisions, a public-private relationship is a contract, not a collaboration. The crucial question concerns just *how* dis-cretion is shared' (Donahue and Zeckhauser, 2011: 45, italics in original). The degree to which societal actors participate in public decision-making, or what Donahue and Zeckhauser call the division of discretion is clearly essential to the collaboration, but it raises other equally important questions about the democratic nature of the collaboration and its accountability. Collaborative strategies in the execution of policies and programs would appear to be consistent with liberal democracy, but when organized interests, NGOs, private businesses and stakeholders – all non-elected – gain access to decision-making those values may be jeopardized.

New public service

The democratic aspects of public administration are also central to the 'new public service' approach, outlined primarily by Robert and Janet Denhardt (2000, 2003). Similar to the previous approaches, the new public service wants to move beyond both conventional (or 'old') public administration and NPM. The basic argument is that government's first responsibility is to cater to the interests of its owners, the citizens, and to make service provision a priority. Thus, the approach of the Denhardts addresses issues related to public management and bureaucracy from a distinct normative perspective. In their view, citizenship and liberal democracy are the normative pillars on which the new public service should be built. This is in marked contrast to the emphasis on efficiency that is at the center of marketized approaches to public administration.

Public value

The final vision for the future of public administration we will mention is the 'public value' approach which has been advanced by Mark Moore (1995; see also Alford and O'Flynn, 2009). The approach is focused on service delivery and the provision of 'public value' to the public. While the precise meaning of 'public value' is still debated (Bryson, Crosby and Bloomberg, 2015), the overall idea is that such value is produced whenever clients receive high-quality, tailored service from the public sector.

Mark Moore (1994), in the early days of public value research and teaching, suggested that the 'public value' framework was inspired by the observation that people usually do not associate the public sector with value creation. However, such value is constantly produced and the mission of this approach is to outline the ideal preconditions for public value creation. To that effect, the framework focuses on public sector managers, arguing that empowering those managers is a precondition for public value creation. The political level of government – referred to as 'the authorizing environment' – is marginalized in the framework; the key driving agent producing public value is the autonomous, empowered manager. The public value paradigm of public service delivery has ramifications beyond service productions; it speaks to the larger governance arrangements as well; while Moore's main concern is with the former aspects of public value, there are also important normative issues related to the public value perspective (Bryson, Crosby and Bloomberg, 2014). In a critical review, Rhodes and Wanna (2007) show how the high degree of managerial autonomy in the public value framework triggers questions about the accountability of the officials delivering public service.

Consequences for the autonomy of the public administration

The four models of embeddedness of the public bureaucracy briefly discussed here tend to agree that the future of public service lies not in maintaining autonomy and separation from society but rather the opposite: in increased engagement with an array of societal actors. However, the models downplay the need to formalize these exchanges. All four models also depart from an almost identical diagnosis of the problems with the contemporary public service. The common argument is that neither traditional public administration nor NPM offers an organizational framework that enables the public sector to strategically engage an increasingly complex society. Furthermore, all four perspectives depart from more or less rejecting conventional public administration and NPM, and from there proceed to outline a new, future model of public service. Finally, all four models seem to agree that the future of the public service will witness a further divorce between the political level of government and the bureaucracy. Perhaps the most extreme position in this brief presentation of approaches to modernize public administration is the public value framework, although essentially all models focus on face-to-face interactions between the public service and its clients.

What does all this mean for the future autonomy and integrity of the public administration? Clearly, in both the debate on the future of public administration and in the reform strategies we see in many countries there is a priority on integrating the public administration with society, not on preserving its autonomy. Furthermore, the more limited role of elected officials – either as goal-setters or as accountable actors when public bureaucracies underperform – suggests a growing emphasis on output-related legitimacy. The future public administration will not seek to legitimize its costs or its rulings by referring to its critical role in democratic governance but rather to its role as a service provider. Indeed, many scholars and practitioners seem to believe that the future of the public sector is concealing the fact that it is in fact *public* administration. These are not altogether new developments. The emergence of NPM in the 1990s was predicated on – to some extent – ignoring the public nature of public organizations and to bring in managerial models from the corporate sector. Also, the growing interest in output legitimacy is a further step away from the conventional model of public administration where due process, transparency, neutrality and accountability are sustained values and norms.

Are there any downsides to this gradual shift towards delivery and output legitimacy as the main sources of legitimacy? One obvious danger in focusing on output-related factors is that we forget who is responsible for bureaucratic failure and malfeasance. By neglecting the public nature of public administration we will hold service providers to account, which often is missing the point that frontline staff do not get to make priorities or decisions pertaining to public services; we would be shooting the proverbial messenger. Another important concern is whether an increasingly embedded public service has the integrity and capacity to enforce regulation in pursuit not of customers' interests but of the larger public interest (Brewer, 2007; Sundström, 2016). Objectives such as relaxing hierarchies, entering collaborative arrangements with societal actors and adapting services to clients' needs could be a recipe for what regulation theory calls 'regulatory capture' (Ayres and Braithwaite, 1995). Such capture occurs when the regulator over time comes to share the worldviews, objectives and strategies of the organizations they regulate. The deeper the public service is embedded in societal networks, the more difficult it gets to regulate those segments of society.

Concluding Discussion

The dimension between integration and autonomy has been a feature of public administration theory since it first emerged. Recent reprioritizations within the public sector have brought these issues back to the forefront of the debate about the future of the public service. Ironically, output-based legitimacy emerged in institutional contexts suffering from (perceived or actual) democratic deficits such as the EU, yet raising output legitimacy to the preferred organizational strategy will only exacerbate those problems by further marginalizing the role of the political leadership of the public service. This is, of course, not to say that everything was better before, because it was not. Recent public management reform has been successful in developing public services and to increase the efficiency in the delivery of those services. But public administration is about more than keeping your customers happy: it is about having the ability to make decisions that will leave clients disappointed when their requests are not supported by legislation or regulation; or ensuring equal treatment among clients despite varying needs; or implementing policies and programs that may not be palatable to the targets of those policies; or having the integrity to deliver auditing reports that are likely to embarrass politicians and bureaucrats. In short, a public bureaucracy needs the capacity, autonomy and integrity to deliver unpopular rulings.

All of this means that the current vogue of having public entities partnering with key societal actors may prove to be a double-edged sword; what is gained in capacity to deliver programs may come at the expense of a loss of integrity.

9

Rationality Versus Incrementalism: Funding Public Organizations

We discussed the contrast between rationality and incrementalism when we discussed decision-making (Chapter 7). While those different manners of making choices are apparent in all areas of governing, they are especially relevant in public budgeting. And public budgeting is especially relevant to all the activities of public administration. Making the budget is in many ways the most important annual activity for public organizations: while government organizations may have been created by law or through the actions of ministers, their lifeblood comes from the budget. Without funding there is little or nothing the organization can do, whether that is paying their personnel, purchasing necessary supplies or providing services to their clients.

The budget is also a fundamental political act. The public budget is a statement of political priorities expressed in dollars and cents, or euros and cents. Therefore, political leaders may be as concerned about the outcomes of the budget process as are the public organizations being funded through the process. The allocation itself is not only among the competing agencies within government, but it is also between the public and the private sectors. Politically, different political parties and leaders advocate that the public sector should be more or less extensive. Furthermore, different political parties and leaders will be more or less willing to accept a public sector deficit. Given the importance of the budget process for all the participants, and for the society as a whole, there have been numerous efforts to make the process more effective. But reformers may differ over which kinds of reform are the more desirable. On the one hand, the traditional budget process was designed largely to ensure the capacity of legislatures and ministers to monitor and control spending. A number of reforms have, however, attempted to enhance the comprehensive, or 'synoptic' rationality of the process in order that public spending produce the most 'bang for the buck'. And still other reforms have been directed at simply preventing budget deficits and alleged overspending by the public sector.

As with many reforms in the public sector, there is some movement back and forth between competing values in the budget process. On the one hand, democratic values argue that elected officials should have control over spending the public's tax money. On the other hand, a more technocratic approach that maximizes the utility of that spending is also valuable. These competing values may be more or less dominant, based on the state of the economy, and the politics of the time. The optimism about the capacity of rational decision-making in government also influences the choice of budget procedures. This chapter will first discuss the basic dynamics and issues in public budgeting. While the budget may appear to be a highly technical issue it is, as already noted, intensely political, so much of this discussion will be on the political dimension.[1] These politics are perhaps more institutional than they are partisan politics, but there are still struggles for power, and clear winners and losers. We will then proceed to discuss alternative strategies for reform and conclude with a discussion of the continuing problems that face public budgeting, especially in an era of resource constraint.

Fundamental Issues in Budgeting

As mentioned briefly above, there are three fundamental issues in the budget, both involving allocations between competing purposes. The first question is the macro-level allocation of resources between the public and the private sector. This allocation is a political and ideological question, but it is expressed in the framing of the budget. How much should government tax and spend? As well as the left versus right competition over the level of public spending, there is a more practical question of whether the public budget is going to be used as an instrument of fiscal policy to stimulate the economy, or perhaps to reduce inflation.

The second fundamental question in budgeting is the micro-allocation among the many competing purposes for which the scarce resources can be spent. Every decision to provide funds for one organization involves a decision not to allocate those funds to others, and therefore budget decisions inherently benefit some clients of the public sector and do not benefit others. And given that these expenditures are being funded primarily through tax revenues, the budget process as a whole involves large-scale redistributions of resources within the society.[2] The micro-allocation stage of budgeting therefore involves creating numerous

---

[1] This political dimension of budgeting was explicated most clearly by Aaron Wildavsky (1975) in the United States, but appears in all settings, even in nondemocratic regimes that also must cope with institutional politics when making their resource allocations.

[2] That redistribution may not be as great, however, as some believe – especially those on the political right. Given that taxes such as value-added tax (VAT) hit all consumers, and numerous benefits accrue disproportionately to the affluent, then the public budget in most countries is only moderately redistributive.

winners and losers, and is extremely important politically, as well as being crucial for the delivery of services to the public.

The role of taxation in funding public expenditure raises the third fundamental issue in budgeting, which is the balance between revenue and expenditure. This balance is important for several reasons. First, the fiscal balance is a means of managing the economy, based on the concepts of Keynesian economics.[3] Second, the deficit often reflects significant institutional failures in government, with taxing and spending decisions often being made by different institutions and at different times. And finally the deficit is a political symbol, especially for the political right, who may argue that the public budget and the individual's household budget should follow the same principles, that is the government should act like a good Swabian housewife (White and Wildavsky, 1989; *The Economist*, 2014).

Although phrased as distinct questions there, these three questions are closely linked and in practice may be difficult to disentangle. For example, the micro-allocation stage may drive the macro-allocation rather than vice versa, as it may appear more logical. Budget-makers may add up what they consider they have to spend to fund existing programs and to meet their political commitments, and that amount may exceed what they might have wanted to spend to maintain the public sector at a particular size relative to the total economy. But in these negotiations over the budget, politics trumps, and if there are commitments the money will generally be spent.

The Budget Process

Although the names of the actors will be different, and their patterns of interaction will be different, there are three basic sets of actors involved in the process of making the public budget (see Good, 2007). The first, as mentioned above, are the spending organizations, which are by far the most numerous actors involved in making the budget. Whether the money is being spent for social welfare, for building highways, or for defense, the spending organizations want and need their money from this process and hence exert pressures on the other actors for more money. And these organizations almost always do want more, to demonstrate their political power if for no other reason.

The second group involved in the process are the 'guardians'; those organizations, actors and individuals who attempt to control spending and to maintain a balanced budget. These are typically ministries of finance, or the treasury, or perhaps individual legislators with a commitment to what they

---

[3]The logic is that if there is a budget deficit then more money is put into the economy, increasing demand and therefore stimulating the economy. Conversely, if governments want to control inflation they extract more money through taxation than they spend, which should slow the economy and control inflation. Although few politicians now use the Keynesian model explicitly, in practice they do, for example, the stimulus package in the United States after the financial collapse in 2008 was Keynesian in all but name (see Kickert, 2012).

consider fiscal probity. The minister of finance may sit in cabinet with his or her colleagues but typically will be defending the public treasury against cabinet colleagues. The rules of some cabinets give the finance minister, along with the prime minister, additional powers over expenditure decisions. Even if the finance minister does not have special powers she or he must maintain the confidence of the prime minister (Savoie, 1999).

The third group of actors involved in the budget process are experts and depoliticized institutions responsible for advising government, and perhaps making decisions on their own, for example the Council of Economic Advisors in the United States, or the 'Five Wise Men' of economic policy in Germany (Potrafke, 2013). These groups, and analogous groups in other countries, are well-regarded economists who are charged with providing government with independent advice. This does not mean that government will take the advice, or that independence can be maintained easily,[4] but it does mean that governments will have access to advice about how best to make their budgets,

The other group of actors that fall into this expert group are central banks (see Schick, 2009). Although responsible directly for monetary policy, the views, and the actions, of the banks are important for the budget process. If for no other reason, the banks are important because inadequate coordination between monetary and fiscal policy will make both ineffective. This role for the banks is especially important when the banks are directly tied to government and in essence function as another arm of economic policymaking for the government of the day.

These three sets of actors exist in almost any political system, but their interactions may be markedly different in different settings. For example, in presidential regimes, notably the United States, the legislature may play the role of both guardian and expert, and may perceive a need to control the spending of the executive. The legislature also may develop organizations such as the Congressional Budget Office to provide independent advice concerning the economic implications of the budget, at both the macro and the micro levels.[5] In parliamentary regimes, cabinet rules will provide different levels of power to the finance minister, and also may empower the independent experts to a greater or lesser extent.

The behavior of these actors in less developed countries is different still. As Wildavsky (1984) pointed out, these countries often engage in 'repetitive budgeting' (see also Tarschys, 2003), that is, their economic uncertainty means that governments need to continuously revise budgets to match unforeseen

---

[4]Murry Weidenbaum, once chair of the Council of Economic Advisors (CEA), noted that the CEA would be asked to adapt their projections of economic events to match the political priorities of the President.

[5]As parliamentary regimes become increasingly presidentialized and the budget process is dominated by the executive, legislatures may divert some of these control activities to *ex post* review of spending rather than *ex ante* attempts to control the budget process. One example is the role of the select committees in the United Kingdom (Russell and Benton, 2011).

circumstances.[6] This style of budgeting may introduce even greater uncertainty into the economy, thus exacerbating the very conditions that lead to repetitive budgeting in the first place. In addition, in these regimes the roles of guardian and expert may be assumed, at least in part, by international donor organizations such as the World Bank and the International Monetary Fund.

Although the formal rules for interaction may differ, the actors will interact in relatively similar ways when considered more analytically. The experts tend to make the first move, setting the parameters for the budget process by making estimates of economic performance for the coming time period. Obviously if the economy is performing well, more tax money will be coming in and there will be less spending on social programs, so the government has more latitude to spend. When the economy is performing poorly there will be less capacity to spend than the spending organizations might like. Although these experts on economics and the budget are meant to be independent, they must still function in a political environment and may adjust their forecasts at least somewhat to the preferences of political leaders. This can be seen in part in the systematic tendency of these forecasts to overestimate economic growth, thus providing the government of the day greater latitude to spend. And that latitude is important because voters tend to like spending programs and dislike taxation, so any clever politician is attempting to spend. This is true even if political systems that say they want balanced budgets – that balance is fine so long as favorite programs are fully funded.

In most budget processes the next stage, whether formalized or not, is for the spenders to prepare requests for funds for the next time period. This part of the budget process tends to bubble up from the bottom, although fiscal constraints often lead to more top-down patterns of decision-making. Spending organizations know what their clients want and need, whether those clients are the unemployed or the armed forces, and will advance their claims on the public purse on behalf of those clients. These spending proposals when collected typically will be much in excess of the available resources, but it is the responsibility of the spenders to fight for their ministries and its clients. Faced with the numerous demands for public spending, the guardians now must become involved in evaluating those claims and deciding which to support and which to trim. This stage often involves additional analysis, albeit at a more micro than macro level. That is, civil servants working in the guardian organizations may perform systematic analyses of the costs and benefits of the alternative expenditures. That said, however, as we will argue below (pp. 125–7), the magnitude of the typical public budget may reduce the possibilities of extensive analysis. In addition, all the analysis possible cannot overcome the dominance of political criteria in the selection of spending priorities.

After the guardians have done their work and have developed a prospective budget, those choices must be legitimated. In parliamentary systems, that legitimation is made first in cabinet and then in parliament. This legitimation process may be more difficult in multi-party systems in which the cabinet may be less

---

[6]During the financial crisis beginning in 2008, many more developed countries had to engage in the same style of budgeting.

unified than in majoritarian systems, but in any regime the budget eventually must be adopted by parliament. In presidential regimes the legitimation process is even more complex with an independent legislature that may or may not be controlled by the same party as the executive. In the relatively few 'transformative legislatures' even in presidential systems (Polsby, 1968), the legislature will be even more active in monitoring and evaluating the public budget.

As the budget is being executed, and especially after the end of the budget year, public expenditures are audited. The audit is another means through which the legislature can control the executive, given that almost all auditing organizations in the world are legislative organizations. Increasingly the control is not just about the financial probity of the expenditures but it is also concerned with the efficiency of the expenditures, and the public policies funded by those expenditures. Then the process begins again, with the results from the last budget year constituting the frame within which the next year's budget negotiations will occur.

Problems in Public Budgeting

The processes through which the budget is made and implemented have been well institutionalized over the years, or centuries, but they still present some important problems that affect the quality of the decisions being made. These problems are hardly secret, and some of the reforms discussed below are designed explicitly to address the issues, yet they persist. This persistence may be in part path dependency, but it also reflects the politics of budget-making, and the attempts of the several institutions involved in the process to maintain their powers within the process.

One of the persistent issues in budgeting is that it is an annual process. While that may appear logical as a way of demarcating the time span of budgeting, for many programs, and even for effective control of spending, one year does not make a great deal of sense. Programs need to be able to plan, and budget controllers need to be able see the longer-term implications of budget choices made in any one year. But the tradition of the annual budget persists, despite efforts to introduce multi-year budgets. When there are multi-year budgets, the figures after the first year may not be taken seriously, or may be seen only as planning statements. The other consequence of the annual nature of the budget process is that it forces spending organizations to allocate all, or at least most, of their money before the end of the budget year, and therefore perhaps to 'invest' in programs that they would not do otherwise. The usual budget game (see below) is that one needs to spend all the money that is allocated, or the assumption from the 'guardians' will be that the budget was too large. In addition to the political dimensions of annual budgeting, the move toward more continuous budgeting also can be used to integrate budgeting with the policy planning process (Hou, 2006).

As well as being annual, budgets are often managed in cash terms. That is, what is being budgeted is the amount of money that will actually be spent during the 12-month period, and the amount of revenue that will actually be received. Another important reform in the budgetary process has been to think in terms of *accruals* rather than cash. That is, how much money will actually be spent over the life of a program, or at least over several years, because of a decision in any one year? For example, initiating a social program may cost very little during the first year but it may cost significant amounts as it gets going and accumulates clients. If we go beyond the distinction between the cash and accrual basis of budgeting, the fact that budgeting is conducted in terms of money can itself be considered a problem. What budgets and spending are for is to create public services, whether military defense, highways or social services. Therefore, budgeting might be considered in terms of the volume of service produced, as the British government did in the 1970s (see Wolfe and Moran, 1993). While volume budgeting may make sense in terms of understanding the performance of government, it may reduce the capacity of political leaders to control spending, and may also make the budget process less accessible to citizens.

The traditional budget is also a line-item budget. When the budget money is allocated to an organization through a line-item budget, it is provided in categories such as personnel, equipment, and the like. While those categories are useful for control by auditors and the legislature, they constitute straight-jackets for managers who are attempting to deliver services. Those managers would generally like to have the capacity to move money around, and then to be assessed on how well they have met their program goals. As New Public Management (NPM) has emphasized the capacity of public managers to control their programs and to be held accountable for the results, the traditional form of budgeting can reduce that managerial capacity. Finally, public budgets tend to be allocated on the basis of organizations. While organizations are the building blocks of governments, they are also another set of barriers to effective budgeting. As we will point out below when discussing program budgeting reforms, major activities in government are not all contained within a single organization. For example, if we were to catalog organizations in the US or Canadian governments that deal with health, we would find a large number of organizations that existed in many cabinet departments. And those numbers might be understated because they do not include organizations dealing with issues such as food security. Especially in federal systems, the fiscal autonomy of levels of government may limit the capacity to use budgets for Keynesian economic policy. Even if central government budgets are substantially larger than those of subnational governments, provincial or state budgets can still influence the overall aggregates of taxing and spending. In some federal systems such as Germany (Lübke, 2005) and Austria, budgets at all levels of government are coordinated, so there is a global target for spending and the deficit.

In sum, the traditional budget process may have worked well when government was relatively simple and provided a limited range of programs. As the range and complexity of public services have increased, the traditional budgeting process makes effective service delivery and program management more difficult. But the one thing that the traditional budget is particularly good at is enabling the legislature, and even ordinary citizens, to see what government is spending and for what. That accountability, and the more or less commonsense nature of the traditional budget helps to let at least some features of the traditional budget process to persist (Wildavsky, 1978).

Incrementalism in Budgeting

The above description of the budgetary process, and the sheer volume of contemporary public budgets, tends to produce incremental processes. As discussed in the chapter on decision-making, there are normative arguments on behalf of making incremental rather than comprehensive decisions in the public sector. The continuous adjustment of policies, or budget allocations, in an incremental process has been argued to permit better decisions in the long run (but see Forester and Spindler, 2006). And in particular incremental solutions may avoid significant losses from making large, incorrect decisions. The budget process may produce incremental outcomes for more empirical reasons. Each budget involves thousands of decisions and if each decision were considered rationally, the budget might never be completed. Therefore, decision-makers may tend to rely on considering only the changes from previous allocations, and even then the decision-making task remains significant.[7] Therefore, to simplify the process, decision-makers tend to develop simple rules of thumb that facilitate their reaching decisions. Those rules of thumb tend to be stable across time and may differ across the agencies being funded.

The incremental interpretation of public budgeting has been supported by a good deal of empirical evidence. This empirical work began with the study of federal budgeting in the United States (Davis, Dempster and Wildavsky, 1966). They found that they could predict budget allocations in a year t with extremely high levels of accuracy on the basis of allocations in year $t–1$ plus a fixed percentage increase. In other words, budget-makers appear to have stable decision rules that make their own tasks easier, and also create a rather stable environment for public agencies being funded through the process. Another version of bounded rationality can also be used to explain the apparent stability of budget decisions – the incremental outcome. Rather than having decision-makers rely on relatively simplistic decision rules and be dominated by expenditures in previous years – the base – Padgett (1980; see also B. D. Jones, Zalanyi and Erdi, 2014) argues that this outcome can be explained more effectively by the aspirations and search behavior of those decision-makers. If we assume that decision-makers when making the annual budget have an aspiration level of additions or cuts and search for program changes that will fulfill those goals, then relatively similar empirical results can be obtained.

The theory of incrementalism in budgeting is based on American experiences, and even there the findings are somewhat contested. For example, the level of incrementalism in allocations drops dramatically if the data are examined at the level of the program rather than the agency (Natchez and Bupp, 1973). In addition, it has been argued that the observation of stability in appropriations is a function of the limited opportunities for change, given the large proportion of the budget that is uncontrollable. Previous commitments to

---

[7]In the case of France, prior to the passage of budgetary reforms in 2001 (Catheau, 2013), the French budget process considered only new spending as it was assumed that previous expenditures would continue unchanged (Lord, 1973).

programs, and obligations such as debt interest provide little latitude for changes in the budget. And if a broader array of countries, and time periods, is considered the experience of incrementalism does not appear to be as pervasive. Incrementalism depends on predictability, both in the resource base and the political system. Many political systems do not have that luxury, and their budgeting is more erratic and less predictable. Perhaps more importantly, assumptions about budgeting based on incrementalism and stability are being threatened by the fiscal crises of many countries. At least since the fiscal crisis of 2008, thinking about budgeting has been as much about decrementalism as about incrementalism, that is, why do budgets go down as well as up? But there is yet no viable theory about decrementalism (Tarschys, 1984). This is in part because the patterns of incremental growth are deeply engrained in the public sector. Also, cutting budgets tends to be considered a one-time event rather than what may become a continuing issue in the public sector.

The available literature that comes closest to addressing the need for decrementalism has been addressed to cutback management. The first round of this literature emerged during the 1970s, when the long period of post-war economic growth came to an end and there was a need, especially for local governments, to reduce spending (Levine, 1978). The second round of cutback management followed the 2008 fiscal crisis, and the associated decline in revenues for the public sector (Cepiku and Savignon, 2012). In both of these waves of the cutback management literature, as is true for the limited literature on decrementalism, there is more description than analytic or theoretical development concerning how to overcome incremental pressures.

Reforming the Budget and the Budget Process

The numerous issues and problems associated with the budget process have led to several attempts to reform budgeting. Some of these reforms have attempted to enhance the rationality of the process, and to overcome the seemingly simple rules used to allocate resources. Other reforms were also interested in overcoming incrementalism, but more in order to reduce levels of expenditure rather than to enhance synoptic rationality. Indeed, some of the reforms associated with reducing expenditures may be less rational than the simple incremental models normally used in making budget decisions. And, as already noted, the incremental model of decision-making tends to be associated with more affluent countries, with governments that have relatively stable revenue streams. Patterns of budgeting in less-fortunate countries often are more erratic than incremental, and may reflect the need to have something on paper, rather than a firm plan for taxing and spending. And these budgets may be revised again and again, as more realistic financial data comes in during implementation – what Wildavsky called 'repetitive budgeting'.

Like all aspects of public administration, the budget process has been the subject of numerous efforts at reform. Given the numerous problems inherent in more traditional forms of budgeting, it is hardly surprising that there have been a wide range of reform proposals. Although there are a large number of such proposals, they can be placed into three major categories. One addresses the fundamental problem of incrementalism and the low level of rationality of the process. A second category is composed of reforms that attempt to produce greater control over spending, and especially to reduce spending. And finally there have been some attempts at reform that attempt to minimize the centralized and technocratic elements of budgeting in favor of more political influence over the decisions.

The Search for Rationality

The dominant strand of reform in the budget process has been to find more comprehensively rational means of allocating resources, even when the circumstances of making decisions appear to require much more simplistic means of making decisions. Many attempts have been made to address incrementalism and to improve the rationality of the decisions. One spate of rationalist reforms was during the 1970s and early 1980s – a period of hubris about policy analysis and the capacity of the state to perform effectively and efficiently. A second wave of these reforms has been associated with attempts to link performance measures to the budget process (see Robinson and Brumby, 2003).

Program budgeting

Program budgeting, or planning, programming, and budgeting system (PPBS), was the most extreme attempt to introduce rational analysis into the budget process (see Novick, 1967). Borrowed from the private sector, this budget mechanism addressed several problems of the traditional budget process. First, rather than being based on organizations, program budgeting asked the question of what government was doing and how did individual organizations contribute to those basic programs of the public sector. Budgets therefore were to be allocated to the fundamental programs, for example health or education, rather than to the organizations. Furthermore, the allocation was to be justified through the outputs produced by those programs. Second, rather than depending on simple rules of thumb, PPBS required heavy investments in analysis, and attempts to identify the optimal of scarce resources. That analysis, in turn, requires identification of alternative uses of those resources, something that breaks with the incremental logic of accepting the existing patterns of allocation and only considering changes from (additions to) that pattern. As well as requiring the use of extensive analytic resources, this approach required organizations potentially to undermine their own established programs and patterns of work.

Program budgeting was primarily an American innovation, although versions were adopted in France (Lord, 1973) and Sweden. Even within the United States, this method was implemented more fully in the department of defense more than in other parts of government, in large part because Robert McNamara, as secretary of defense, was the primary advocate. Also, measuring outcomes or outputs in defense was more difficult than in many domestic policy areas, and somewhat paradoxically, the analysis of alternatives was somewhat less constrained by awkward information.

Zero-based budgeting

While many scholars have dismissed zero-based budgeting as excessively simplistic, it was an attempt to overcome some of the problems of traditional incremental budgeting. Most importantly, as the name implies, this method of budgeting attempted to undermine the idea that there was a budgetary base that was not subject to discussion, as was true in the incremental model. The method in reality did not require justification of all expenditures in every year, but it did force organizations to identify how much money they needed to continue to survive, and how much they needed to continue to provide the existing levels of service. Another aspect of zero-based budgeting was that it did not think of additions of budgets in percentage terms but rather in terms of packages of services. The argument, quite accurately, was that simply adding a little bit here and a little bit there might not add to levels of service, while thinking in terms of levels of additional services would make the process more rational. This form of budgeting therefore had some relationship to the volume budgeting that was in place in the United Kingdom during the 1970s (Heclo and Wildavsky, 1974). In this budget system decisions were made in terms of services provided rather than money, although this produced significant problems in financial accountability for governments.

Accrual budgeting

Many countries have now replaced annual cash budgeting with accrual budgeting. As discussed above, cash budgeting tends not to take adequate account of the longer-term implications of decisions made in any one year. In addition, cash accounting does not take into account adequately the assets and liabilities that are created by public programs. By including an analysis of the full costs of public programs, in any one year and across time, decision-makers can make more informed decisions about the implications of expenditures as well as about revenues. While accrual budgeting is generally lauded as a means of increasing the comprehensive rationality of the budget process, it has also been questioned because it may reduce the control of governments, and perhaps especially parliaments over public spending. Like the experiments with volume budgeting in the United Kingdom, once decisions are made they appear to be institutionalized and not considered adequately in subsequent years. For this reason, among others, Germany dropped accrual budgeting after an experiment over approximately a decade (R. Jones and Luder, 2011).

In addition to the political issues that are associated with accrual budgeting there are significant measurement issues that may reduce the utility of the approach (see also below for performance budgeting). Perhaps the most important concerns social insurance programs, especially pensions. While it may appear obvious that governments have long-term obligations to provide pensions to their citizens, governments tend not to treat them as liabilities in accrual systems. The logic is that, at least in principle, governments as sovereigns could choose to reduce or eliminate these obligations (Blondal, 2003).

Performance budgeting

Performance budgeting is the contemporary approach to budget reform that most closely approximates some of the earlier attempts at increasing synoptic rationality (see Robinson and Brumby, 2003). As was true for PPBS, the allocation of funds is justified through the outputs of government programs. Furthermore, those outputs are quantified, and levels of change from one time period to the next can be utilized to assess the performance of the public organization and to make budget allocations. At first glance this approach to budgeting appears to be an extremely good way to budget. It focuses on what government does, and it can be used to motivate greater effectiveness and efficiency in government. Although this may appear to be a positive approach, there are also some significant questions. Perhaps the most basic is measurement (see Bouckaert and Peters, 2002). If performance budgeting is to function we need to be able to measure the outputs and outcomes of government programs This appears relatively easy for some programs such as building roads but is much more difficult for defense or for regulatory policy.

Also, performance budgeting, as is true for other reforms coming from NPM, emphasizes efficiency more than other important values within the public sector. This emphasis on efficiency privileges programs that can be more easily measured, and for which efficiency gains are more feasible. In particular it may disadvantage social programs that depend more on providing citizens personal services that involve high labor costs. Performance budgeting also privileges programs that have benefits that appear relatively quickly, whereas some successful programs may have sleeper effects that may not appear for years or even decades (Salamon, 1979). Finally, even if we could do all the technical measurements, what would we do with the information? Should organizations who perform poorly be punished with lower budgeted resources, or perhaps they should be given more resources in order to improve their performance. Both possible answers appear reasonable. Thus, while this approach to budgeting may emphasize what governments do, there is no clear way to link budget decision-making to the information that becomes available.

The Search for Control

Although rationality is an important value for making budget decisions, in some instances it may be important simply to gain some control over spending. One particularly good example of that imperative occurred in the United Kingdom when the rational approach of volume budgeting was replaced by cash limits designed to reassert control over public spending. More recently, the fiscal crisis beginning in 2008 produced a need to impose controls over spending. In general, however, control is difficult to maintain given the uncontrollable nature of many expenditures, and the political commitments that are embedded in the base budgets of most organizations.

Although politicians are always attempting to control the bureaucracy, and public spending, there have been two major periods with governments attempt to achieve greater control. The first came in the 1970s and early 1980s during which discussions of 'cutback management' were important for understanding transformations in the public sector (Levine, 1978; see Bozeman, 2010). After decades of economic growth and growth in public spending, a significant slow-down in the economy produced a perceived need to control spending. At the time this was perceived to be a short-term event, but concerns with control have persisted. The second major wave of reductions in budgets have been related to the economic crisis beginning in 2008. This period of austerity has utilized many of the same approaches to reducing expenditures as in the previous period, and has had many of the same political conflicts over cuts (Lodge and Hood, 2012). What may have distinguished this period, however, was that it came after some decades of attempts to manage public spending, when there was relatively little slack left in public budgets.

We cannot go through all the various devices used in all the countries which have been facing the fiscal crisis (but see Raudla, Savi and Randma-Liiv, 2013). We should note, however, that many of these mechanisms were about as far away from the rational model as could be imagined. Most involved rather sim-ple across-the-board cuts in spending, albeit often protecting social programs and uncontrollable expenditures such as debt interest. These expenditure cuts were about just that – cutting – rather than attempting to devise some optimal use of public funds.

The Search for Political Responsibility

The third dimension of budget reform emphasizes the desire to move budgeting away from the technocracy that has characterized the process in some settings, and has been sought in many more. The purpose of these reforms has been to emphasize political control and political involvement. The budget is a central political document, and it is important to emphasize the responsibility of politi-cal leaders for this allocation of public resources. And if it is not the political leaders who are involved, it may be the public who attempt to control funding of programs through more direct public participation.

Envelopes

The budgetary process has tended to focus on allocations to individual organizations, and even individual programs. While this focus gives those directly involved in the budget process a great deal of influence over alloca-tions, it does not provide the ministers responsible for administering the budget as much control. The envelope system of budgeting, in which the ini-tial allocation of resources is to broad areas of policy, permits ministers and other political actors to shape the final allocation. This system of budgeting, which was used in Canada for a significant period of time, not only forces political decisions about the relative priorities of various components of, for example, the social and health policy domain, but it also requires offsetting of spending in one area if there are to be increases in others. An analogous system, called portfolio budgeting, has been used in Australia, with an emphasis on controlling total expenditures in a particular area (Xavier, 1997). Similarly, the 'pay as you go' system in the United States (PAYGO) required decision-makers to offset increased expenditures with either cuts in other programs or increased revenues (Blondal, Kraan and Ruffner, 2003).

Participatory budgeting

While envelope budgeting has emphasized greater political involvement of ministers and perhaps legislators in the budget process, a growing movement has been emphasizing more direct popular involvement in making spending decisions. While there are still relatively few opportunities for direct participation at the national level, the involvement of the public has been institutionalized in local government in a number of countries. This form of deliberative democracy began in Brazil, more specifically in the city of Porto Allegre (Wampler, 2010). In this model there are a series of meetings beginning in neighborhoods and then moving upward to the city level in which priorities for public spending are discussed and voted on. While fixed expenditures such as pensions and debt service are not considered in this process, other spending – perhaps notably infrastructure – is discussed and largely determined. Although the exact procedures may vary, across countries or even across cities, the general pattern of beginning at the neighborhood and then moving upward is common.

The participatory budget process appears to have produced some benefits in the allocation of resources, especially infrastructure spending (Shah, 2007), but it is far from a panacea for the problems of budgets. In the first place, a significant portion of the budget cannot be covered, given that they are on-going commitments. Perhaps more importantly, despite the openness of the process, the most impoverished members of society tend not to participate, so that this process may not be as democratic as it appears. Furthermore, this process tends to separate the organizations who will have to implement the budget from its creation, and perhaps to make implementation through the public bureaucracy more difficult. Finally, although the process may be democratic, it may not necessarily produce the most effective use of public resources. As in many other alternatives among processes, there does appear to be a tradeoff between 'democracy' and 'rationality'.

Summary and Conclusions

The budget is a central process for government in general, and for the public bureaucracy in particular. This is one of the oldest activities in the public sector, and despite those centuries of the process, there are continuing issues and problems. But there are also continuing efforts to reform the process and to find some balance between issues of rationality, the capacity to make timely decisions, and political control. While developing a more effective budget process may appear a relatively simple task, the magnitude of the task and the numerous competing political and economic values makes finding an effective process difficult.

   Perhaps the most important finding from all the budgetary research is that the process can never be, nor should perhaps it aspire to be, fully rational. There are too many aspects of programs that cannot be measured adequately, and there are too many important political factors involved, to ever permit a simple rational calculation. At best (from a rationalist perspective), the decisions about the budget will be made through bounded rationality, reflecting the complexity of the tasks, the extent to which those tasks are embedded in organizational and political contexts, and the range of possible goals involved.

10

Authority Versus Democracy

Government organizations require executive capacity to deliver the programs and services of which they have been placed in charge. Such capacity to act – getting things done – is paramount to these organizations, in part because executing the government's decisions is a matter of democratic significance. Governments are elected to make and implement policy. Executive capacity is also important because such delivery is often assumed to be integral to the legitimacy of those institutions. 'Executive capacity' in the context of the public sector is the sum of its human, financial and organizational resources, combined with a legal mandate specifying jurisdiction and authority. At the same time, the political power from which such executive capacity is delegated to political leaders and institutions from the people in general elections. As we have noted several times in this book, the public bureaucracy has major powers over citizens and clients, ranging from charging fines and fees to incarceration and extradition. Thus, the public bureaucracy represents a major challenge to democracy because it is composed of a large number of unelected, permanent officials with substantial expert knowledge and substantial capacity to make decisions that may have a profound impact on the lives of its clients. This challenge is resolved by extensive processes and frameworks of accountability, which mean that any bureaucrat using public authority will be accountable for those actions.

The dichotomy or dilemma that this chapter will explore is whether we want constitutional and institutional design to cater primarily to goals related to authority, that is, the capacity of public institutions to deliver policy and programs, or whether instead we prioritize political and societal responsiveness. Most would probably want both; there is obvious virtue and logic to both of these objectives. The constitutional strategy across most of the Western world to accommodate the tensions between authority and democracy has been to design the relationship between public institutions so as to ensure internal (i.e. inter-institutional) control and accountability; the US system of 'checks and balances' between the legislature, the presidency and the judiciary is a good example. In terms of external control, the single most important arrangement to ensure that the capabilities that are accorded collective institutions – which is essential to their capacity to govern – by the public is electoral accountability. Indeed, as Mulgan (2000: 563) points out, if the key issue of democracy is to ensure that government is responsive to the needs and preferences of the public, then democracy becomes primarily a system put in place to ensure accountability. The electoral mandate alone will not suffice to ensure such responsiveness; there has to be some means of holding elected officials to account for their actions or inactions as well.

Accountability is in vogue, or, as Bovens, Goodin and Schillemans put it, 'the buzzword of modern governance' (2014a: 1, for an overview, see Shedler, 1999; Mulgan, 2000; Bovens, 2007; Bovens, Goodin and Schillemans, 2014b). As often happens with issues that are widely studied and debated, there has been some conceptual 'stretching' (Sartori, 1970), and accountability research is no exception to this rule. Mark Bovens makes a useful distinction between 'narrow' and 'broad' accountability, where the former category refers to the issues that are most immediately associated with holding elected or administrative officers to account while the latter category includes transparency, legal security and all other values that we tend to associate with good government (Bovens, 2007; see also Mulgan, 2000).

Also, 'broad' accountability is an evaluative, more than an analytical version of accountability, whereas 'narrow' accountability defines in a formal-legal sense what accountability is and how it is to be exercised. That is, broad accountability is not concerned with detailed analysis of specific issues but more with general patterns of responsiveness within the public sector. The problem, as Bovens (2007) points out, is that much of the contemporary debate about accountability is about 'broad' and not 'narrow' accountability, something which has further confused the debate on this topic. A related problem is that while public administration emphasizes formal-legal and electoral accountability, New Public Management (NPM) reform advocates performance-based accountability (see Chapter 1). The argument here is that NPM offers clearer and more immediate accountability related to performance and delivery where customers through choice can voice their preferences and thus hold service providers to account.

The chapter first discusses different aspects of accountability before we turn to an analysis of the growing complexity of accountability that has emerged in the wake of NPM reform and how different types of accountability can be exercised (Willems and van Dooren, 2012). The tasks of accountability have become even more difficult as governments have increasingly come to use a variety of instruments involving social and market actors to deliver public services. Therefore, this chapter will consider a wide variety of types of accountability and accountability instruments as well as their possible effects. We will also consider the possibilities of enhancing direct public involvement in accountability.

The Many Shapes and Forms of Accountability

Accountability is a fundamental concept in the study of public administration as well as in democratic government more broadly. The exercise of administration may have profound impact on clients and the public and must therefore be subject to close scrutiny from a legal perspective. Such control is not only essential to the legitimacy of the bureaucracy; it is also a key component in the democratic embeddedness of the administration, given the executive capacity which the administration controls. One of the key mechanisms of such control of authority is, as mentioned, accountability. However, the meaning of accountability has significantly grown over the past couple of decades. In the 'broad' meaning of accountability as defined by Bovens (2007), accountability is today given a multitude of different meanings, and strengthening accountability is sometimes advocated as the panacea to the wide range of problems facing contemporary governments. Accountability may be used to address issues of efficiency as well as legality of actions, and also can be seen as a source of legitimacy when other sources of legitimacy are weak. We will discuss conventional formal-legal accountability before we briefly introduce other types of accountability.

Mark Bovens (2007) emphasizes the interactive nature of accountability. He suggests that accountability could be defined as 'a relationship between an actor and a forum, in which the actor has an obligation to explain and to justify his or her conduct, the forum can pose questions and pass judgement, and the actor may face consequences' (Bovens, 2007: 450). This definition captures the core elements of accountability: it is actor-centered; it is set in some kind of forum, implying that holding someone to account is a public process; judgments will be passed; and potential consequences may be levied on the actor that has broken the rules defining his or her position (see also Mulgan, 2000). To these criteria for accountability we might also add that the forum is independent of the actor whose actions are being assessed.

Accountability, then, refers to the processes and instruments by which the political level of government can ensure that the public administration acts within its constitutionally and legally defined boundaries, and that its actions are conducted in the prescribed manner. The elected officials, in turn, are accountable to the public so that abuse of public office may well cost a politician his or her re-election (see Day and Klein, 1987). Thus, accountability is sometimes a direct, sometimes an indirect process, a sequential process of internal and external control. The theory of accountability thus may look fairly straightforward. However, holding institutions and bureaucrats accountable represents a major challenge to elected officials and to the public more generally. To some extent, as we will discuss throughout this chapter, the fundamental problem can be described as a principal–agent problem, where the agent is accountable to the principal, who in turn is accountable to a more senior level of the administration or to the public. Problems occur as a result of the information asymmetry between the principal and the agent, meaning that the principal will not have complete knowledge of the agent's action while remaining accountable for those actions.

Formal-legal accountability

In a public administration perspective, the most important type of accountability is formal-legal accountability (Peters, 2014). Such accountability is conducted when the performance of a public servant is assessed against the rules that define legal administrative conduct, mainly during the exercise of legal authority. If the public servant is found to be acting in conflict with those rules, he or she will be reprimanded by senior levels of the bureaucracy. This could include a range of sanctions such as a fine, suspension, termination of employment or initiating a criminal justice procedure.

The severity of the committed act is thus one aspect of formal-legal accountability. In some jurisdictions, formal-legal accountability also distinguishes between different types of issue. In Sweden, the main legal charge against a public servant abusing public office (*tjänstefel*) was redefined in the 1970s, so that henceforth it only applied to public services where legal authority is being exercised. This type of accountability is in many ways the most straightforward and unambiguous type of accountability. The rules against which administrative action is reviewed, for instance administrative law or statutes defining appropriate action by public sector employees, refer to what could be considered to be cases of severe malfeasance, such as corruption or abuse of public office.

In most countries there is some form of administrative law that defines how administrators should apply the law and how they should make and adjudicate law. For example, the Administrative Procedures Act in the United States expresses rules of rule-making and for the conduct of administrative courts (Kerwin and Furlong, 2011). While these rules for the bureaucracy may still produce constitutional issues, administrative law is generally applied and adjudicated within the bureaucracy itself, and tends to focus on process more than substance. That said, countries in the Napoleonic tradition use institutions such as the *Conseil d'Etat* to ensure that actions within administration are also substantively legal.

Political and democratic accountability

Formal-legal accountability is used to assess whether public servants have conducted their work in accordance with the formal rules that define the modus operandi of the bureaucracy. Political and democratic – sometimes the concept 'electoral' is used – accountability refers to the exercise whereby the public evaluate the performance of elected officials. The key issues in this type of accountability are not so much related to the legality of an elected politician's performance but are more concerned with the degree to which he or she has delivered on the promises that were made during the election campaign (Naurin, 2011). In order for this type of accountability to be effective, elected officials have an obligation to explain their actions and to deliver 'answerability' more broadly (Shedler, Diamond and Plattner, 1999; Bovens, 2007). Answerability means that the elected official in question should be committed to engaging the electorate, either directly or via the media (see more on the media below) and to provide explanation and justification for his or her actions. This may appear rather obvious but politicians sometimes have incentives not to be so candid about their performance. Sometimes the end result of answerability is an exchange between an assertive journalist determined to expose a politician's faults and bad judgments on the one hand, and a media-trained politician 'staying on message' on the other, to the detriment of clarification and democratic accountability.

Democratic accountability is an exceedingly complicated process. Interestingly, elected officials have been found to fulfill the commitments they made in the election campaign to a large extent, perhaps larger than many observers would have guessed (Naurin, 2011). In terms of accountability, perhaps the biggest problem is to decide to what degree undelivered promises can be justified. For instance, during the global financial crisis starting in 2007, most governments had to reassess their spending and implement drastic budget cuts. This policy change often meant deviating from electoral commitments, or at least indicated a significant change in policy that had not been announced during the election campaign. The question that voters will have to analyze in this situation when they hold politicians to account is whether the response to the crisis was sufficient justification for breaking the election promise. Indeed, the argument could be made that not responding forcefully to the crisis would have been a neglect of political responsibility. Thus the relationship between election campaign pledges, party strategy and changes in the preconditions for the delivery of those pledges is complex, and analyzing that relationship in order to establish accountability requires more detailed information and analytical skills than the average voter possesses.

These problems are exacerbated by the politics of accountability. Opposition parties will accuse incumbent parties for breaking their promises to the voters, while incumbents will make the case that the opposition issue unrealistic promises which, if implemented, will jeopardize the economy of the country. Again, the average voter will find it difficult to make sense of the issues and the debate. In addition, the opposition parties may focus on relatively minor deviations to embarrass a government while perhaps ignoring some of the more basic political and policy issues.

In sum, while democratic or electoral accountability is an integral component of democratic governance it is also a challenging process. The circumstance that political parties have incentives to exaggerate their achievements and downplay their failures only adds complexity to this task. These political forms of accountability are, furthermore, complemented by legal mechanisms that can also be used to hold public administration accountable for their actions.

Accountability, responsibility and the ethics of public administration

We will now return to the internal accountability processes within the public administration in order to discuss another type of accountability that occurs in cases when a public servant may not necessarily have acted in conflict with formal rules but nonetheless behaved inappropriately. For instance, acting out of poor judgment when dealing with a client might be inappropriate administrative behavior, but it is not illegal. This means that there are several gray zones in this type of accountability, where it is less obvious whether a particular action by a bureaucrat should render some form of sanction. When these less serious (but arguably more common) cases of administrative malpractice are addressed in terms of accountability we find that mechanisms other than formal laws or other rules matter more and more. The daily work of public servants is not only guided by formal laws and rules but also by codes of ethics. Public sector employees are socialized into roles defined by subtle values and rules, or what March and Olsen (1989) call a 'logic of appropriateness'. This is a continuous process, reproduced through peer interactions and adapted to changes over time in the nature of the issues that the organization handles, its clients' needs, other agencies' programs, and so on. The key point here is that these socialization processes articulate the normative aspects of public administration, that is, the prescribed administrative behavior.

In addition, most public organizations today have a code of ethics or code of conduct to supplement regulatory frameworks that apply to all public organizations. Such codes of ethics assist the legal framework of public administration in securing accountability. Kinchin (2007) identifies five values – fairness, transparency, responsibility, efficiency and conflict of interest – which are the core ethical values that link directly to accountability. These values are extremely difficult to define in legal terms, yet they are central to the public ethos and conduct and also to accountability. Prior to NPM, these norms and values were sustained within the public bureaucracy. However, as the public bureaucracy became exposed to market-based values, that internal process was challenged in favor of more market-based values such as efficiency.

Thus, the early NPM reform in the1990s triggered an extensive debate about ethics in the public administration (see, for instance, Frederickson, 1993). This may in part be due to injection of market-based values and ideas that NPM entailed, and in part to the closer linkages between the public sector and the private business sector, for instance through contracts. NPM advocates would, however, disagree with the critique that market-based management complicated accountability (see Chapter 2). Their counterargument was that NPM strengthened accountability: not in relation to senior levels of the bureaucracy or to the elected officials, but rather through market-based choice exercised by empowered customers. We will return to this discussion later in this chapter.

The political controls over bureaucracy and the normative controls imposed through codes of ethics may at times conflict, forcing the individual public servant to make difficult choices. The most obvious example is when a civil servant is given an order by a political superior, which the public servant believes to be illegal or unethical. Which form of accountability is more important, and which should the individual comply with? Similarly, the public servant may feel responsibilities both to the clients of a program and to the laws being administered, a problem which arises most frequently for 'street-level' bureaucrats who interact with the public on a daily basis (Meyers and Vorsanger, 2003).

Accountability through public involvement

The final type of accountability we will discuss in this section is the notion of strengthening accountability by bringing in representatives of the public into policy-making and to some extent administration. A large number of countries around the world have for decades experimented with opening up for citizen engagement in different forms and forums. Such engagement caters to several objectives for government: it facilitates new input on policy issues; builds trust and legitimacy for government; allows government to tap into specialized expertise outside government; and increases popular understanding for the problems governments face with making budget allocations among important projects, just to name a few (Blomgren Bingham, Nabatchi and O'Leary, 2005).

The type of accountability that public involvement can offer falls into what Bovens (2007) calls 'broad' accountability; it creates new arenas and channels for transparency and responsiveness, probably to a greater extent than accountability in a more formal sense. Even so, however, experiences have often been positive and public involvement, for instance in participatory budgeting, has become institutionalized in many cases. Beginning in cities in Brazil, this mechanism provides citizens the opportunity to shape at least some aspects of the public budget, and also to comment on previous actions of government. Social media and the internet have further assisted the development of new forums where the public can give input on public service and policy choice. Many government programs now use online citizen (or customer) satisfaction surveys as a matter of course, and are open to a range of other electronic communications. As we mentioned in Chapter 1, local governments in some Australian jurisdictions use online services to facilitate citizens' input on budget-related issues. In China and Indonesia, smartphone apps can be used to report poor quality of public service or suspected cases of corruption (for an overview see M. B. Brown, 2006). These forms of participation and accountability appear to be especially important for more authoritarian regimes where the usual mechanisms for participation are absent or ignored.

Accountability or authority?

The public in most countries appear to be more concerned with increasing the accountability of government than ensuring that government has the authority and capacity it requires to deliver governance. This drive for a search for more control of public office may be a manifestation of a lack of trust in government and elected officials. At the same time, however, that same public will turn to government in times of crisis (Hibbing and Theiss-Morse, 2002). Thus, ensuring that government has the necessary legal, financial and organizational resources to deliver its programs is in itself a contested issue. It should be noted that many governments over the past couple of decades have implemented cutbacks in their own core staff, a strategy which might appear strange, given the increasing complexity of issues that these governments face and a growing need for coordination (Peters and Savoie, 1998).

The issue here is that although there is no zero-sum game per se between government capacity and the level of accountability, a growing amount of that capacity is found in the executive branch of government or is being contracted out to private actors and societal partners, where power and control are negotiated and accountability in its conventional form therefore becomes a more complex process compared with in-house capacity building. Emphasizing government capacity may thus jeopardize accountability whereas strengthening accountability may lead government to conduct more service delivery in-house, which could drive costs. We will now see how some of the issues we have discussed above play out in contemporary public administration. Again, our focus is not just on accountability as such but also how contemporary governments develop executive authority and capacity, and the degree to which that reform aides or confuses accountability.

Exercising accountability

The literature on accountability has proliferated over the past two decades (see Mulgan, 2000; Bovens, Goodin and Schillemans, 2014b). Scholars and practitioners are more preoccupied with accountability issues today than perhaps ever before. There is today also a wider range of such issues than we saw earlier. This dramatic increase in accountability has several explanations. Some, as we have already mentioned, are related to NPM reform that implicitly (sometimes explicitly) challenges the specificity of public sector organizations not only in managerial but also in normative terms.

Accountability and New Public Management reform

One important reason for the growing interest in accountability has been different types of public management reform. Given that conventional accountability within the public bureaucracy is conducted from the bottom and up, and from the bureaucracy to the political leadership, reform that empowers middle-level managers and autonomous, operative institutions will also impact the process of accountability.

NPM reform aimed at creating a public service that differs in many respects from conventional public administration (Goldfinch and Wallis, 2009; Christensen and Laegreid, 2011a; see also Chapter 2). This reform has a number of different elements, which in different ways have entailed a more complex accountability. The common denominator has been the separation of policy from operations which has introduced a principal–agent problem between elected officials and the bureaucracy and thereby also a potential accountability problem. With the growing number of actors, often drawn from different segments of society, and a separation of policy-making and the operative element of government, accountability becomes an extremely complicated process (Jantz and Jann, 2013). The main problem is that conventional accountability processes flow from the lower to the higher levels of the bureaucracy and from the top level of the administration to the political level. This process ensures that elected officials are ultimately responsible for the bureaucracy's decisions and actions.

One example of NPM reform has been the creation of autonomous, executive agencies to deliver programs and policy (Pollitt and Talbot, 2004; Pollitt et al., 2005; Verhoest et al., 2012). This reform has been guided by a belief that separating policy from operations will clarify these respective roles, help empower public service managers and also open up new points of contact between government and society. However, despite their autonomy, agencies remain, at least in theory, accountable to their respective parent department and delegating authority does not remove that accountability. Delegation, however, significantly complicates accountability; how can we, for instance, establish whether a failed program should be blamed on the principal, that is, the department, or the agent, that is, the agency (see Pressman and Wildavsky, 1974)? In terms of public management, the problem here is that if departments were to choose the opposite strategy and grant these agencies only limited discretion to monitor closely their activities, that strategy would largely defeat the purpose of the reform. Another, albeit related, type of accountability problem has emerged as a consequence of the increasing usage of organizations situated at the border between the public and private spheres of society. Such 'hybrid organizations' serve to provide a structure to partnerships, networks or other forms of public–private collaboration. There are a host of such structures in terms of the cast of actors involved and the organizational strength of the collaborative arrangement, as well as in terms of the purpose of the 'hybrid' organization.

The most familiar example of such organizations is public–private partnerships, where public and private actors pool resources towards some shared objective. Public–private partnerships are frequently used both at the global level (Bexell and Mörth, 2010) and the local level of the political system (Pierre, 1998). In these partnerships, accountability is even more difficult to sustain. The basic logic of a public–private partnership is to merge public and private resources, but this strategy greatly complicates accountability, as political actors have only indirect means of controlling how the partnership spends public money or uses public authority (see Acar, Chao and Yang, 2008). Most importantly, contracting out, competitive tendering and the externalization of the operative elements of the public sector have driven accountability problems (Mulgan, 1997). Contracting out as a strategy for service delivery takes the principal–agent problem to even higher levels since it includes not only the separation between decision-making and execution but also that this arrangement traverses the border between the state and the market. Bringing in contractors into public service delivery can often be an efficient strategy to cut costs, just as relying on temporary staff rather than having all expertise continuously on the public payroll creates a more flexible workforce and may help cut salary costs. The downside is that it makes accountability far more complicated. If a contractor has delivered services which are found to be of inferior quality, how can we ascertain whether this is the result of poor public procurement, or poor contract management, or whether it is because the private contractor simply did not deliver what was stated in the contract?

Perhaps even more fundamentally it is difficult to write contracts in policy areas such as social services that can detail adequately the types of care and attention which social workers need to use when dealing with vulnerable populations of clients. Effective contracting depends on being able to detail the requirements for the contractor, and enforcing 'specific performance', in the courts if necessary. This may be easy to do for building a road or even designing a fighter plane, but is extremely difficult for human services when the 'product' is rather vague and the raw material (people) is highly variable. Again, at the heart of these problems is a principal–agent arrangement that separates decision-making from executive capacity. Conventional accountability, as already mentioned, allows politicians to control senior bureaucrats who, in turn, can hold lower-level public servants to account. Autonomous agencies and private contractors break that chain of conventional responsibility and accountability. If thus NPM has complicated conventional accountability, has it also offered some alternative mechanisms through which service providers and elected officials can be held to account in the NPM administrative landscape? Let us now turn to that issue.

New Public Management as an Alternative Accountability Process

NPM clearly offers accountability but it is a different type of accountability compared with conventional accountability, which is mainly concerned with how government and the public bureaucracy conduct their deliberation and decision-making. Accountability in the NPM model of administration is primarily oriented toward what the political system delivers (see Heinrich, 2002). True, a public bureaucracy shaped by NPM reform will still be diligent to punish administrative malfeasance and rule-breaking (Peters, 2003), but the emphasis will be on measuring performance and present the customers of public services with performance data and choice among competing service providers. Performance measurement and management has been rightly criticized from a number of different perspectives for causing pathologies in public management (see, for instance, Christensen and Laegreid, 2001, 2011a, 2011b; Heinrich, 2002; Radin, 2006). Focusing on performance means focusing on what is being measured (Bevan and Hood, 2006), and indeed the whole idea of measurement in public service delivery can be questioned. These critical comments notwithstanding, it does seem clear that NPM has helped politicians, bureaucrats and probably also the public focus on performance, delivery and quality of public services.

NPM has also driven an increase in the number of agencies whose sole mission is to assess the performance of other agencies. Online availability of performance data on, for instance, schools or hospitals can help clients make informed choices about which services to use. Parents can base their decisions about which school to send their children on these performance reports, just as a patient can choose among different hospitals for a procedure based on performance data. Thus we can think of performance measurement as a form of performance-based demand-side accountability; high-performing entities are rewarded by increasing demand and more generous budget procurements while entities with a poorer performance record will note decreasing demand and budget cutbacks. It is a more immediate accountability process compared with the more tedious process where underperforming service providers are reported to the political leadership which, in turn, is accountable to the electorate.

Such processes where inspections 'name, shame and blame' underperforming service providers have, however, proven to cause widely different responses within the targeted service providers, ranging from mobilization to panic or resignation (for schools, see Elstad, 2009). The problem, in brief, is that some service providers operate in more challenging societal environments than others or are better geared to address such challenges than others. Naming and shaming a school reporting low-grade averages, to continue the case of schools, may be to punish a public institution without giving full consideration to the preconditions for its service delivery. It could also be a way for politicians and bureaucrats to remove themselves from accountability for not addressing those challenging social preconditions in the first place (Radin, 2006). Thus, for all the pathologies that performance management entails, it does appear as if we have never had a better account of government performance than we do today, and this knowledge is an essential prerequisite for accountability (Heinrich, 2002). The pathologies are mainly associated with performance management, that is, using performance data and the collection of that data as an indirect instrument to steer and control service providers, and less with the collection of data measuring performance per se.

A closely related accountability arrangement is called accountability by customer satisfaction. Public service providers increasingly use surveys among their clients to measure the degree of client satisfaction. Just as in the case with performance data, such survey results are often posted on an agency's website. Data on client satisfaction can also be used as a variable in the wage-setting process, giving employees an incentive to ensure that their clients are happy with the service they receive. As is also the case with using performance data to punish or reward service providers who do an exceptionally good or bad job, surveys provide politicians and managers with instant feedback from the recipients of public services. For the clients, surveys are opportunities to voice complaints or satisfaction with such services. Again, rather than approaching elected officials in an attempt to improve service quality, the appeal of surveys is that they allow the client to deliver instantaneous feedback. This instantaneous feedback may not be, however, a substitute for more in-depth analysis and evaluation of policy issues.

How important, however, is customer satisfaction in public service delivery? We need to be aware of the diversity of such services. Client satisfaction with services provided by, for instance, schools and hospitals would appear fairly (but not entirely) appropriate to measure with surveys, but what about courts or agencies issuing building permits and other areas where the public service exercises legal authority? Furthermore, we need to recognize the difference between the interests of individual clients and the larger public interest. A client who has his or her building application approved by a municipal board is likely to be a satisfied client, but the construction may leave a large group of citizens deeply dissatisfied. Brian Brewer (2007) makes the important argument that 'the consumerist model is based on a narrow perspective of what constitutes public accountability. By placing too much attention on customer satisfaction, important values of fairness and due process, which are fundamental to good governance and the citizenship status of individuals in their societies, may be undermined' (Brewer, 2007: 555; see also Pierre, 1995b; Aberbach and Christensen, 2005).

In sum, NPM has in many ways strengthened accountability, or at least opened up new channels through which elected officials and public servants can be held to account. However, this new type of accountability is primarily 'broad' accountability in Bovens' terminology; it is not concerned with formal-legal accountability, but rather deals with clients' usage of performance data and whether clients are satisfied with the quality of services. Similarly, from a democratic viewpoint we can see that NPM has increased the number of points of contact between clients and the public sector and thus helped increase citizens' engagement with the state. But we also see that this is a more atomistic, individualized type of engagement and not a public discourse of democracy.

The changing role of media

Along with the continuing development of NPM, particularly performance measurement and management, the media have become more important agents in the accountability process. The media have always been essential to democratic accountability and have an essential role in democratic governance to scrutinize politicians and bureaucrats (Schillemans, 2012; S. Jacobs and Schillemans, 2016; Peters, 2016). This conventional role of the media has over time been supplemented by a wider scope of scrutiny which dovetails with the emergence of NPM (Djerf-Pierre, Ekström and Johansson, 2013). Here, performance measurement and the online posting of performance data has significantly aided media coverage of the public sector. The 'name, shame and blame' strategy to identify underperforming service providers (Elstad, 2009) has helped drive the expansion of media coverage.

In terms of accountability, the 'mediatization' of not just politics but of society at large has had a significant impact on the relationship between the media and elected officials (Esser and Strömbäck, 2014). Although the mediatization argument is extensive and complex, the present analysis is focused on the struggle between politicians and media in terms of who should define the format of the media's coverage, and thus whether mediatization caters to conventional accountability (see Schillemans, 2012; S. Jacobs and Schillemans, 2016). Overall, over the past few decades the media have become more assertive and less submissive to authority and have been largely successful in imposing their format on the political scene rather than vice versa. If 20 years ago the media would come to press meetings when summoned by politicians, nowadays it is more politicians who schedule their press conferences to fit with the media schedule. Again, this is an extensive research field, but the balance of control appears to have shifted towards the media. This development speaks directly to the capacity of the media to hold politicians and bureaucrats to account. For instance, there now appears to be more attention to the spectacular reporting of scandals or errors committed by politicians, and less focus on more in-depth analysis of the execution of public office (Djerf-Pierre, Ekström and Johansson, 2013). Much of the news on broadcast media now consists of short soundbites, rather than any attempt to explain complex issues and expand the public debate on those issues.

Furthermore, since much of electoral accountability is de facto exercised through the media, this changing strategy of the media may weaken that particular form of accountability. Media reporting of politics and administration is biased according to a medium's format, preferences and media logic in terms of what professional journalists consider to be worthy news reports, which might not include the issues that would contribute to electoral accountability.

Thus, the new forms of accountability that NPM, shaped by the media format, have entailed are essentially accountability as it is exercised in the market, not in the political sphere of society. Alfred Hirschman, in his seminal analysis of how clients and customers in different areas of society respond to decline in services and goods (Hirschman, 1970), noted with some frustration that 'voice' – which he viewed as 'political action par excellence' – was used so sparingly while 'exit' was the preferred strategy; 'a person less well trained in economics might naïvely suggest that the best way of expressing views is to express them!' (Hirschman, 1970: 16–17). In other words, conventional accountability is mainly about exercising voice whereas the NPM version draws on market theory and thus emphasizes exit.

Summary and Conclusions

Accountability in the contemporary debate is often seen as the sum of all the positive values that we accord government: transparency, legality and control of politicians and bureaucrats. We have never had as much data and information on public administration as we do today, which means that the preconditions for effective accountability should be good. Indeed, performance measurement, a keystone of NPM, identifies over- and underperforming public institutions and allows clients and customers to strategically choose which service provider they will use. Overall, public service is more transparent than perhaps ever before. A common denominator between the emerging, alternative accountability mechanisms is that they focus strictly on public sector performance and the capacity of clients and customers to improve that performance by strategically choosing among different service providers. There appears to be little concern about the dilemma that we identified in the introduction to this chapter between building government capacity and authority on the one hand and holding that authority to account on the other hand. This might be related to the general trend in many countries of a decreasing trust in government and elected officials; the weaker the institutional trust, the more tentative will citizens be to allow government to strengthen its executive capacity and the more will those citizens want to strengthen accountability.

The distinction between public administration and public management (see Chapter 2) correlates to a significant extent with that between input- and output-based legitimacy. On the one hand, in the conventional model of public administration, where there is close political supervision of the bureaucracy, and services are delivered with a minimum of collaboration with societal partners, legitimacy is derived overwhelmingly on the input side of the political system. In the public management context, on the other hand, where collaborative arrangements are common and managers enjoy more autonomy in their relationship to the political leadership, legitimacy is generated mainly from satisfaction with services and opportunities for customers to engage service providers directly.

In this chapter, we highlight the tension between the need for government to build and reproduce capacity and authority to govern on the one hand, and the development of accountability to monitor how that capacity and authority is exercised on the other hand. The government's capacity to govern is to a growing extent contingent on its ability to mobilize actors in its external environment. Meanwhile, accountability remains firmly focused on public office and the use of public authority and funds. Here lies a growing problem, given the increasingly collaborative nature of governance and service delivery; public service and to some extent also authority is derived from collaboration with societal actors who cannot be held to account. Thus, to some extent we know more than ever before about matters which seem to become less and less relevant for effective and valid accountability.

11

Conclusions: The New Public Administration

This final chapter provides a summarizing overview of the analysis so far and reflects on what all this means in terms of where the development of public administration is headed. Although this discussion by necessity will be speculative, we believe that the trajectory of change thus far provides clues as to which aspects of the organization and key roles of public bureaucracy are most likely to be the focus of future reform. Equally important, we must recognize that this is a normative as much as an empirical analysis, involving questions about what would be a desirable objective of such reform. To some extent, entering such a normatively charged discussion has some value in itself, as we believe that much of the reform of the bureaucracy over the past two decades has ignored the normative aspects of the public service: its objectives; its relationship to citizens and politicians; its distinctive features that differentiate it from other organizations; its modus operandi; and the professional values that it fosters. We cannot identify the flaws in current administration, just as we cannot say what will happen (or indeed what we think would be a desirable course of development) without departing from those normative aspects of public administration.

We furthermore believe that the debate about the future of public administration as a research field must return to concern itself with what Christopher Pollitt (2016) calls 'the big picture'. Pollitt's concern is that public administration research over the past decade or so has taught us 'more and more about less and less'. Although this research has embraced advanced quantitative approaches and methods, it has at the same time become concerned with an understanding of the public bureaucracy as a normatively defined structure performing critical roles in democratic governance. This plea is more than just a group of senior scholars ranting about the novelties brought into their research field by younger generations of students. There is a tendency in contemporary public administration research to divorce itself from the foundational questions concerning public administration. This research typically relies on datasets and methodologies that might lead to publications in leading journals, but such an approach often fails to address issues related to the specificity of public sector organizations, the normative dimensions of public administration and its contributions to democratic governance (Pollitt, 2016; Peters and Pierre, 2017).

One significant component of the 'big picture' in public administration is that these individuals and organizations are involved in governance. What they do is much more than management, especially management as conceived in rather generic terms to be equivalent to management in the private sector. Therefore, public administration must take into account political values and be open to political influence, while maintaining a commitment to public service broadly defined. Maintaining the balance of the political and the professional, and between political responsiveness and neutrality, represents a continuing challenge for public administration. As we have argued throughout this book, the public bureaucracy in most countries has undergone major, if not fundamental, changes over the past couple of decades. Bureaucracies around the world display a track record of reform and change, which effectively dispels the myth about the rigidity of public sector organizations. This manifestation of the bureaucracy's capacity to change, coupled with what appears to be an increasing pace of change in society, raises an intriguing question about what the public administration will look like in 10 or 20 years, and what we normatively speaking want it to look like in the future.

The most obvious hypothesis is that public administration will continue to look much like it has looked in the past. Although there are technological changes, and changing policy problems to be addressed, many of the basic processes of government are unchanged. There will still be the need to provide public services to citizens and to provide policy and management advice to political leaders. Indeed, despite all the changes and reforms that have been experienced, in many ways, public administration remains the essential craft that was known by Weber and Wilson (see van de Walle et al., 2017). The alternative hypothesis is that public administration will be fundamentally transformed. This could come about through technological advances, with citizens able to manage much of their own business with the public sector without the assistance of public employees. When assistance will be needed that may come from private sector contractors, or social partners, rather than from direct public employees. The advent of big data and other online sources of information may reduce the policy advice function of senior public administrators, and in the process further politicize governing.

The reality of the future will most likely be neither of these extreme alternatives, but more likely some blending of these two, combined with a gradual evolution of practice in the face of a changing environment. Whatever that future may be like, many of the fundamental dilemmas of administration that we have discussed above are likely to persist and to require continuing debate and effort.

Dilemmas of Public Administration

In this book we have argued that contemporary public administration is struggling to accommodate a series of dilemmas or tradeoffs between values that are central to good public administration and ultimately to democratic governance. These different dilemmas and the values they represent have oscillated between oblivion and prioritized issues, over time and across different countries.

The first, and arguably the most important of the dilemmas we address in the book is that between administration and management. At its core, this dilemma juxtaposes the basic values of administration, such as rule following, legal security, due process and accountability against efficiency-related values. Pursuing the latter values has ramifications for the former values. For example, many of the procedures associated with due process take a great deal of time and may appear to be inefficient, but are essential to a truly public version of public administration.

The second dilemma focused on the public sector's personnel: that is, between the roles of bureaucrats and service providers. These roles correspond to some extent with the previous dilemma between administration and management; we would associate the traditional role of the bureaucrat with administration and the service provider with management. However, this dilemma also incorporates other aspects of the roles of public servants. We thus discuss the distinction between responsibility and responsiveness of public servants, and the degree to which public servants identify mainly with the rules and norms of their parent organization or whether they primarily engage their clients and respond to their needs.

The third dilemma is between political neutrality and responsiveness of public servants. This dimension concerns the relationship between the public bureaucracy and the political levels of government. Should the bureaucracy primarily provide 'neutral competence' or should it be geared to be as responsive to political directives as possible? While the traditional model of public administration emphasizes the merit system and neutrality, public servants also need to provide faithful service to their political 'masters' and to demonstrate some commitment to the goals of government.

We then turned to the fourth dilemma, related to coordination and specialization; how do we square the growing need for coordinated policies and program on the one hand with the need for expertise and specialization on the other? Both of these tendencies are considered to be high priorities by contemporary governments. Given the complexities of the tasks facing the public service, it requires specialization to deliver good policy advice and to implement programs, but improved coordination across jurisdictional and organizational borders may improve the overall performance of the public sector (see Bianchi and Peters, 2018).

The fifth dilemma we have studied is that between simplicity and complexity. The issue here is closely related to policy-making and implementation. While there is agreement that most policy problems tend to become increasingly complex, there has been more debate concerning the best strategy to respond to that complexity in terms of policy design. The programs implemented to solve or accommodate those problems could attempt to either reflect the complexity of the problem or instead use a much less complex design in order to simply cut through the complexities of society and societal problems.

Sixth, we turned to how decisions are made in the public bureaucracy. We described a dilemma between a search for rationality on the one hand, and routine-based decisions on the other. It is easy to see the rationale for wanting decisions to be made in a rational fashion. However, administrative decisions often tend to be a process of applying the law to a specific case, and are thus made in a routine fashion. There is virtue in that procedure, however, there is also a need for ensuring that administrative decision-making is conducted in a rational style.

The seventh of our dilemmas is that between the autonomy and societal integration of the public bureaucracy. Autonomy is seen as essential to impartiality, integrity and high-quality public administration. At the same time, we see administrative institutions at all levels of government engaging various forms of collaborative arrangements with societal actors in service delivery. Such collaboration is generally heralded, because it allows the bureaucracy to tap into the expertise, funds and societal penetration of NGOs and other partners. But this strategy comes at a price; public institutions engaging in collaboration must be willing to negotiate the design of programs, perhaps even be willing to invite their partners to the decision-making process, hence compromising the integrity and autonomy of the bureaucracy.

The eighth and final dilemma we explored is that between authority and democracy. Bureaucracies require significant organizational capabilities to deliver on their basic mission, but as key components of a democratic system of government, they are also expected to be loyal and responsive to the political leadership and attentive to clients' needs. The executive capacity of a bureaucracy is delegated authority from politicians and ultimately from the people. How do we find the sweet spot, if indeed there is one, between delegated authority, democracy and individual freedom?

Again, these dilemmas are essentially conflicts between values, each of which are an integral part of the normative framework of public administration. Furthermore, as we observe administrative reform over time, we can see that these values have been accorded different degrees of significance in different reform eras. For example, administrative autonomy was heralded a century ago by scholars such as Wilson and Weber, only to be challenged in the mid-twentieth century by reformist political movements who saw the 'apolitical' bureaucracy as an indirect obstacle to social reform (Rothstein, 1998). And, closer to the present day, 'politicization' is back on the no-no's of administrative reform as it is believed to damage the integrity of the bureaucracy and engender corruption (Rothstein and Teorell, 2008). The same view is articulated by NPM reform, albeit for different reasons; in the NPM vernacular, depoliticization is a prerequisite for managerial control of the delivery of public service. We can see similar patterns of oscillation between other reform objectives, too, for instance, between centralization and decentralization, delegating authority and retracting that authority, or between political control and professional autonomy (see Aucoin, 1990). While there is some logic to this pattern – when problems in any given arrangement emerge there will be calls for returning to the previous order – it also seems clear that these pendulum movements may sometimes prevent progress. We will return to this issue later in this chapter.

One strategy to cope with these seemingly inconsistent or contradictory expectations of the public bureaucracy is to focus on the relationship between formal and informal institutions. For instance, formal institutions emphasize the autonomy and neutrality of the bureaucracy, but, in most countries, informal institutions both allow and encourage a range of informal, political exchanges between the two sides of the politico-administrative dichotomy. Similarly, public management reform stresses the importance of managerial autonomy, but as we have discussed earlier in this book that autonomy is often curtailed by growing political presence, again without any reassessment of formal institutional design. Thus, whereas public administration relies heavily on institutional arrangements that define not only the relationship with politicians and with clients but also the internal work of the bureaucracy, informal institutions may help overcome some of the apparent conflict between different values.

We can utilize the typology developed by Helmke and Levitsky (2004) to help understand the relationships between formal and informal institutions in administration (Figure 11.1). They argue that even when formal institutions are effective, informal institutions can complement the activities of those formal institutions, or the two can find means of working together to accommodate their different preferences. When formal institutions of governing are not effective, however, informal institutions can substitute for the formal, or perhaps create real competition over services. For public administration in most developed countries, the formal and informal institutions involved in implementation complement each other and provide alternative means of pursuing public goals. In less developed countries, these relationships may be more complex and alternative arrangements for making and delivering public programs may compete as much as they complement. This is especially true when the institutions of the state lack full legitimacy, and social actors, whether not-for-profits, market actors or clans, provide an alternative set of mechanisms for governing.

Outcomes	Effective informal Institutions	Ineffective informal institutions
Convergent	Complementary	Substitutive
Divergent	Accommodating	Competing

Figure 11.1   Formal and informal institutions

Source: Helmke, G. and S. Levitsky (2004), 'Informal Institutions and Comparative Politics: A Research Agenda', *Perspectives on Politics* 2:725–40.

Back to the Future?

The preceding discussion, where reform is portrayed as a pendulum movement between end values on different dimensions, might suggest to some readers that the future of public administration is behind us, displaying a combination of values which has already been tried but dismissed after some period of time. That is perhaps too simple a view, given that the acceptability of one side or the other of these dilemmas is contingent on changing conditions in the political and administrative systems, as well as changing ideas about what constitutes 'good governance' (Grindle, 2017). In our view, the most salient of the dilemmas discussed earlier is that between administration and management, and the broader issue of how to reconcile managerialism and governance as we begin to discuss what a future public administration, and a public sector, should look like. There appears to be a search currently in many countries for a reform paradigm that secures the improvements in efficiency delivered by the New Public Management (NPM) reform while at the same time rearticulating the foundational purpose of the bureaucracy in democratic governance (see Halligan 2010; Pollitt and Bouckaert, 2011). Striking that balance between management and impartial, professional and administration catering to governance would thus be an important first objective. Not only does this dilemma address an overarching issue about the role and modus operandi of the public service, but the norms and values that are prioritized on that dimension also determine where we come down on several of the other dilemmas.

Before we go further into that discussion, however, we must consider the likely scenario for the public service and the challenges it offers to the bureaucracy. Let us now turn to that discussion.

New challenges

Several of the old, seemingly chronic problems – the 'silo' syndrome, the lack of coordination and long-term planning, just to name a few – have not gone away while more recent problems such as growing complexity and international exposure will create, or exacerbate, the contingencies to which the public service must relate. In many ways, the bureaucracy may be more exposed to these changes than are political leaders, given the need of the bureaucracy to provide advice on these issues and provide services for citizens in rapidly changing environments.

First, over the next couple of decades, most societies in the developed world are likely to experience increasing ethnic diversity. The bureaucratic staff in most of these countries did not mirror the ethnic composition of their respective jurisdiction even prior to the current growth in migration; this issue will pose a growing problem over the years to come. Moreover, not only do bureaucracies need to be representative of ethnic diversity; other dimensions such as gender and social class will need to be considered, and increasing ethnic and social diversity will prompt the bureaucracy at all levels of government to rethink policy and program design in order to better match the needs of clients. It is likely to drive new forms of collaborative service delivery or governance, as the conventional instruments for public service delivery may fail to reach these new groups of clients. In high-trust societies, the public service will have adapt to the fact that many immigrants – often for good reason – probably do not trust government, politicians and bureaucrats. Public servants, not least in local government, will require proper training in intercultural communication and learn ways to engage distrusting clients.

The second set of challenges likely to emerge is in the form of deepening international interdependence and exchange of ideas about the public bureaucracy. NPM was not the first international campaign on public sector reform – there was a similar diffusion of ideas in the 1960s and 1970s related to program budgeting and evaluation – nor is it likely to be the last one. We will probably see new reform concepts gaining international currency, promoted by international institutions, urging national administrative systems to adopt those ideas. But these reforms may well not be suitable for all administrative systems; matching reforms and their potential settings remains a significant challenge.

A third challenge for the public administration is how to design a framework of administrative reform that combines increased efficiency and cost-cutting with the foundational norms of public administration. As was the case with previous such campaigns, the normative foundation of reform will sit more comfortably with some administrative tradition than with others. The next set of reform concepts is not likely to be as clearly neoliberal as NPM, but may instead emphasize community-based ideas about collaborative strategies for public service delivery. The Denhardts, in their discussion of the new public service, reject both conventional hierarchies and the market as foundations for the future public sector. They argue that such a foundation should be a reaffirmation of citizenship, democracy and shared values across the public–private border, with service and the public interest as the key purposes and objectives of such collaboration (J. V. Denhardt and Denhardt, 2011). The rationale for this model of reform is that it allows the public sector to diversify its services and to share the costs of public service with other actors in society without bringing in the market to the same extent as was case with NPM. The merit of the model is that it outlines an alternative strategy for enhancing the efficiency of public service delivery while engaging the targets of those services. The NPM strategy certainly made some gains in these respects, but they should not be exaggerated (Hood and Dixon, 2015).

A fourth challenge, finally, concerns the future support, trust and legitimacy of the public administration among its clients and the polity more broadly. Citizens' trust in conventional channels of input-based legitimacy, such as politicians and political parties, has been decreasing in most countries for a long time while different forms of single-issue involvement on an individual base have gained popularity. At the same time, output-based legitimacy is a dangerous strategy to pursue as it implies that clients are basically content with public service providers as long as they receive what they want, with no regard to wider notions about public interest (Scharpf, 1999, 2009; Brewer, 2007). Furthermore, legitimizing the public sector through output-related support is a strategy that is sensitive to changes in the economy. For example, governments around the world have wrestled with the downfall of the global financial crisis of 2007–2008. In many instances, the choice has been between significant cuts in public services and tax increases. Neither of these choices is likely to foster output legitimacy. Even when governments were able to avert much more severe consequences for citizens through budget cuts, they appeared to get little credit for their judgment or their courage.

Thus, over the past several decades the public sector in many countries – perhaps with the exception of the high-trust systems in Scandinavia – has witnessed a gradual erosion of trust among its clients, both on the input side and the output side. Rothstein and Teorell (2008) would argue that the best strategy to counter this development is for the state to deliver throughput, that is, the process of deliberation and decision-making in public organizations, which is transparent and accountable and conducted with a high degree of institutional integrity and impartiality. That argument notwithstanding, we suggest part of the problem lies in the denial of any major differences between public and private services, which has been a defining feature of NPM reform. The public bureaucracy can never be as responsive, flexible and service-minded as a private service provider because it has to cater not just to the present customer but also to the interest of all clients, that is, to defend the public interest. And, it implements the law in a transparent and accountable process, something a market-based organization does not have to worry about.

The new public administration is thus more different from the bureaucracy we see today primarily in terms of how it interacts with its external environment than in terms of how it conducts its internal work. Those internal procedures for deliberation and decision-making are, however, essential to build external trust, as mentioned earlier. Clients who have good reason to believe that the public administration delivers procedural justice and that their matters are addressed properly, swiftly and in accordance with the law, are likely to trust the bureaucracy. In contrast, clients who suspect that bureaucrats are corrupt or stretch formal rules will display a lower level of trust in public institutions. We may well be underway towards a context where trust is perceived as similar to customer satisfaction, but that would be missing a major point about public administration: it is *public* administration.

References

Aberbach, J. D. and T. Christensen (2005), 'Citizens and Consumers: An NPM dilemma', *Public Management Review* 7:225–45.

Aberbach, J. D., R. D. Putnam and B. A. Rockman (1981), *Bureaucrats and Politicians in Western Democracies* (Cambridge, MA: Harvard University Press).

Acar, M., G. Chao and K. Yang (2008), 'Accountability When Hierarchical Authority is Absent: Views from Public-Private Partnership Practitioners', *American Review of Public Administration* 38:3–23.

Agranoff, R. and M. McGuire (2004), *Collaborative Public Management: New Strategies for Local Government* (Washington, DC: Georgetown University Press).

Albrow, M. (1987), 'The Application of the Weberian Concept of Rationalization to Contemporary Conditions', in S. Lash and S. Whimster (eds), *Max Weber, Rationality and Modernity* (Abingdon: Routledge), 164–82.

Alexander, E. (1989), 'Improbable Implementation: The Pressman-Wildavsky Paradox Revisited', *Journal of Public Policy* 9:451–63.

Alford, J. (2009), *Engaging Public Sector Clients: From Service-Delivery to Co-Production* (Basingstoke: Palgrave).

Alford, J. and J. O'Flynn (2009), 'Making Sense of Public Value: Concepts, Critiques and Emergent Meanings', *International Journal of Public Administration* 32:171–91.

Allison, G. T. (1983), 'Public and Private Management: Are They Fundamentally Alike in All Unimportant Respects?', *Policy* 1:14–29.

Andres, G. J. (2009), *Under the Influence* (New York, NY: Routledge).

Ansell, C. and A. Gash (2007), 'Collaborative Governance in Theory and Practice', *Journal of Public Administration and Theory* 18:543–71.

Arrow, K. (1974), *The Limits of Organization* (New York, NY: Norton).

Aucoin, P. (1990), 'Administrative Reform in Public Management: Paradigms, Principles, Paradoxes and Pendulums', *Governance: An International Journal of Policy, Administration, and Institutions* 3:115–37.

Ayres, I. and J. Braithwaite (1995), *Responsive Regulation: Transcending the Deregulation Debate* (Oxford: Oxford University Press).

Barberis, P. (1998), 'The New Public Management and a New Accountability', *Public Administration* 76:451–70.

Bardach, E. (1998), *Getting Agencies to Work Together: The Practice and Theory of Managerial Craftsmanship* (Washington, DC: The Brookings Institution).

Bellfield, C. and H. M. Levin (2005), 'Vouchers and Public Policy: When Ideology Trumps Evidence', *American Journal of Education* 111:548–671.

Bemelmans-Videc, M.-L., R. C. Rist and E. Vedung (eds) (1998), *Carrots, Sticks and Sermons: Policy Instruments and their Evaluation* (New Brunswick, NJ: Transaction Publishers).

Bertelli, A, M. (2007), 'Determinants of Bureaucratic Turnover Intention: Evidence from the Department of the Treasury', *Journal of Public Administration Research and Theory* 17:235–58.

Bevan, G. and C. Hood (2006), 'What's Measured is What Matters: Targets and Gaming in the English Public Health Care System', *Public Administration* 84:517–38.

Bexell, M. and U. Mörth (eds) (2010), *Democracy and Public-Private Partnerships in Global Governance* (Basingstoke: Palgrave).

Bianchi, C. and B. G. Peters (2018), 'Measuring Coordination and Coherence', in E. Bianchi, E. Borgonovi, E. Anessi and E. Pessina (eds), *Outcome-Based Performance Management in the Public Sector* (Zurich: Springer International Publishing).

Binmore, K. (2009), *Rational Decisions* (Princeton, NJ: Princeton University Press).

Blais, A. and S. Dion (1991), *The Budget-Maximizing Bureaucrat: Appraisal and Evidence*. (Pittsburgh, PA: University of Pittsburgh Press).

Blomgren Bingham, L., T. Nabatchi and R. O'Leary (2005), 'The New Governance: Practices and Processes for Stakeholder and Citizen Participation in the Work of Government', *Public Administration Review* 65:547–58.

Blondal, J. R. (2003), 'Accrual Accounting and Budgeting: Key Issues and Recent Development', *OECD Journal of Budgeting* 3:43–59.

Blondal, J. R., D.-J. Kraan and M. Ruffner (2003), 'Budgeting in the United States', *OECD Journal of Budgeting* 3:7–15.

Bo, E. D. (2006), 'Regulatory Capture: A Review', *Oxford Journal of Economic Policy* 22:203–25.

Bogason, P. and M. Brans (2008), 'Making Public Administration Teaching and Theory Relevant', *European Political Science* 7:84–97.

Borghe, L. E., T. Falch and P. Tovmo (2008), 'Public Sector Efficiency: The Role of Political and Budgetary Institutions, Fiscal Capacity, and Democratic Participation', *Public Choice* 136:475–95.

Börzel, T. A. and T. Risse (2010), 'Governance Without a State: Can It Work?', *Regulation and Governance* 4:113–34.

Bouckaert, G. and J. Halligan (2008), *Managing Performance: International Comparisons* (Abingdon: Routledge).

Bouckaert, G. and B. G. Peters (2002), 'Performance Measurement and Management: The Achilles' Heel of Administrative Modernization', *Public Performance & Management Review* 25:359–62.

Bouckaert, G., B. G. Peters, and K. Verhoest (2010), *The Coordination of Public Sector Organizations: Shifting Patterns of Public Management* (Basingstoke: Macmillan).

Bourgault, J. and K. Van Dorp (2013), 'Management Reforms, Public Service Bargains, and Top Civil Service Identity', *International Review of Administrative Sciences* 79:49–70.

Bovens, M. (2007), 'Analysing and Assessing Accountability: A Conceptual Framework', *European Law Journal* 13:447–68.

Bovens, M. (2010), 'Accountability as a Virtue and as a Mechanism', *West European Politics* 33:946–67.

Bovens, M., R. E. Goodin and T. Schillemans (2014a), 'Public Accountability', in M. Bovens, R. E. Goodin and T. Schillemans (eds), *The Oxford Handbook of Public Accountability* (Oxford: Oxford University Press), 1–20.

Bovens, M., R. E. Goodin and T. Schillemans (eds) (2014b), *The Oxford Handbook of Public Accountability* (Oxford: Oxford University Press).

Bowen, E. (1982), 'The Pressman-Wildavsky Paradox: Four Addenda, or Why Models Based on Probability Theory can Predict Implementation Success and Suggest Useful Tactical Advice to Implementers', *Journal of Public Policy* 2:1–21.

Bozeman, B. (2007), *Public Values and Public Interest* (Washington, DC: Georgetown University Press).

Bozeman, B. (2010), 'Hard Lessons from Hard Times: Reconsidering and Reorienting the "Managing Decline" Literature', *Public Administration Review* 42:509–15.

Bozeman, B. (2013), 'What Organization Theorists and Policy Researchers Can Learn from One Another: Publicness Theory as a Case in Point', *Organization Studies* 34:169–88.

Brans, M. and B. G. Peters (eds) (2011), *Rewards for High Public Office in Europe and North America* (Abingdon: Routledge).

Breeden, A. (2016), 'French Inquiry Urges Changes to Intelligence Agencies in Light of Failures', *New York Times,* 5 July.

Brehm, J. O. and S. Gates (1997), *Working, Shirking and Sabotage: Bureaucratic Response to a Democratic Public* (Ann Arbor, MI: University of Michigan Press).

Bresser-Pereira, L. C. (2004), *Democracy and Public Management Reform* (Oxford: Oxford University Press).

Brewer, B. (2007), 'Citizen or Customer? Complaints Handling in the Public Sector', *International Review of the Administrative Sciences* 73:549–56.

Brown, M. B. (2006), 'Survey Article: Citizen Panels and the Concept of Representation', *Journal of Political Philosophy* 14:203–25.

Brown, T. L., M. Potoski and D. M. van Slyke (2006), 'Managing Public Service Contracts: Aligning Values, Institutions, and Markets', *Public Administration Review* 66:323–31.

Bryson, J. M. (2012), 'Strategic Planning and Management', in B. G. Peters and J. Pierre (eds), *Handbook of Public Administration*, 2nd edn. (London: Sage), 147–62.

Bryson, J. M., B. C. Crosby and L. Bloomberg (2014), 'Public Value Governance: Moving Beyond Traditional Public Administration and the New Public Management', *Public Administration Review* 74:445–56.

Bryson, J. M., B. C. Crosby and L. Bloomberg (eds) (2015), *Public Value and Public Administration* (Washington, DC: Georgetown University Press).

Burns, J. P., L. Wei and B. G. Peters (2013), 'Changing Governance Structures and the Evolution of Public Service Bargains in Hong Kong', *International Review of Administrative Sciences* 79:131–48.

Campbell, C. and B. G. Peters (1988), 'The Politics/Administration Dichotomy: Death or Merely Change', *Governance* 1:79–99.

Campbell, C. and G. Szablowski (1979), *The Superbureaucrats: Structure and Behaviour in Central Agencies* (Toronto: Macmillan of Canada).

Carter, P. (2012), 'Policy as Palimpsest', *Policy & Politics* 40:423–43.

Catheau, D. (2013), *Finances Publiques de l'Etat* (Paris: Hachette).

Cepiku, D. and A. B. Savignon (2012), 'Governing Cutback Management: Is there a Global Strategy for Public Administrations?', *International Journal of Public Sector Management* 25: 428–36.

Chisholm, D. (1989), *Coordination Without Hierarchy: Informal Structures in Multiorganizational Systems* (Berkeley, CA: University of California Press).

Christensen, T. and P. Laegreid (eds) (2001), *New Public Management: The Transformation of Ideas and Practices* (Aldershot: Ashgate).

Christensen, T. and P. Laegreid (eds) (2006), *Autonomy and Regulation* (Cheltenham: Edward Elgar).

Christensen, T. and P. Laegreid (2008), 'NPM and Beyond: Structure, Culture and Demography', *International Review of Administrative Sciences* 74:7–23.

Christensen, T. and P. Laegreid (eds) (2011a), *The Ashgate Research Companion to New Public Management* (Aldershot: Ashgate).

Christensen, T. and P. Laegreid (2011b), 'Democracy and administrative policy: contrasting elements of New Public Management (NPM) and post-NPM', *European Political Science Review* 3:125–46.

Christensen, T., P. Laegreid, P. G. Roness and K. A. Rovik (2007), *Organization Theory and the Public Sector* (Abingdon: Routledge).

Chun, Y. H. and H. G. Rainey (2005), 'Goal Ambiguity in US Federal Agencies', *Journal of Public Administration Research and Theory* 15:1–30.

Clark, P. B. and J. Q. Wilson (1961), 'Incentive Systems: A Theory of Organizations', *Administrative Science Quarterly* 6:129–66.

Cohen, M. D., J. G. March and J. P. Olsen (1971), 'A Garbage Can Model of Organizational Choice', *Administrative Science Quarterly* 17:1–25.

Craft, J. and B. G. Peters (2015), 'Comparing Policy Work at the Center: A Framework for Comparing Central Agencies', paper presented at the Biennial Conference of the International Public Policy Association, Milan, Italy.

Crozier, M. (1964), *The Bureaucratic Phenomenon* (Chicago, IL: University of Chicago Press).

Dahl, R. A. and C. E. Lindblom (1953), *Politics, Economics and Welfare: Planning and Politico-Economic Systems Resolved into Their Basic Social Processes* (New York, NY: Harper and Row).

Dahlström, C., B. G. Peters and J. Pierre (eds) (2011), *Steering from the Centre: Strengthening Political Control in Western Democracies* (Toronto: University of Toronto Press).

Damaska. M. R. (1986), *The Faces of Justice and State Authority* (New Haven, CT: Yale University Press).

Davis, O. A., M. A. H. Dempster and A. Wildavsky (1966), 'A Theory of the Budgetary Process', *American Political Science Review* 60:529–57.

Day, P. and R. Klein (1987), *Accountabilities* (London: Tavistock).

de Graaf, G. (2010), 'The Loyalties of Top Public Administrators', *Journal of Public Administration Research and Theory* 21:285–306.

De Zwart, F. (2000), 'The Logic of Affirmative Action: Caste, Class and Quotas in India', *Acta Sociologica* 43:235–48.

Dempster, M. A. H. and A. Wildavsky (1979), 'On Change, Or There is no Magic Size for an Increment', *Political Studies* 27:371–89.

Denhardt, R. B. and J. V. Denhardt (2000), 'The New Public Service: Serving Rather Than Steering', *Public Administration Review* 60:549–59.

Denhardt, R. B. and J. V. Denhardt (2003), *The New Public Service: Serving, not Steering* (Armonk, NY: M. E. Sharpe).

Denhardt, J. V. and R. B. Denhardt (2011), *The New Public Service: Serving, not Steering*, 2nd edn. (Abingdon: Routledge).

Derlien, H.-U. (1991), 'Historical Legacy and Recent Developments in the German Federal Civil Service', *International Review of Administrative Sciences* 57:385–401.

Derlien, H.-U. (1999), 'On the Selective Interpretation of Max Weber's Concept of Bureaucracy in Organization Theory and Administrative Science, in P. Ahonen and K. Palonen (eds), *Disembalming Max Weber* (Jyväskylä: Sophia Press), 56–77.

Derlien, H.-U. and B. G. Peters (eds) (2008), *The State at Work* (Cheltenham: Edward Elgar).

Diefenbach, T. (2009), 'New Public Management in Public Sector Organizations: The Dark Side of Managerial "Enlightenment"', *Public Administration* 87:892–909.

Djerf-Pierre, M., M. Ekström and B. Johansson (2013), 'Policy failure or moral scandal? Political Accountability, Journalism and New Public Management', *Media, Culture and Society* 35:960–76.

Donahue, J. D. and R. G. Zeckhauser (2011), *Collaborative Governance: Private Roles for Public Goals in Turbulent Times* (Princeton, NJ: Princeton University Press).

Doornbos, M. (2004), 'Good Governance: The Pliability of a Policy Concept', *Praxis* 8:272–88.

Dowding, K. and P. John (2012), *Exits, Voices and Social Investment: Citizens' Reaction to Public Services* (Cambridge: Cambridge University Press).

Downs, A. (1967), *Inside Bureaucracy* (Boston, MA: Little, Brown).

Draca, M. (2014), *Institutional Corruption? The Revolving Door in American and British Politics* (Warwick: SMF-Cage Perspectives).

Dunleavy, P. (1985), 'Budgets, Bureaucrats and the Growth of the State: Reconstructing an Instrumental Model', *British Journal of Political Science* 15:299–328.

Dunlop, C. A. (2014), 'The Possible Experts: How Epistemic Communities Negotiate Barriers to Knowledge Use in Ecosystems Service Policy', *Environment and Planning C: Government and Public Policy* 32:208–28.

The Economist (2014), 'Hail the Swabian Housewife', 1 February.

Elmore, R. F. (1979), 'Backward Mapping: Implementation Research and Policy Decisions', *Political Science Quarterly* 94:601–16.

Elmore, R. F. (1985), 'Forward and Backward Mapping: Reversible Logic in the Analysis of Public Policy', in K. F. Hanf and T. A. J. Toonen (eds), *Policy Implementation in Federal and Unitary Systems* (Dordrecht: Springer), 33–63.

Elstad, E. (2009), 'Schools which are Named, Shamed and Blamed by the Media: School Accountability in Norway', *Educational Assessment, Evaluation and Accountability* 21:173–89.

Entwistle, T. and S. Martin (2005), 'From Competition to Collaboration in Public Service Delivery: A New Agenda for Research', *Public Administration* 83:233–42.

Esser, F. and J. Strömbäck (eds) (2014), *Mediatization of Politics* (Basingstoke: Palgrave).

Etzioni, A. (1967), 'Mixed Scanning: A Third Approach to Decision-Making', *Public Administration Review* 27:385–92.

Etzioni, A. (1986), 'Mixed Scanning Revisited', *Public Administration Review* 46:8–14.

Eymeri-Douzanes, J.-M., X. Boix and S. Mouton (2015), *Le règne des entourages: Cabinets et conseillers de l'exécutif* (Paris: Presses de Sciences Po).

Falleti, T. G. (2010), *Decentralization and Subnational Politics in Latin America* (Cambridge: Cambridge University Press).

Fayol, H. (1917), *General and Industrial Management* (London: Pitman).

Forester, J. P. and C. J. Spindler (2006), 'Budgeting Theory Through "Relational Learning"', *Journal of Organization Theory and Behavior* 4:107–31.

Frederickson, H. G. (ed.) (1993), *Ethics and Public Administration* (London: Routledge).

Frederickson, H. G. (2005), 'Whatever Happened to Public Administration? Governance, Governance Everywhere', in E. Ferlie, L. E. Lynn and C. Pollitt (eds), *The Oxford Handbook of Public Management* (Oxford: Oxford University Press), 282–304.

Freeman, J. (2003), 'Extending Public Law Norms through Privatization', *Harvard Law Review* 116:1285–352.

Freidson, E. (1986), *Professional Powers: A Study of the Institutionalization of Formal Knowledge* (Chicago, IL: University of Chicago Press).

Fry B. R. and L. G. Nigro (1996), 'Max Weber and US Public Administration: The Administrator as Neutral Servant', *Journal of Management History* 2:37–46.

Gailmard, S. and J. Patty (2007), 'Slackers and Zealots: Civil Service, Policy Discretion, and Bureaucratic Expertise', *American Journal of Political Science* 51:873–89.

Galaz, V. (Forthcoming) (ed.), *Handbook on Global Challenges, Governance and Complexity* (Cheltenham: Edward Elgar).

Gallo, N, and D. E. Lewis (2012), 'The Consequences of Presidential Patronage for Federal Agency Performance', *Journal of Public Administration Research and Theory* 22:219–43.

Geddes, B. (1994), *Politician's Dilemma: Building State Capacity in Latin America* (Berkeley, CA: University of California Press).

Gerth, H. H. and C. W. Mills (1946), *From Max Weber: Essays in Sociology* (New York, NY: Oxford University Press).

Gilley, B. (2009), *The Right to Rule: How States and Win and Lose Legitimacy* (New York, NY: Columbia University Press).

Gist, J. R. (1977), '"Increment" and "Base" in the Congressional Appropriations Process', *American Journal of Political Science* 21:341–52.

Goggin, M. L. (1990), *Implementation Theory and Practice: Toward a Third Generation* (Glenview, IL: Scott, Foresman).

Goldfinch, S. F. and J. L. Wallis (eds) (2009), *International Handbook of Public Management Reform* (Cheltenham: Edward Elgar).

Goldfinch, S. F. and J. L. Wallis (2010), 'Two myths of convergence in public management reform', *Public Administration* 88:1099–115.

Good, D. A. (2007), *The Politics of Public Money: Spenders, Guardians, Priority Setters and Financial Watchdogs Inside the Canadian Government* (Toronto: University of Toronto Press).

Goodsell, C. T. (2011), *Mission Mystique: Belief Systems in Public Agencies* (Washington, DC: CQ Press).

Gormley, W. T. (1989), *Taming the Bureaucracy: Muscles, Prayers and Other Strategies* (Princeton, NJ: Princeton University Press).

Grindle, M. S. (1997), 'Divergent Cultures?: When Public Organizations Perform Well in Developing Countries', *World Development* 35:481–95

Grindle, M. S. (2012), *Jobs for the Boys* (Cambridge, MA: Harvard University Press).

Grindle, M. S. (2017), 'Good Governance, R. I. P.: A Critique and an Alternative', *Governance* 30:17–22.

Gulick, L. and L. Urwick (1937), *Papers on the Science of Administration* (New York, NY: Public Administration Clearing House).

Gustavsen, A., A. Röiseland and J. Pierre (2014), 'Procedure or Performance? Assessing Citizens' Attitudes Towards Legitimacy in Swedish and Norwegian Local Government', *Urban Research and Practice* 7:200–12.

Haeder, S. F. and D. L. Weimer (2013), '"You Can't Make Me Do It": State Implementation of Exchanges Under the Affordable Care Act', *Public Administration Review* 73:524–47.

Hall, P. (2011), *Managementbyråkrati* [Management bureaucracy] (Stockholm: Liber).

Hall, P. A. (1993), 'Policy Paradigms, Social Learning and the State: The Case of Economic Policymaking in Britain', *Comparative Politics* 25:275–96.

Halligan, J. (2010), 'Reforming Management and Management Systems', in J. Pierre and P. Ingraham (eds), *Comparative Administrative Change and Reform* (Montreal: McGill-Queen's University Press), 139–58.

Halligan, J. A. (2001), 'Politicians, Bureaucrats and Public Sector Reform in Australia and New Zealand', in B. G. Peters and J. Pierre (eds), *Politicians, Bureaucrats and Public Sector Reform* (London: Routledge), 157–68.

Hammond, T. H. (1990), 'In Defense of Luther Gulick's "Notes on the Theory of Organization"', *Public Administration* 68:143–73.

Hanusch, H. (1980), *An Anatomy of Government Deficiencies* (Berlin: Springer Verlag).

Hayes, M. T. (2006), *Incrementalism and Public Policy* (Lanham, MD: University Press of America).

Head, B. and J. Alford (2015), 'Wicked Problems: Implications for Public Policy and Management', *Administration & Society* 47:711–39.

Heclo, H. and A. Wildavsky (1974), *The Private Government of Public Money* (Berkeley, CA: University of California Press).

Heinrich, C. J. (2002), 'Outcomes-based Performance Management in the Public Sector: Implications for Government Accountability and Effectiveness', *Public Administration Review* 62:712–25.

Helmke, G. and S. Levitsky (2004), 'Informal Institutions and Comparative Politics: A Research Agenda', *Perspectives on Politics* 2:725–40.

Hennessey, P. (1993), *Never Again: Britain 1945–51* (New York, NY: Pantheon).

Heritier, A. (2013), 'Covert Integration of Core State Powers: Renegotiating Incomplete Contracts', in P. Genschel and M. Jachtenfuchs (eds), *Beyond the Regulatory Polity: The European Integration of Core State Powers* (Oxford: Oxford University Press), 230–48.

Heritier, A. and D. Lehmkuhl (2008), 'The Shadow of Hierarchy and New Modes of Governance', *Journal of Public Policy* 28:1–17.

Hibbing, J. R. and E. Theiss-Morse (2002), *Stealth Democracy* (Cambridge: Cambridge University Press).

Hill, M. and P. L. Hupe (2015), *Implementing Public Policy: An Introduction to the Study of Operational Governance*, 3rd edn. (London: Sage).

Hirschman, A. O. (1970), *Exit Voice and Loyalty: Responses to Decline in Firms, Organization and States* (Cambridge, MA: Harvard University Press).

Hjern, B. and D. O. Porter (1981), 'Implementation Structures: A New Unit of Organizational Analysis', *Organization Studies* 2: 211–27.

Hofstede, G., G. J. Hofstede and M. Minkov (2010), *Culture's Consequences: The Software of the Mind* (New York, NY: McGraw-Hill).

Hogwood, B. W. and B. G. Peters (1984), *Policy Dynamics* (Brighton: Wheatsheaf).

Hollibaugh, G. E. (2015), 'The Political Determinants of Ambassadorial Appointments', *Presidential Studies Quarterly* 45:445–66.

Hollibaugh, G. E., G. Horton and D. E. Lewis (2014), 'Presidents and Patronage', *American Journal of Political Science* 58:1024–42.

Hood, C. (1974), *The Tools of Government* (Chatham, NJ: Chatham House).

Hood, C. (1976), *The Limits of Administration* (New York, NY: Wiley).

Hood, C. (1991), 'A Public Management for all Seasons?', *Public Administration* 69:3–19.

Hood, C. (2005), 'Public Management: The Word, the Movement, the Science', in E. Ferlie, L. E. Lynn and C. Pollitt (eds), *The Oxford Handbook of Public Management* (Oxford: Oxford University Press), 7–26.

Hood, C. (2011), *The Blame Game: Spin, Bureaucracy and Self-Preservation in Government* (Princeton, NJ: Princeton University Press).

Hood, C. and R. Dixon (2015), *A Government that Worked Better and Cost Less? Evaluating Three Decades of Reform in UK Central Government* (Oxford: Oxford University Press).

Hood, C. and M. Lodge (2006), *The Politics of Public Service Bargains* (Oxford: Oxford University Press).

Hood, C. and B. G. Peters, with G. O. M. Lee (2002), *Reward for High Public Office in Asia and Pacific Rim Countries* (London: Routledge).

Hou, Y. (2006), 'Budgeting for Fiscal Stability over the Business Cycle: A Countercyclical Fiscal Policy and Multiyear Budgeting', *Public Administration Review* 68:631–48.

House, R. S. and E. Araral (2014), 'The Institutional Analysis and Development Framework', in Araral, E., S. Fritzen, M. Howlett, M. Ramesh and X. Wu (eds), *Routledge Handbook of Public Policy* (London: Routledge), 175–88.

Huber, J. D. and C. R. Shipan (2002), *Deliberate Discretion? The Institutional Foundations of Bureaucratic Autonomy* (Cambridge: Cambridge University Press).

Hupe, P. (2013), 'Dimensions of Discretion: Specifying the Objects of Street-level Bureaucracy Research', *Der Moderne Staat* 6:425–40.

Hupe, P. and M. Hill (2015), '"And the Rest is Implementation": Comparing Approaches to What Happens in Policy Processes Beyond Great Expectations', *Public Policy and Administration* 31:103–21.

Hupe, P., M. Hill and A. Buffat (eds) (2015), *Understanding Street-Level Bureaucracy* (Bristol: Policy Press).

Hyden, G. (2013), 'Culture, Administration and Reform in Africa', *International Journal of Public Administration* 36:922–31.

Jacobs, A. M. (2011), *Governing in the Long-term: Democracy and the Politics of Investment* (Cambridge: Cambridge University Press).

Jacobs, S. and T. Schillemans (2016), 'Media and Public Accountability: Typology and Exploration', *Policy and Politics* 44:23–40.

Jacobsen, D. I. (2006), 'The Relationship Between Politics and Administration: The Importance of Contingency Factors, Formal Structures, Demography and Time', *Governance* 19:303–23.

Jantz, B. and W. Jann (2013), 'Mapping accountability changes in labour market organizations: From concentrated to shared accountability?', *International Review of Administrative Sciences* 79:227–48.

Jerome-Forget, M., J. White and J. M. Weiner (1995), *Managing Health Care Through Internal Markets* (Montreal: Institute for Research on Public Policy).

John, P. and M. Johnson (2008), 'Is there still a public service ethos?', in A. Park, J. Curtice, K. Thomson, M. Philips, M. Johnson and E. Clery (eds), *British Social Attitudes: The 24th Report* (London: Sage), 105–26.

Jones, B. D. (1999), 'Bounded Rationality', *Annual Review of Political Science* 2:297–311.

Jones, B. D., L. Zalanyi and P. Erdi (2014), 'An Integrated Theory of Budget Politics and Some Empirical Tests: The US National Budget 1791–2010', *American Journal of Political Science* 58:561–78.

Jones, R. and K. Luder (2011), 'The Federal Government of Germany's Circumspection concerning Accrual Budgeting and Accounting', *Public Money & Management* 31:265–70.

Jordan, A. and A. Lenschow (2010), 'Environmental Policy Integration: A State of the Art Review', *Environmental Policy and Governance* 20:147–58.

Kaufman, H. (1956), 'Emerging Conflicts in the Doctrine of Public Administration', *American Political Science Review* 50:1057–72.

Kaufman, H. (1977), *Red Tape: Its Origins, Uses and Abuses* (Washington, DC: The Brookings Institution).

Kennedy, B. A. (2013), 'Sorting Through: The Role of Representation in Bureaucracy', *Journal of Public Administration Research and Theory* 21:791–816.

Kennedy, B. A. (2014), 'Unraveling Representative Bureaucracy: A Systematic Analysis of the Literature', *Administration & Society*, 46:395–421.

Kerwin, C. M. and S. Furlong (2011), *Rulemaking: How Government Agencies Write Law and Make Policy*, 4th edn. (Washington, DC: CQ Press).

Kettl, D. F. (1997), 'The Global Revolution in Public Management: Driving Themes, Missing Links', *Journal of Policy Analysis and Management* 16:446–62.

Kettl, D. F. (2015), 'The Job of Government: Interweaving Public Functions and Private Hands', *Public Administration Review* 75:210–29.

Kickert, W. J. M. (2012), 'State Responses to the Fiscal Crisis in Britain, Germany and the Netherlands', *Public Management Review* 14:299–309.

Kinchin, N. (2007), 'More than Writing on a Wall: Evaluating the Role that Codes of Ethics Play in Securing Accountability of Public Sector Decision-Makers', *Australian Journal of Public Administration* 66:112–20.

Kingdon, J. W. (2003 [1985]), *Agendas, Alternatives and Public Policies*, 2nd edn. (New York, NY: Longman).

Kingsley, J. D. (1944), *Representative Bureaucracy* (Yellow Springs, OH: Antioch Press).

Kirschen, E. S. et al. (1964), *Economic Policy in Our Time* (Dordrecht: North-Holland).

Kiser, L. L. and E. Ostrom (2000), 'The Three Worlds of Action: A Metatheoretical Synthesis of Institutional Approaches', in M. D. McGinnis (ed.), *Polycentric Games and Institutions* (Ann Arbor, MI: University of Michigan Press), 56–88.

Klijn, E.-H. (2008), 'Complexity Theory and Public Administration', *Public Management Review* 10:299–317.

Knill, C. (1999), 'Explaining Cross-National Variance in Administrative Reform: Autonomous versus Instrumental Bureaucracies', *Journal of Public Policy* 19:113–39.

Kohler-Koch, B. and B. Finke (2007), 'The Institutional Shaping of EU-Society Relations: A Contribution to Democracy via Participation?', *Journal of Civil Society* 3:205–21.

Kooiman, J. (ed.) (1993), *Modern Governance: New Government-Society Interactions* (London: Sage).

Koppenjan, J. and E.-H. Klijn (2004), *Managing Uncertainties in Networks: A Network Approach to Problem-Solving and Decision Making* (London: Routledge).

Kramer, R. (1999), 'Weaving the Public into Public Administration', *Public Administration Review* 59:89–92.

Laegreid, P. and T. Christensen (eds) (2013), *Transcending New Public Management: The Transformation of Public Sector Reforms* (Aldershot: Ashgate).

Laegreid, P. and K. Verhoest (eds) (2010), *Governance of Public Sector Organizations: Proliferation, Autonomy and Performance* (Basingstoke: Macmillan).

Le Grand, J. (2013), *Motivation, Agency and Public Policy: Of Knights and Knaves, Pawns and Queens* (Oxford: Oxford University Press).

Lee, K.-H. and J. Raadschelders (2008), 'Political-Administrative Relations Impacts and Puzzles in Aberbach, Putnam and Rockman, 1981', *Governance* 21:419–38.

Levin, K., B. Cashore, S. Bernstein and G. Auld (2012), 'Overcoming the Tragedy of Super Wicked Problems: Constraining our Future Selves to Ameliorate Global Climate Change', *Policy Sciences* 45:121–52.

Levine C. H. (1978), 'Organizational Decline and Cutback Management', *Public Administration Review* 38:316–25.

Lewis, M. W., C. Andriopoulos and W. K. Smith (2014), 'Paradoxical Leadership to Enable Strategic Agility', *California Management Review* 56:58–77.

Light, P. C. (2005), *Thickening Government: Federal Hierarchy and the Diffusion of Accountability* (Washington, DC: The Brookings Institution).

Lindblom, C. E. (1965), *The Intelligence of Democracy: Decision-Making Through Mutual Adjustment* (New York, NY: The Free Press).

Linder, S. H. and B. G. Peters (1989), 'Implementation as a Guide to Policy Formulation: A Question of "When" Rather than "Whether"', *International Review of Administrative Sciences* 56:631–52.

Lindgren, K.-O. and T. Persson (2010), 'Input and Output Legitimacy: Synergy or Trade-Off? Empirical Evidence from an EU Survey', *Journal of European Public Policy* 4:449–67.

Lipsky, M. (1980), *Street-Level Bureaucracy: Dilemmas of the Individual in Public Services* (New York, NY: Russell Sage Foundation).

Lipton, E., I. Austen and S. Lafreniere (2013), 'Tension and Flaws before Health Website Crash', *New York Times*, 22 November.

Lodge, M. and C. Hood (2012), 'Into an Age of Multiple Austerities: Public Management and Public Service Bargains in the OECD Countries', *Governance* 25:79–101.

Lord, G. (1973), *The French Budgetary Process* (Berkeley, CA: University of California Press).

Lowi, T. J. (1969), *The End of Liberalism* (New York, NY: W. W. Norton).

Lübke, A. (2005), 'Fiscal Discipline Between Levels of Government in Germany', *OECD Journal of Budgeting* 5:23–38.

Lundqvist, L. J. (1980), *The Hare and the Tortoise: Clean Air Policies in the United States and Sweden* (Ann Arbor: University of Michigan Press).

Lynn, L. E. (2005), 'Public Management: A Concise History of the Field', in E. Ferlie, L. E. Lynn and C. Pollitt (eds), *The Oxford Handbook of Public Management* (Oxford: Oxford University Press), 27–50.

Mahoney, J. and K. Thelen (2010), *Explaining Institutional Change: Ambiguity, Agency and Power* (Cambridge: Cambridge University Press).

Makkai, T. and J. Braithwaite (1992), 'In and Out of the Revolving Door: Making Sense of Regulatory Capture', *Journal of Public Policy* 12:61–78.

Mann, C., J.-P. Voss, N. Amelung, A. Simons, T. Runge and L. Grabner (2014), 'Challenging Futures of Citizen Panels: Critical Issues for Robust Forms of Public Participation' (Berlin: Technische Universität [TU] Berlin).

Manning, N. (2001), 'The Legacy of the New Public Management in Developing Countries', *International Review of Administrative Sciences* 67:296–310.

Maor, M. (2014), 'Policy Persistence, Risk Estimation and Policy Underreaction', *Policy Sciences* 47:425–43.

March, J. G. (1994), *Primer on Decision-Making: How Decisions Happen* (New York, NY: The Free Press).

March, J. G. and J. P. Olsen (1989), *Rediscovering Institutions: The Organizational Basis of Politics* (New York, NY: Free Press).

Marsh, D., M. J. Smith and D. Richards (2000), 'Bureaucrats, Politicians and Reform in Whitehall: Analysing the Bureau-shaping Model', *British Journal of Political Science* 30:461–82.

Maynard-Mooney, S. and M. Musheno (2012), 'Social Equities and Inequities in Practice: Street-level Workers as Agents and Pragmatists', *Public Administration Review* 72:16–23.

McCubbins, M. D., R. Noll and B. Weingast (1989), 'Structure and Process, Politics and Policy: Administrative Arrangements and the Political Control of Agencies', *Virginia Law Review* 75:431–82.

McGerr, M. (2005), *A Fierce Discontent: The Rise and Fall of the Progressive Movement in America, 1870–1920* (New York, NY: Oxford University Press).

Merton, R. K. (1936), 'The Unanticipated Consequences of Purposeful Social Action', *American Sociological Review* 1:894–904.

Metcalfe, L. (1994), 'International Policy Co-ordination and Public Management Reform', *International Review of Administrative Sciences* 60:271–90.

Meyer-Sahling, J. and T. Veen (2010), 'Governing the Post-Communist State: Government Alternation and Senior Civil Service Politicization in Central and Eastern Europe', *East European Politics* 28:4–22.

Meyers, M. K., and V. L. Nielsen (2012), 'Street-Level Bureaucrats and the Implementation of Public Policy', in B. G. Peters and J. Pierre (eds), *Handbook of Public Administration*, 2nd edn. (London: Sage), 245–56.

Meyers, M. K. and S. Vorsanger (2003), 'Street-Level Bureaucrats and the Implementation of Public Policy', in B. G. Peters and J. Pierre (eds), *Handbook of Public Administration* (London: Sage), 153–63.

Miller, G. J. (2005), 'The Political Evolution of Principal-Agent Models', *Annual Review of Political Science* 8:203–25.

Milward, B., L. Jensen, A. Roberts, M. I. Dussauge-Laguna, V. Junjan, R. Torenvlied, A. Boin, H. K. Colebatch, D. Kettl and R. Durant (2016), 'Is Public Management Neglecting the State?', *Governance* 29:311–34.

Moore, M. H. (1994), 'Public Value as the Focus of Strategy', *Australian Journal of Public Administration* 53:296–303.

Moore, M. H. (1995), *Creating Public Value: Strategic Management in Government* (Cambridge, MA: Harvard University Press).

Moe, T. M. (1989), 'The Politics of Bureaucratic Structure', in J. E. Chubb and P. E. Peterson (eds), *Can the Government Govern?* (Washington, DC: The Brookings Institution), 267–329.

Moe, T. M. (1991), 'Politics and the Theory of Organization', *Journal of Law, Economics & Organization* 7: 106–29.

Moynihan, D. P. (2008), *The Dynamics of Performance Management: Constructing Information and Reform* (Washington, DC: Georgetown University Press).

Mueller, D. C. (2003 [1979]), *Public Choice*, 3rd edn. (Cambridge: Cambridge University Press).

Mulgan, R. (1997), 'Contracting Out and Accountability', *Australian Journal of Public Administration* 56:106–16.

Mulgan, R. (2000), 'Accountability: An Ever-Expanding Concept?', *Public Administration* 78:555–83.

Natchez, P. B. and I. C. Bupp (1973), 'Policy and Priority in the Budgetary Process', *American Political Science Review* 67:951–63.

Naurin, E. (2011), *Election Promises, Party Behaviour and Voter Perceptions* (Basingstoke: Palgrave).

Neuhold, C., S. Vanhoonacker and L. Verhey (2013), *Civil Servants and Politics: A Delicate Balance* (Basingstoke: Macmillan).

Nilsson, L. (2004), 'Medborgarna och den Offentliga Sektorns Gränser', in S. Holmberg and L. Weibull (eds), *Ju mer vi är tillsammans* (Gothenburg: SOM Institutet), 41–50.

Niskanen, W. A. (1971), *Bureaucracy and Representative Government* (Chicago, IL: Aldine, Atherton).

Noordegraaf, M. (2015), *Public Management: Performance, Professionalism and Politics* (Basingstoke: Palgrave).

Norman, R. (2001), 'Letting and Making the Managers Manage: the Effect of Control Systems on Management Action in New Zealand's Central Government', *International Public Management Journal* 4:65–89.

North, D. C. (1993), 'Institutions and Credible Commitment', *Journal of Theoretical and Institutional Economics* 149:11–23.

Novick, D. (1967), *Program Budgeting: Program Analysis and the Federal Budget* (Cambridge, MA: Harvard University Press).

Olivier de Sardan, J.-P. (2014), 'The Delivery State in Africa: Interface Bureaucrats, Professional Cultures and Bureaucratic Modes of Governance', in T. Bierschenck and O. de Sardan (eds), *State at Work: Dynamics of African Bureaucracies* (Leiden: Brill), 156–74.

Olsen, J. P. (2006), 'Maybe it Is Time to Rediscover Bureaucracy', *Journal of Public Administration Research and Theory* 16:1–24.

Olsen, J. P. (2008), 'The Ups and Downs of Bureaucratic Organization', *Annual Review of Political Science* 11:13–37.

Ongaro, E. (2010), 'The Napoleonic Tradition and Public Management Reform in France, Greece, Italy, Portugal and Spain', in M. Painter and B. G. Peters (eds), *Tradition and Public Administration* (Basingstoke: Macmillan), 174–90.

Osborne, D. and T. Gaebler (1993), *Reinventing Government: How the Entrepreneurial Spirit is Tranforming the Public Sector* (New York, NY: Plume).

Osborne, S. P. (2006), 'The New Public Governance', *Public Management Review* 8:377–87.

Osborne, S. P. (ed.) (2010), *The New Public Governance: Emerging Perspectives on the Theory and Practice of Public Governance* (London: Routledge).

Ostrom, E. (2007), 'Institutional Rational Choice: An Assessment of the Institutional Analysis and Development Framework', in P. A. Sabatier (ed.), *Theories of the Policy Process*, 2nd edn. (Boulder, CO: Westview Press), 21–63.

O'Toole, L. J. (2000), 'Research on Policy Implementation: Assessments and Prospects', *Journal of Public Administration Research and Theory* 10:263–88.

Padgett, J. (1980), 'Bounded Rationality in Budgetary Research', *American Political Science Review* 74:354–72.

Page, E. C. (1985), *Political Authority and Bureaucratic Power* (Brighton: Wheatsheaf).

Page, E. C. (2003), 'Civil Servant as Legislators: Law-Making in British Administration', *Public Administration* 81:651–79.

Page, E. C. (2010), 'Accountability as a Bureaucratic Minefield: Lessons from a Comparative Study', *West European Politics* 33:1010–29.

Page, E. C. (2012), *Policy without Politicians: Bureaucratic Influence in Comparative Perspective* (Oxford: Oxford University Press).

Painter, M. and B. G. Peters (eds) (2010), *Tradition and Public Administration* (Basingstoke: Palgrave).

Panizza, F., C. Ramos and G. Schleris (2016), 'Counselors, Cadres and Clients: The Politics of Patronage in Argentina and Uruguay Under Two Left of Center Governments', paper presented at International Political Science Association Conference, Poznan, Poland, July.

Parry, R. (2003), 'The Influence of Heclo and Wildavsky's *The Private Government of Public Money*', *Public Policy and Administration* 18:3–19.

Payan, T. (2006), *Cops, Soldiers and Diplomats: Explaining Agency Behavior in the War on Drugs* (Lanham, MD: Lexington Books).

Perry, J. L. (1996), 'Measuring Public Service Motivation: An Assessment of Construct Reliability and Validity', *Journal of Public Administration Research and Theory* 6:5–22.

Peters, B. G. (1987), 'Politicians and Bureaucrats in the Politics of Policymaking', in J. E. Lane (ed.), *Bureaucracy and Public Choice* (London: Sage), 256–82.

Peters, B. G. (2001), *The Future of Governing* (Lawrence, KS: University of Kansas Press).

Peters, B. G. (2003), 'Administrative Traditions and the Anglo-American Democracies', in J. A. Halligan (ed.), *Civil Service Systems in Anglo-American Countries* (Cheltenham: Edward Elgar), 10–26.

Peters, B. G. (2009), *The Politics of Bureaucracy*, 6th edn. (London: Routledge).

Peters, B. G. (2010a), 'Bureaucracy and Democracy', *Public Organization Review* 10:209–22.

Peters, B. G. (2010b), *The Future of Governing: Four Emerging Models*, 2nd edn. (Lawrence, KS: University Press of Kansas).

Peters, B. G. (2014), 'Accountability in Public Administration', in M. Bovens, R. E. Goodin and T. Schillemans (eds), *The Oxford Handbook of Public Accountability* (Oxford: Oxford University Press, 2014), 211–25.

Peters, B. G. (2015a), *Pursuing Horizontal Management: The Politics of Public Sector Coordination* (Lawrence, KS: University Press of Kansas).

Peters, B. G. (2015b), 'What is so Wicked About Wicked Problems?', paper presented at International Public Policy Association's conference, Milan, Italy, July.

Peters, B. G. (2016), 'Governance and the Media: Exploring the Linkages', *Policy and Politics* 44:9–22.

Peters, B. G. (2017), *The Politics of Bureaucracy*, 7th edn. (London: Routledge).

Peters, B. G. (Forthcoming) *Administrative Traditions and Administrative Reform.* Oxford: Oxford University Press.

Peters, B. G. and J. A. Hoornbeek (2005), 'The Problem of Policy Problems', in P. Eliadis, M. Hill and M. Howlett (eds), *Designing Government* (Montreal: McGill/Queens University Press), 77–105.

Peters, B. G. and J. Pierre (eds) (2004), *The Politicization of the Civil Service: The Quest for Control* (London: Routledge).

Peters, B. G. and J. Pierre (2016), 'Two Roads to Nowhere: Appraising Thirty Years of Public Administration Research', *Governance: An International Journal of Policy, Administration, and Institutions* 30:11–16.

Peters, B. G. and J. Pierre (2017), *Comparative Governance* (Cambridge: Cambridge University Press).

Peters, B. G., J. Pierre and T. Randma-Liiv (2011), 'Global Financial Crisis, Public Administration and Governance: Do New Problems Require New Solutions?', *Public Organization Review* 11:13–27.

Peters, B. G. and D. J. Savoie (eds) (1998), *Taking Stock: Assessing Public Sector Reform* (Montreal and Kingston: McGill-Queens University Press).

Peters, B. G., E. Schröter and P. von Maravić (2015), *Representative Bureaucracy in Action: Country Profiles from the Americas, Europe, Africa and Asia* (Cheltenham: Edward Elgar).

Pierre, J. (1995a), 'Governing the Welfare State: Public Administration, State and Society in Sweden', in J. Pierre (ed.), *Bureaucracy in the Modern State* (Cheltenham: Edward Elgar), 140–60.

Pierre, J. (1995b), 'The Marketization of the State: Citizens, Customers and the Emergence of the Public Market', in B. Guy Peters and Donald J. Savoie (eds), *Governance in a Changing Environment* (Montreal and Kingston: McGill-Queens University Press), 47–69.

Pierre, J. (ed.) (1998), *Partnerships in Urban Governance: European and American Experience* (Basingstoke: Macmillan).

Pierre, J. (2011), 'Stealth Economy? Economic Theory and the Politics of Administrative Reform', *Administration and Society* 43:672–92.

Pierre, J. (2012), 'Governance and Institutional Flexibility', in D. Levi-Faur (ed.), *Oxford Handbook in Governance* (Oxford: Oxford University Press), 187–200.

Pierre, J. (2013a), 'Democratizing Regional Economic Development in Sweden: Why? Did it Make a Difference?', in J. Bickerton and B. Guy Peters (eds), *Governing: Essays in Honour of Donald J. Savoie* (Montreal: McGill-Queen's University Press, 2013), 291–305.

Pierre, J. (2013b), *Globalization and Governance* (Cheltenham: Edward Elgar).

Pierre, J. and M. Painter (2010), 'Why legality Cannot Be Contracted Out: Exploring the Limits of New Public Management', in M. Ramesh, E. Araral Jr and X. Wu (eds), *Reasserting the Public in Public Services: New Public Management Reforms* (London: Routledge), 49–62.

Pierre, J. and B. G. Peters (2000), *Governance, Politics and the State* (Basingstoke: Macmillan).

Pierre, J. and B. G. Peters (2017), 'The shirking bureaucrat: A Theory in Search of Evidence?', *Policy and Politics* 45:157–72.

Pierre, J. and A. Röiseland (2016), 'A 'Choice Revolution'? Exit and Voice in Local Government Reconsidered', *Public Administration* 94:738–53.

Pierre, J., A. Röiseland and A. Gustavsen (2013), 'Legitimitet gjennom prestasjon?' [Legitimacy through Performance?], in H. Oscarsson, L. Weibull and A. Bergström (eds), *Vägskäl* [Crossroads] (Gothenburg: The SOM Institute, 2013), 269–80.

Pierre, J., A. Röiseland and A. Gustavsen (2015), 'Accountability by professionalism or managerialism? Exploring attitudes among Swedish and Norwegian local government leaders', *International Journal of Public Administration* 38: 689–700.

Pierre, J., A. Röiseland, B. G. Peters and A. Gustavsen (2015), 'Comparing Local Politicians' and Bureaucrats' Assessments of Democratic Participation: The Cases of Norway and Sweden', *International Review of Administrative Sciences*. Published online ahead of print: DOI: https://doi.org/10.1177/0020852315598214.

Pierre, J. and S. Schütt (2005), 'Regionalisering och ekonomisk utveckling: Västra Götalandsregionens utvecklingspolitik' [Regionalization and Economic Development: The Politics of Economic Development in the Västra Götaland Region], in L. Nilsson (ed.), *Svensk Samhällsorganisation i Förändring: Västsverige vid Millennieskiftet* [*The Changing Societal Organization in Sweden: West Sweden at the Turn of the Millennium*] (Gothenburg: CEFOS), 415–40.

Pierre, J. and G. Sundström (eds) (2009), *Samhällsstyrning i Förändring: Regeringskansliet och nya governanceformer* [The Changing Societal Governance: The Central Government Office and New Forms of Governance] (Malmö: Liber).

Piven, F. F. and R. A. Cloward (1993), *Regulating the Poor: The Functions of Public Welfare*, 2nd edn. (New York, NY: Vintage Books).

Poguntke, T. and P. Webb (eds) (2007), *The Presidentialization of Politics: A Comparative Study of Modern Democracies* (Oxford: Oxford University Press).

Pollitt, C. (1990), *Managerialism and the Public Services: The Anglo-American Experience* (Oxford: Blackwell).

Pollitt, C. (1993), *Managerialism and the Public Services: Cuts or Cultural Change in the 1990s?* (Oxford: Blackwell).

Pollitt, C. (2003), 'Performance Audit in Western Europe: Trends and Choices', *Critical Perspectives on Accounting* 14:151–70.

Pollitt, C. (2016), *Advanced Introduction to Public Management and Administration* (Cheltenham: Edward Elgar).

Pollitt, C. and G. Bouckaert (2011), *Public Management Reform: A Comparative Analysis – New Public Management, Governance, and the Neo-Weberian State* (Oxford: Oxford University Press).

Pollitt, C., J. Caulfield, A. Smullen and C. Talbot (2005), *Agencies: How Governments do Things Through Semi-Autonomous Organizations* (Basingstoke: Palgrave).

Pollitt, C. and C. Talbot (eds) (2004), *Unbundled Government: A Critical Analysis of the Global Trend Toward Agencies, Quangos and Contractualization* (London: Routledge).

Polsby, N. W. (1968), 'The Institutionalization of the US House of Representatives', *American Political Science Review* 62:144–68.

Porter, D. O., and B. Hjern (1981), 'Implementation Structures: A New Unit of Administrative Analysis', *Organization Studies* 2:211–27.

Potrafke, N. (2013), 'Minority Positions in the German Council of Economic Experts', *European Journal of Political Economy* 31:180–7.

Pressman, J. L. and A. Wildavsky (1974), *Implementation* (Berkeley, CA: University of California Press).

Quah, J. S. T. (2003), 'Paying for the "Best and Brightest"', in C. Hood, B. G. Peters and G. O. M. Lee (eds), *Rewards for High Public Office: Asia and Pacific Rim* (London: Routledge), 145–62.

Radin, B. A. (2006), *Challenges to the Performance Movement: Accountability, Complexity and Democratic Values* (Washington, DC: Georgetown University Press).

Rainey, H. G. (2009), *Understanding and Managing Public Organizations* (New York, NY: John Wiley).

Ramesh, M., E. Araral Jr. and X. Wu (eds) (2010), *Reasserting the Public in Public Services: New Public Management Reforms* (London: Routledge).

Raudla, R., R. Savi and T. Randma-Liiv (2013), *Literature Review on Cutback Management* (Erasmus University: Department of Public Management).

Rhodes, R. A. W. (1997), *Understanding Governance: Policy Networks, Governance, Reflexivity and Accountability* (Buckingham: Open University Press).

Rhodes, R. A. W. and J. Wanna (2007), 'The Limits to Public Value, or Rescuing Responsible Government from the Platonic Guardians', *Australian Journal of Public Administration* 66:406–21.

Rittel, H. W. J. and M. M. Webber (1973), 'Dilemmas in the General Theory of Planning', *Policy Sciences* 4:155–69.

Robinson, M. and J. Brumby (2003), *Does Performance Budgeting Work?* (Washington, DC: International Monetary Fund).

Room, G. (2012), *Complexity, Institutions and Public Policy: Agile Decision-making in a Turbulent World* (Cheltenham: Edward Elgar).

Rose, R. (1980), 'Government against sub-governments: A European perspective on Washington', in R. Rose and E. N. Suleiman (eds), *Presidents and Prime Ministers* (Washington, DC: American Enterprise Institute for Public Policy Research), 284–327.

Rosenbloom, D. H. (2000), 'Retrofitting the Administrative State to the Constitution: Congress and the Judiciary's Twentieth-Century Progress', *Public Administration Review* 60:39–46.

Rothstein, B. (1998), *The Social Democratic State: The Swedish Model and the Bureaucratic Problem of Social Reform* (Pittsburgh, PA: University of Pittsburgh Press).

Rothstein, B. (2009), 'Creating Political Legitimacy: Electoral Democracy Versus Quality of Government', *American Behavioral Scientist* 53:311–30.

Rothstein, B. and J. Teorell (2008), 'What is Quality of Government? A Theory of Impartial Government Institutions', *Governance: An International Journal of Policy, Administration, and Institutions* 21:165–90.

Russell, M. and M. Benton (2011), *Selective Influence: The Policy Impact of the House of Commons Select Committees* (London: The Constitution Unit, University College London).

Saetren, H. (2005), 'Facts and Myths About Research on Public Policy Implementation: Out-of-Fashion, Allegedly Dead, but Still Very Much Alive and Relevant', *Policy Studies Journal* 33:559–82.

Saetren, H. (2014), 'Implementing the Third Generation Research Paradigm in Policy Implementation Research: An Empirical Assessment', *Public Policy and Administration* 29:84–105.

Salamon, L.M. (1979), 'The Time Dimension in Policy Evaluation: The Case of New Deal Land Reform', *Public Policy* 27:129–83.

Salomonsen, H. H. and T. Knudsen (2011), 'Changes in Public Service Bargains: Ministers and Civil Service Bargains in Denmark', *Public Administration* 89:1015–35.

Sanchez-Delgado, R. (2014), 'Rebalancing EU Interest Representation? Associative Democracy and EU Funding of Civil Society Organizations', *Journal of Common Market Studies* 52:337–53.

Sandfort, J. and H. B. Milward (2009), 'Collaborative Service Provision in the Public Sector', in S. Cropper, C. Huxham, M. Ebers, and P. S. Ring (eds), *The Oxford Handbook of Inter-organizational Relations* (Oxford: Oxford University Press), 142–74.

Sartori, G. (1970), 'Concept Misformation in Comparative Politics', *American Political Science Review* 64:1033–53.

Savoie, D. J. (1999), *Governing from the Centre: The Concentration of Power in Canadian Politics* (Toronto: University of Toronto Press).

Schaffer, B. (1973), *The Administrative Factor* (London: Frank Cass).

Scharpf, F. W. (1988), 'The Joint Decision Trap: Lessons from German Federalism and European Integration', *Public Administration* 66:239–78.

Scharpf, F. W. (1997), *Games Real Actors Play: Actor-Centered Institutionalism in Policy Research* (Boulder, CO: Westview).

Scharpf, F. W. (1999), *Governing in Europe: Effective and Democratic?* (Oxford: Oxford University Press).

Scharpf, F. W. (2009), 'Legitimacy in the Multilevel European Union', *European Political Science Review* 1:173–204.

Schick, A. (2009), 'Crisis Budgeting', *OECD Journal on Budgeting* 9:119–32.

Schillemans, T. (2012), *Mediatization of Public Services: How Organizations Adapt to News Media* (Frankfurt a. M.: Peter Lang).

Schmitter, P. C. and T. L. Karl (1991), 'What Democracy Is ... And Is Not', *Journal of Democracy* 2:75–88.

Schön, D. A. and M. Rein (1994), *Frame Reflection: Solving Intractable Policy Disputes* (New York, NY: Basic Books).

Schulman, P. R. (1980), *Large-Scale Policymaking* (New York, NY: W. W. Norton).

Selden, S. C. (1997), *The Promise of Representative Bureaucracy: Diversity and Responsiveness in a Government Agency* (Armonk, NY: M. E. Sharpe).

Shah, A. (2007), *Participatory Budgeting* (Washington, DC: The World Bank).

Shaw, R. and C. Eichbaum (2014), 'Ministers, Minders and the Core Executive: Why Ministers Appoint Special Advisors in Whitehall Contexts', *Parliamentary Affairs* 67:584–616.

Shedler, A. (1999), 'Conceptualizing Accountability', in A. Shedler, L. Diamond and M. F. Plattner (eds), *The Self-Restraining State: Power and Accountability in New Democracies* (Boulder: Lynn Rienner), 13–28.

Shedler, A., L. Diamond and M. F. Plattner (eds) (1999), *The Self-Restraining State: Power and Accountability in New Democracies* (Boulder: Lynn Rienner).

Simon, H. A. (1947), *Administrative Behavior* (New York, NY: Macmillan).

Simon, H. A. (1973a), 'Applying Information Technology to Organizational Design, *Public Administration Review* 33:268–78.

Simon, H. A. (1973b), 'The Structure of Ill-Structured Problems', *Artificial Intelligence* 4:181–201.

Simon, H. A. (1991), 'Partitioning of Unstructured Problems in Parallel Processing', *Computing Systems in Engineering* 2:135–48.

Simon, H. A. (1995), 'Rationality in Political Behavior', *Political Psychology* 16:45–61.

Smith, S. R. (2012), 'Street-Level Bureaucracy and Public Policy', in B. G. Peters and J. Pierre (eds), *Handbook of Public Administration*, 2nd edn. (London: Sage), 354–65.

Sørensen, E and J. Torfing (2007a), 'Theoretical Approaches to Governance Network Dynamics', in E. Sørensen and J. Torfing (eds), *Theories of Democratic Network Governance* (Basingstoke: Macmillan), 25–42.

Sørensen, E. and J. Torfing (2007b), 'Theoretical Approaches to Metagovernance', in E. Sørensen and J. Torfing (eds), *Theories of Democratic Network Governance* (Basingstoke: Palgrave), 169–82.

Soss, J., R. C. Fording and S. E. Schram (2011), *Disciplining the Poor: Neoliberalism and the Persistent Power of Race* (Chicago, IL: University of Chicago Press).

Steinmo, S., K. A. Thelen and F. Longstreth (eds) (1992), *Structuring Politics* (Cambridge: Cambridge University Press).

Steurer, R. (2013), 'Disentangling Governance: A Synoptic View of Regulation by Government, Business and Civil Society', *Policy Sciences* 46:387–410.

Streeck, W. and K. Thelen (2005), *Beyond Continuity: Institutional Change in Advanced Political Economies* (Oxford: Oxford University Press).

Streeck, W. and K. Thelen (eds) (2009), *Institutional Change in Advanced Political Economies* (Oxford: Oxford University Press).

Suleiman, E. (2003), *Dismantling Democratic States* (Princeton: Princeton University Press).

Sundström, A. (2016), 'Violence and the Costs of Honesty: Rethinking Bureaucrats' Choices to Take Bribes', *Public Administration* 94:593–608.

Svallfors, S. (2015), 'Who Loves the Swedish Welfare State? Attitude Trends 1980–2010', in J. Pierre (ed.), *The Oxford Handbook of Swedish Politics* (Oxford: Oxford University Press), 22–36.

Svara, J. (2001), 'The Myth of the Dichotomy: Complementarity of Politics and Administration in the Past and Future of Public Administration', *Public Administration Review* 61:176–83.

't Hart, P. (2006), 'Ministers and Top Officials in the Dutch Core Executive: Living Together, Growing Apart?', *Public Administration* 84:121–46.

Tahvilzadeh, N. (2012), *Representativ Byråkrati* (Gothenburg: School of Public Administration, University of Gothenburg).

Tarschys, D. (1984), 'Good Cuts, Bad Cuts: The Need for Expenditure Analysis in Decremental Budgeting', *Scandinavian Political Studies* 7:241–59.

Tarschys, D. (2003), 'Time Horizons in Budgeting', *OECD Journal on Budgeting* 3:77–103.

Teodoro, M. P. (2011), *Bureaucratic Ambition: Careers, Motives and Bureaucratic Ambition* (Baltimore, MD: The Johns Hopkins University Press).

Thalen, R. W. and C. R. Sunstein (2008), *Nudge: Improving Decisions About Health, Wealth and Happiness* (New Haven, CT: Yale University Press).

Thomas, J. (1999), 'Bringing the Public into Public Administration: The Struggle Continues', *Public Administration Review* 59:83–88.

Thompson, J. R. (2006), 'The Federal Civil Service: The Demise of an Institution', *Public Administration Review* 66:496–503.

Thompson, J. D. and A. Tuden (1959), *Strategy, Structure and Process in Organizational Design, in Comparative Studies in Administration* (Pittsburgh: University of Pittsburgh Administrative Studies Center).

Thompson, V. A. (1961), *Modern Organization* (University: University of Alabama Press).

Torfing, J., B. G. Peters, J. Pierre and E. Sørensen (2011), *Interactive Governance: Advancing the Paradigm* (Oxford: Oxford University Press).

Torfing, J. and P. Triantafillou (2013), 'What's in a Name? Grasping New Public Governance as a Political-Administrative System', *International Review of Public Administration* 18:9–25.

Tsebelis, G. (2002), *Veto Players: How Political Institutions Work* (Princeton, NJ: Princeton University Press).

Tummers, L. and V. Bekkers (2014), 'Policy Implementation, Street Level Bureaucracy and Discretion', *Public Management Review* 16:527–47.

Tummers, L. L. G., V. Bekkers, E. Vink and M. Musheno (2015), 'Coping During Public Service Delivery: A Conceptualization of Systematic Review of the Literature', *Journal of Public Administration Research and Theory* 25:1099–126.

van de Walle, S., G. Hammerschmid, R. Andrews and P. Bezes (eds) (2017), *Public Administration Reforms in Europe: The View from the Top* (Cheltenham: Edward Elgar).

van Hulst, M. and D. Yanow (2016), 'From "Frames" to "Framing": Theorizing a More Dynamic Political Approach', *American Review of Public Administration* 40:92–112.

Vandenabeele, W. (2008), 'Government Calling: Public Service Motivation as an Element in Selecting Government as an Employer of Choice', *Public Administration* 86:1089–105.

Vandenabeele, W., G. A. Brewer and A. Ritz (2014), 'Past, Present and Future of Public Service Motivation Research', *Public Administration* 92:779–89.

Vaughn, J. S. and J. D. Villalobos (2015), *Czars in the White House: The Rise of Policy Czars as Presidential Management Tools* (Ann Arbor, MI: University of Michigan Press).

Vercesi, M. (2012), 'Cabinets and Decision-Making Processes: Reassessing the Literature', *Journal of Comparative Politics* 52:4–27.

Verhoest, K., S. van Thiel, G. Bouckaert and P. Laegreid (eds) (2012), *Government Agencies: Practices and Lessons from 30 Countries* (Basingstoke: Palgrave).

Waldo, D. (1968), 'Scope of the Theory of Public Administration', in J. C. Charlesworth (ed.), *Theory and Practice of Public Administration: Scope, Objectives, and Methods* (Philadelphia: American Academy of Political and Social Sciences/American Society for Public Administration).

Waldo, D. (2007 [1948]), *The Administrative State: A Study of the Political Theory of American Public Administration* (Brunswick, NJ: Transaction Publishers).

Wampler, B. (2010), *Participatory Budgeting in Brazil: Contestation, Cooperation and Accountability* (University Park: Pennsylvania State University Press).

Weible, C. and H. Jenkins-Smith (2016), 'The Advocacy-Coalition Framework', in B. G. Peters and P. Zittoun (eds), *Contemporary Approaches to Public Policy* (London: Macmillan), 16–34.

White, J. and A. Wildavsky (1989), *The Deficit and the Public Interest: The Search for Responsible Budgeting in the 1980s* (New York, NY: Russell Sage Foundation).

Wildavsky, A. (1975), *Budgeting: A Comparative Theory of the Budgetary Process* (Boston, MA: Little, Brown).

Wildavsky, A. (1978), 'A Budget For All Seasons? Why the Traditional Budget Lasts', *Public Administration Review* 38:501–9.

Wildavsky, A. (1984), *Budgeting: A Comparative Theory of the Budgetary Process* 2nd edn. (New Brunswick, NJ: Transaction).

Willems, T. and W. van Dooren (2012), 'Coming to Terms with Accountability: Combining Different Forums and Functions in a Multidimensional Way', *Public Management Review* 14:1011–36.

Wilson, W. (1887), 'The Study of Administration', *Political Science Quarterly* 2:197–222.

Wolfe, P. R. and D. W. Moran (1993), 'Global Budgeting in OECD Countries', *Health Care Financing Review* 14:56–76.

Workman, S. (2015), *The Dynamics of Bureaucracy in US Government: How Congress and Federal Agencies Process Information and Solve Problems* (Cambridge: Cambridge University Press).

Xavier, J. A. (1997), 'Portfolio Budgeting in Australian Portfolios – Principles and Practices', *Public Budgeting and Finance* 17:88–103.

Zahardis, N. (2014), 'Ambiguity and Multiple Streams', in P. A. Sabatier and C. M. Weible (eds), *Theories of the Policy Process*, 3rd edn. (Boulder, CO: Westview Press), 25–58.

Index